Praise for *We Don't Need Permission*

'Eric's advice will help change all our futures for good.'
Sir Lenny Henry

'This book is a manifesto for much-needed radical and
overdue change.'
**Ric Lewis, founder and chairman of Tristan
Capital Partners**

'Razor-sharp lessons for under-represented entrepreneurs,
paired with his burning passion for advancing communities of
colour, manifest in a recipe for unapologetic success.'
**Kathryn Finney, investor, philanthropist,
author of *Build the Damn Thing***

'With one in two Black British families living below the
poverty line today, Eric's book is the generational
game-changer we need.'
David Harewood, author of *Maybe I Don't Belong Here*

'Eric expands our vision to see how Black innovators,
entrepreneurs, and business owners have changed the world, and
gives us a powerful plan to realize a better future for everyone.'
**Greg Hoffman, author of *Emotion by Design*
and former Nike CMO**

'Collins convincingly argues that we possess all the
aptitude, experience and resources needed to leverage
business tools to achieve equality. The book's lessons are
applicable to everyone in a big rush to change the
world or themselves.'
Rob Pierre, founder and CEO of Jellyfish

D1350849

www.penguin.co.uk

WE DON'T NEED PERMISSION

HOW BLACK BUSINESS CAN CHANGE OUR WORLD

Eric Collins

with Mim Eichler Rivas

bantam

TRANSWORLD PUBLISHERS
Penguin Random House, One Embassy Gardens,
8 Viaduct Gardens, London SW11 7BW
www.penguin.co.uk

Transworld is part of the Penguin Random House group of companies
whose addresses can be found at global.penguinrandomhouse.com

Penguin
Random House
UK

First published in Great Britain in 2022 by Bantam
an imprint of Transworld Publishers

The following quotations reproduced by kind permission: Gary Younge p. 33
courtesy the *Guardian*; Michael Mamas p. 62 courtesy Entrepreneur.com © 2022
Entrepreneur Media Inc. All rights reserved. Used under licence; Brad Stone p. 65
courtesy Penguin Random House; Benjamin Zephaniah p. 181 courtesy the
Hackney Gazette; Imran Khan p. 183 courtesy the *Guardian*; pp. 233–5 courtesy of Barbara Smith.

A CIP catalogue record for this book
is available from the British Library.

ISBNs 9781787635395 (hb)
9781787635401 (tpb)

Typeset in 13/16pt Garamond MT Std by Jouve (UK), Milton Keynes
Printed and bound in Great Britain by Clays Ltd, Elcograf S.p.A.

The authorized representative in the EEA is Penguin Random House Ireland,
Morrison Chambers, 32 Nassau Street, Dublin D02 YH68.

Penguin Random House is committed to a sustainable
future for our business, our readers and our planet. This book
is made from Forest Stewardship Council® certified paper.

MIX
Paper from
responsible sources
FSC® C018179

For Adeline and Henry Collins, my first investors

CONTENTS

PROLOGUE: THE PROMISED LAND

The Savoy
London
15 October 2021

By the time I arrived at the Savoy – where the annual *Powerlist* dinner was being held, and those gathered would discover the hundred names who made the 2022 list – I was running late. My plan had been to arrive early enough to mingle and enjoy the freedom to see the great and the good of Black Britain, with whom I had been starving to spend time for two years. But I had left home later than planned: I had been on a call involving a large potential investment targeting Black UK technology startup companies.

So when I arrived at the hotel, a full hour behind schedule, I assumed that I'd be hurried to my table just as the proceedings were beginning. Fortunately, the organizers realized that this reunion was a pandemic remedy – allowing everyone extra time to reconnect with friends and colleagues and enjoy meeting some of the new members of what had become for many of us an extended family. Having worked and lived in the UK since 2014, I and my family had been embraced by this cohesive community and made to feel at home from the start.

The *Powerlist*, a unique publication, had been founded in 2007 by Michael Eboda in order to celebrate the achievements of Black Britons. Each year a distinguished panel selects the UK's hundred most influential Black people from across a range of fields – including business, science and technology, medicine, law, education, government, sport and the arts.

The dinner that typically accompanies the list's formal launch has always been a celebratory and highly publicized affair. Past keynote speakers include former prime ministers Theresa May, David Cameron and Gordon Brown, as well as the current Mayor of London, Sadiq Khan (the city's first Muslim mayor). Yet as much as it is a celebration of Black power and success, intended to encourage younger people of colour in the UK, it's also a chance to ask ourselves what more we can do to address ongoing struggles faced by far too many Black Britons. In our shared journey towards the Promised Land of true equality, the *Powerlist* gathering reminds us how far we've come and how far we still must go.

The evening of 15 October 2021 did all that and more. After all, this was the first time many of us had seen each other since the Fall of 2019, at the launch for the 2020 list. Not too long afterwards, we got the first mention of an airborne virus called Covid-19. Given the catastrophic events that followed, the lockdowns that ensued and the disproportionate toll on Black Britons, the 2021 list was published more sombrely.

The freedom to move about and congregate with others – following all health precautions, of course – was not to be taken for granted: something we've all learned. It was as if we had all been left to navigate our way through a life-threatening storm. Yet now here we were, alive, some of us still blinking as we walked into the brightness of more promising days. We were not saved, as it were, but there was work to do, and there was a powerful sense of re-energized resolve to get things done immediately because, as we now all knew, another day was not guaranteed.

Like many, I'd felt an urgency to respond in some meaningful way to the tumultuous events happening around the world and, pointedly, to issues of inequality in the UK that for too long had been swept under the rug. Those feelings were intensified when confronted by statistics that we should all find absolutely unacceptable. Especially alarming was a study by the Social Metrics Commission, reported in the *Guardian* in July 2020, which found that 'Black and minority ethnic (BAME) households in the UK are over twice as likely to live in poverty as their white counterparts.' Being a poor person of colour further exposes you to job loss, cuts in pay, and diminishing opportunities to get ahead. With the onslaught of a pandemic, the *Guardian* stated, nearly one in two Black households are living in poverty while less than one in five white families can be classified as poor. That is outrageous.

Covid-19 itself took a disproportionate toll on communities of colour due to racism, discrimination and the kinds of key-worker jobs known to have had higher exposure, illness and death rates. On top of all that is the fact that, around the world, the hardest hit from the start were minority women. So much so that the *New York Times* has pointed out that the face of Covid-19's worst destruction is female and non-white.

You may not remember the precise moment when you first heard of a highly contagious virus spreading across the globe, but you most likely will not forget the first time you saw a video captured on 25 May 2020, when a young woman in Minneapolis, Minnesota, took out her mobile phone and recorded the murder by a white police officer of a Black man named George Floyd. That young woman's action – which she took without needing permission – helped set off a global uprising unlike anything seen in contemporary history, propelled by the activists of Black Lives Matter, joined by millions around the world.

Then, despite support from many quarters, or maybe because of it, came the backlash – energizing efforts already under way in many places to reboot racial caste systems. In the UK, a rising tide of white supremacy was apparent to anyone listening to the rhetoric. The *Independent* reported in August 2020 that Britain's far right was growing more openly racist because of the worldwide support for Black Lives Matter protests. The paper cited a report from Hope Not Hate. In it, the authors warned that white nationalist voices, like the anti-Muslim firebrand Tommy Robinson and the recently formed Patriotic Alternative group (which called for the expulsion of non-white people from the UK), were demonstrating a shift in the direction of much more 'openly racial politics'.

If ever there was a time to write about what I have long believed has been a missing link in truly dismantling institutionalized white supremacy, it is now. The empowering moment for many happened when, in the midst of the pandemic, folks dusted off an underused mantra to 'Buy Black', mobilizing people around the world to support local Black shops, restaurants and service providers in their communities.

The missing link for creating equity and lasting change for people of colour starts as simply as that – by supporting and investing in Black businesses. Empowering entrepreneurs of colour is a key with which to end inequality, grow opportunities and boost local as well as national economies. For Black business to change the world, more than ad hoc action is needed. Deliberate planning is required.

As a venture capitalist – VC for short – I invest in young companies with the goal that they will grow to be massive and make lots of money for all sorts of stakeholders. Knowing that there are tens of thousands of people like me around the world looking for the next big thing, I see an important role that investors can play in promoting greater global equality.

There is much more work to be done.

In 2018, only 3 per cent of VCs in the US were Black. That is only just starting to change. Less than 1 per cent of venture capital goes to Black founders worldwide. Extend Ventures, a not-for-profit whose remit is to democratize access to venture capital, conducted a 2020 study covering more than ten years of UK investing and found that only 0.024 per cent of capital was going to Black entrepreneurs. Only 0.02 per cent went to Black female teams. At the height of the Black Lives Matter protests, it was encouraging to hear investors and corporate spokespeople talk about their commitment to equality. But the money has been slow in coming. In February 2021, Entrepreneur.com reported that VC-backed startups were still predominantly white (71.6 per cent) and male (89.3 per cent), while over a third are still in America's Silicon Valley.

Five months later, a July 2021 CrunchBase had better news. Investment in Black-founded businesses had quadrupled in one year, even if it still represented a disproportionately low percentage when compared to the billions going to male/white-founded startups. A key ingredient in the progress that should be noted has been increasing numbers of VCs of colour and also women. More good news was reported by *Forbes* in May 2021: 17 per cent of Black women were in the process of founding their own business. These are exciting strides. At the same time, we know that the pandemic has forced many women of colour out of the workplace. Our job as investors and change agents is to make sure that these new businesses not only survive, but reach their full potential. We must take purposeful steps and make more resources available for the folks who continue to disproportionately experience job loss and financial hardship.

One message I want to emphasize in this book is that without the harnessing of large-scale capital, the momentum needed for such businesses to achieve their full potential can't be sustained. Unprecedented action is the answer, or nothing will change. With focus, purposeful measures and collaborative/ collective effort, change will happen. Everyone has a role to play, and I hope this book empowers you to set off on your own path.

Like me, you may have grown up with a life plan centred around pursuing a single major professional goal. Like me, you may discover by necessity or choice that you have more than one career in you. I learned early in my adult life that single-employer job security was unlikely to be my path.

My ten steps for empowerment are drawn in part from that experience. They come from my diverse exposure to the power of capital in the many settings where I have lived and worked. Certainly, the years I've spent in the UK, my adopted home, have provided lessons about the power needed to dismantle white supremacy and create lasting change. My many years of experience in the US are an emphatic corollary, along with knowledge gained from working, and sometimes toiling, around the world.

Writing *We Don't Need Permission* has also allowed me to draw on lessons I learned growing up where and how I did. They derive not only from my own business ventures, but also from the examples of entrepreneurs, executives and teams whose successes and failures should be studied. From them we learn how it can be done, or not. Further insights I'll share have resulted from my unexpected adventure as the host of the acclaimed Channel 4 TV series *The Money Maker*, where the same investment, management and turnaround principles used in my work as a VC are applied to smaller UK businesses.

This book is not intended to instruct readers in the nuts and bolts of building a small business. Although the lessons for profitable growth may be the same, Black economic empowerment relies on thinking bigger than you may ever have imagined before. In fact, much bigger. This book aims to revolutionize how we think about ways to harness and control capital by creating Black-founded global Fortune 500 and FTSE 100 companies that are generation-changing (meaning they launch and generate tremendous positive impacts all within our lifetimes) – which, to date, do not exist.

That's what we have to change. And the point is that we don't need permission to change what isn't working. We need Black entrepreneurship to succeed wildly. This book endeavours to supply that prescription.

As the book progresses, I especially want to highlight the underutilized tools of capitalism that should be employed by Black people, women and other communities which have been marginalized. Other well-worn tools still matter – education, community organizing, protest movements and electoral politics, legal action, social, digital and other forms of media and influence. But the missing link, the thing which has not been fully developed and which stunts Black empowerment, is that there are still no consistent, large capital sources to fund a relentless agenda of equality on all fronts. We need to alter our strategies to achieve an inclusive form of capitalism, find new ways of sharing and collaborating, and use our actions for scaling up.

The Promised Land, for me, will be reached by creating the conditions that will make possible the first Black female CEO and founder of the next Netflix and the next Microsoft and the next Amazon and beyond. It is a cause that is good for us as people of colour and for the world – not only because this is how we create true and lasting equality, freedom and self-determination for all, but because it is good business. Among the many ears I hope to reach, my invitation to join in the movement goes out to Black entrepreneurs and all who are poised to become the disruptors and leaders in the worlds of tech and finance, especially Black women, who are now primed to conceive, build and run the next Spotify or Uber. I want to reach current and future business and community leaders from backgrounds that have not traditionally had access to capital and who are ready to end their dependence on receiving permission from others to think on a mass scale. My call is for allies and investors who have meaningful roles to play in the Black empowerment revolution.

My call is, above all, to you, the reader.

In a podcast, 'The Recipe', I've been talking to a range of successful individuals who share their recipes for surviving as well as thriving. At a time of great struggle, felt most acutely by people of colour in the UK and around the world, my sincere desire is that you'll be inspired to find your own formula for a level of success and impact that may have felt out of reach in the past. There is nothing about me that should be seen as exceptional other than that I've learned to put resources to work. If I can do that, so can you, whatever your current standing. You don't need permission.

And you are in good company.

That's the big takeaway I'd like to share with you from the *Powerlist* dinner in October 2021. Celebrated that night were many of the list's top ten – starting with number one, Jacky Wright, the British corporate Vice-President and Chief Digital Officer of Microsoft, whose mission is to connect everyday people around the world to the digital revolution. Footballer Marcus Rashford, number two on the list, was recognized for his anti-bullying activism on behalf of the UK's Black youth. Representing achievement in arts and entertainment were Daniel Kaluuya at number four (new to the list), and at number three Anne Mensah, Vice-President of Content UK at Netflix.

At number six, also new to the list, was Steven Bartlett, founder/ former CEO of tech startup Social Chain, and the youngest Dragon to appear on the perennial TV show for entrepreneurs, *Dragons' Den*. Human rights lawyer Jacqueline McKenzie, at number ten, was applauded for her leadership in migration, asylum and refugee law, but especially for her tireless fight for the rights of the Windrush generation.

When I finally took my seat, just before dinner was served, I made several new friends. Among them was an accountant who handles the affairs of a number of athletes in a variety of sports, sitting next to the head of an African-focused invest- ment firm; and, two seats away, the head of a charity that supports young people transitioning from foster care to inde- pendence. This lawyer-turned-CEO was solving a problem of her lived experience. Her drug-addicted mother could not raise her. She'd entered the child support services sector early in life only to 'graduate' to independence at sixteen with no resources and few life skills. Her charity provides an effective transitional process, and she was being recognized for her pioneering work. All the talk around me was about caring for one another and making the world a better place.

Was I in the right room for people who are changing the world? Absolutely.

Almost everyone who spoke did so with the conviction that we were no longer under the yoke of needing permission. We weren't yet where we needed or wanted to be, but that's where we were headed. The high point for me was the final musical selection for the evening, sung by the choir who rose to prominence after performing at the wedding of the Duke and Duchess of Sussex.

The song, the classic 'Lovely Day' by the late Bill Withers (RIP), brought us all to our feet in a rousing singalong of the chorus. While singing, I knew that I was collectively speaking into reality the truth that the Promised Land must be reached, and pledging to do my bit in getting there as part of this remarkable whole.

The emotion felt by all in that hotel ballroom was, I believe, unexpected and yet so needed. The unexpected is something my experiences have taught me to embrace, as you'll see next, as the first of the ten steps to empowerment.

1

CAPITAL IS THE X FACTOR

Step #1: Embrace the unexpected

People are more comfortable with a familiar discomfort
than they are with an unfamiliar new possibility.

LISA NICHOLS, ENTREPRENEUR, AUTHOR, MOTIVATIONAL SPEAKER

London Gatwick Airport
A departure lounge in the South Terminal
Spring 2018

The phone call that changed the trajectory of my life and altered my thinking about Black economic empowerment came out of the blue. At that moment, I happened to be waiting to board a flight from London to Los Angeles and was reviewing notes for a meeting I had scheduled with one of America's leading medical associations (then run by a wonderfully effective Black woman, Adrienne White-Faines). At that time, I flew so often for business that the airport was practically my home.

Not that I minded. In my varied roles over the years – as entrepreneur, market investor, corporate executive and strategy
consultant to behemoth-sized and smaller businesses, fast-
growing startups, international agencies and government
bodies – I'm always in my element when on the move.

Travel comes with the territory. For many of my peers, constant travel for work, especially when you are crossing multiple
time zones, can be a huge downside of the job. But despite the
inconvenience, the perpetual jet lag and sleep deprivation, I
must confess that I find almost everything about departures
and arrivals fascinating.

Perhaps you've had the same feeling of wonder as you venture through your daily routine, maybe sometimes going outside
your comfort zone. Whom will you meet? What will you see?
What new ideas might come your way? What unforeseen cir-
cumstance might send you off in an unplanned yet possibly
fortuitous direction? Or will your best-laid plans go awry? In
any case, there is something empowering about the promise of
untold opportunity looming ahead – which is why Step #1:
Embrace the unexpected can be your lifeline even in inclement
times.

My appreciation of all kinds of expeditions probably has
something to do with the fact that, from a very young age,
travel was a meaningful part of my life. When I was a child
growing up in North Carolina, my father, Henry Collins, a scientist who left academia to join a Swiss chemical company,
regularly flew for business from the 1970s.

Switzerland was a frequent destination for my dad, and so
was domestic travel to far-flung parts of North America.
Sometimes, if we were lucky enough, my mother, Adeline, an
educator who had been raised in Philadelphia, would take my
two siblings and me to go and see him off at Greensboro's airport. The sight of him embarking on his journey still looms

large in my memory – Dad, always dressed in a suit, with his briefcase and carry-on, tall and imposing, striding purposefully towards the departure gate, one of the few Black passengers I remember seeing. Whenever he returned, my brother, sister and I would bombard him with questions. We were more interested in asking, 'What'd they give you to eat and drink on the plane, Daddy?' than in what he actually did while away in Switzerland. We squabbled over the airplane treats he brought home for us to share, especially those Swiss chocolates.

Dad's job and the importance of his work, which had world-impacting properties, were completely normal to me. The notion became part of my DNA that if you want to prosper and change the world for the better, go off and get to know it. I regularly saw a Black business executive, my father, jetting off for meetings across the Atlantic. That was our life. But it wasn't until I started comparing notes with school friends that I realized how odd others might find this. Even then, I didn't connect my love of travel with an even deeper yearning for the freedom that comes from determining one's own destinations.

Freedom is a longing, I believe, that lies in most of us. Yet it took me years to recognize a self-limiting condition which exists right beside that desire for freedom – what I see as a need for permission from others and from entrenched systems – which afflicts far too many of us in Black communities around the world. We too often feel, somehow, that we need permission to sit in seats of power and control the resources that come with those positions. Seeking permission comes in many subversive forms. I have been guilty of waiting for invitations to be extended by others who begrudgingly give them, looking for recognition to be conferred by others who don't see me as equal, yearning for acceptance from others who feel I am not worthy, being told I'm OK by folks who don't respect me.

In early 2018, with the halcyon days of America's first Black president fading in our rear-view mirror, this awareness was coming into sharp focus. An ascendant right wing, emboldened in the US by Trump and his party, funded by powerful billionaires who controlled vast empires of industry, had already led to the normalization and tacit acceptance of white supremacist mobs. We'd seen them unmasked in Charlottesville, Virginia in the early days of that administration. It was there, in August 2017, that a planned 'Unite the Right' rally of hundreds – including members of the Ku Klux Klan, alt-right, neo-Nazi and other white nationalist groups like the nascent Proud Boys – turned into one of the biggest and most violent such gatherings in decades. Claiming to be there to preserve a statue of Robert E. Lee (the military leader of a failed civil insurrection) that was slated for removal, marchers carried weapons, shields and torches, waved Confederate flags and banners with swastikas, and shouted racist and anti-Semitic slurs.

In the UK, in parallel, there was a similar, noticeable surge of right-wing racism and an uptick in race-related hate crimes – coinciding with tensions roused by the 2016 Brexit referendum. Many leading the charge for the 'Leave' campaign blamed economic instability on Black people and immigrants, and especially immigrants of colour. For some, Brexit seemed to have validated open expression of white supremacy by giving permission to hate speech and race-motivated crime.

The pressure cooker in the UK had been intensifying for more than a decade, dating back to austerity measures established when Conservative leaders came to power in the wake of the global financial crisis of 2009–10. Inflaming the rhetoric in 2018 was none other than the soon-to-become Prime Minister Boris Johnson, who, remember, had for a long time refused to apologize for comments made in a 2002 *Telegraph* column in which he suggested that the Queen had grown to 'love the

Commonwealth' because of the crowds of 'flag-waving pic-caninnies'. He also described Africans as having 'watermelon smiles'. Among ongoing racist and xenophobic slurs over the years, Johnson wrote in another *Telegraph* piece in 2018 that Muslim women in burkas looked 'like letter boxes' and that they could be mistaken for bank robbers. When asked if his refusal to apologize right away was an open invitation to white supremacists and a validation of their cause, Johnson insisted his comments were taken out of context.

Nationalistic equivalents to MAGA (the Trump-made credo of Make America Great Again) appeared to be spreading across Europe and around the world. Signs of the times were deeply troubling. A new and different kind of response was desperately needed, but what that was exactly, I didn't then know.

For decades, centuries really, Black people had been marching in faith to attain basic rights of equal justice, equal opportunity and equal access, making great strides and then being pushed back. Some had achieved positions of stature and wealth, while too many others were continually held back. Deeply resonating with me were the words of the civil rights activist Fannie Lou Hamer, spoken in 1964 after Ku Klux Klan attempts to murder her for the crime of trying to cast a ballot: *I am sick and tired of being sick and tired.*

It occurred to me that in our generations-old struggle for economic equality and justice, the old tools were not enough. We'd employed a range of strategies (cajoling, appealing, demanding, forcing) and had utilized many tactics – educating, working, marching, protesting, taking legal action, voting, electing leaders including, in the US, a president who was in the struggle with us, and more. What else was there?

More to the point: was there something else I could do?

If you have ever had a similar experience when trying to solve a big issue that impacts you and a lot of other people, that thought process meant your entrepreneurial, problem-solving gears were kicking in. Many of the most successful innovations in history have come about in response to the same kinds of questions.

Waiting to board the plane in Spring 2018, I had no ready solutions other than to appreciate how far I'd come personally, with thanks to both of my parents – my ever-empowering mother as well as my globe-trotting father. I thought of the recipe for success shared in our household – God, family and education. The other key ingredient was the Collins credo that whatever opportunities we'd been given ought to be shared, multiplied and paid forward. So many Black people continued to be denied those same opportunities, and I was all too conscious of that. Wasn't there something more I could do to change the equation?

Not sure where to begin such an undertaking, I turned my attention to my own job search. My inbox contained several unanswered emails from recruiters and founders asking me to consider potential CEO and COO (Chief Operating Officer) roles at various promising companies. For the past two years I had served as the COO of Digital Surgery – a bleeding-edge tech company solving the problem of how to get safe surgery to the five billion-plus people worldwide who don't have it. I was at a crossroads, preparing to leave the company that in a few years' time would sell to Medtronic, a medical tech, services and solutions company, for $400 million. My flight plan had been to cut off my electronics and use the ten-hour trip ahead of me to have a long, hard think about what to do next.

Having recently turned fifty-two, I wanted my next role in the right firm to deliver impact, allowing me to take advantage of my UK residency and US citizenship. This status hadn't come about by design. Originally, I'd come to the UK with a sponsored work visa and then received a Tech Nation Tier 1 visa after five years. In year six came indefinite leave to remain. The following year, I successfully applied for citizenship. The happy plot twist had started simply with a job and a bit of serendipity. Behind that adventure had been a reminder to self to follow Step #1 and *Embrace the unexpected*. Now, whatever my next opportunity was going to be, my other priority was to pursue goals that involved using technology as audacious as Digital Surgery's and as impactful as its mission to save the world one successful procedure at a time.

Then came the phone call that forced me to abandon all of that. It changed what was in my head for the next ten hours. Soon enough, it would change my life's priorities.

The lesson here is that, just as you can unexpectedly create opportunities for yourself by solving problems on your own, sometimes those opportunities come for you to solve with other people. The point is – open your ears. You never know.

'Hi Eric, how are you? Do you have a moment to speak?'

The warm voice on the other end of the call belonged to Tom Ilube. A multifaceted British entrepreneur, Tom attended school in Benin City, Nigeria and then went to Oxford University, contributing factors that I believe helped him achieve the meaningful success that he has. Half Nigerian, half British, he grew up in part, as I had, surrounded by individuals who had distinguished themselves. And it had meant that he would too. Tom served on the board of the BBC and is a non-executive director for the marketing giant WPP. He is a fellow at two Oxford colleges, Chair of the Rugby Football Union, and was instrumental in setting up the UK's first internet bank, Egg. Tom also launched the Hammersmith Academy secondary school in west London, considered one of the country's most innovative technology schools, and he founded the African Science Academy, a brilliant STEM school for African girls in

Accra, Ghana. Not surprisingly, Tom Ilube was voted the most influential Black person in Britain in 2018 – back to the *Power-list*. And on top of all that he has been honoured with an OBE.

Already in line to board the flight, I didn't have much time to chat, but Tom is the kind of person whose call you take, no matter what you're doing. He doesn't call often, nor is he one for small talk, so I knew it had to be something important. Tom was direct, as always, yet I also detected an unusual sense of excitement and a touch of urgency in his voice.

'I'm having a get-together at my place,' he began, and went on to say that it had been instigated by Sir Lenny Henry. In attendance would be some of the biggest names in finance, along with investment bankers, institutional investors, fund managers, serial entrepreneurs and luminaries from the world of sport, media, entertainment and the civil service. Then he added, 'Eric, I'd really like you to be there.'

I almost said, 'You had me at Lenny Henry!' but refrained. Lenny, besides being a television icon and British national treasure, known even by an American from the South like me, had for decades agitated for more diverse representation and equality in broadcasting and the entertainment industry. Having co-founded the charity Comic Relief in 1985, which has raised over £1.6 billion in thirty years and helped over 50 million people in the UK and overseas, he is a tireless champion for others. But I immediately wondered what Lenny and Tom were doing convening a hush-hush meeting of influential Black Brits – which included the self-named Black Hand Gang, a group of Black entertainers, athletes and activists – at a house in Richmond, on the outskirts of south-west London. Why the urgency in his tone?

Tom filled me in, first by noting that the invited guests had three things in common. Besides being Black and particularly well established in their careers, every invitee had at some point been on (or associated with) the *Powerlist*. The third and most crucial thread connecting everyone invited to this meeting was that they, like me, were also fed up. Particularly fed up about the lack of progress the Black community was making in Britain despite being permanent fixtures there in large numbers for over half a century.

Many Black British citizens had arrived in the same post-war periods as other non-Blacks who had immigrated from elsewhere, but as far as we could tell they had not made anywhere near the same amount of progress as people from other immigrant communities. There were exceptions, of course, and certain segments of the Black community seemed to be making more strides than others. Yet two decades into the twenty-first century, Black Britons continued to lag behind in terms of meaningful progress – especially with respect to capital access, creation and accumulation.

If you're Black, unless you are a rare exception to the rule, access to paradigm-shifting transformative amounts of money is still almost impossible to come by. Whether the capital is in the form of family gifts, personal savings, inheritance, third-party lending or risk capital, its availability to ambitious folks is limited. In a September 2021 article linking UK home ownership to wealth, the *Independent* cited findings from the Joseph Rowntree Foundation's study on UK housing and the UK Office for National Statistics: British white home ownership stood at 68 per cent, British Indian homeownership was 74 per cent, while only 37 per cent of British Black Caribbeans owned their homes and 30 per cent of British Blacks overall. Home ownership is a major source of wealth accumulation. There remain commonplace and systemic barriers to getting home loans.

Systemic racism is an insidious circle. It ensures limitations to opportunity, resulting in income disparities, which means less money for families, which means fewer assets, leading to a lack of access to capital via investment and borrowing, which means less flexibility in opportunity, fewer safety nets and more limited networks, among other obstacles.

In some ways there was nothing unprecedented about Tom's gathering. We'd met for different reasons in the past; excluding the *Powerlist* galas, we would regularly meet in some form or another at least once a year. Various avenues of collective action were always encouraged. But up until now, there had not been a unifying goal to pursue. The cause of Black economic empowerment was a goal that could not have come at a more timely moment.

On the call, as Tom told me the names of those expected to attend, it struck me that something extraordinary could be made of this situation. Deploying the right resources could yield results in areas for which I have a passion – from collaborating with extraordinary teams to focusing on tools for sustained change, leveraging diverse networks, and reworking existing opportunities to achieve goals the world had never seen before. If we could solve the problem of Black inequality in the UK, we could apply these lessons anywhere. And everywhere.

The meeting was to be a working session – not, under any circumstances, a gathering in which participants bemoaned the issues, sat around pondering how terrible things were while swapping personal anecdotes about examples of racism they'd encountered, or calling out structural prejudice that had thwarted their career paths. No, this session was to be actively, *aggressively* about solutions. No more evidence was needed, no more studies were required, no more commissioned reports necessary. We lived the problems. We had waited a long time, perhaps too long, for other people to fix things, and they'd failed. We'd all come to the awareness that if we wanted things to change, that change would have to come from us, from Black folk. We needed to stop waiting for allies to arrive. We needed to stop waiting for someone else to allow us to start boldly making the world we wanted to see. We needed to stop waiting for permission.

My mind whirled with excitement as I settled into my seat on the plane, sorry to have to end the call so soon. There were unlimited possibilities to be achieved, I was sure, if we harnessed the energy, experience and, above all, the resource muscle of everyone called to assemble. I'd long believed that, in order to change the world, charity, good intentions and benevolence were only a start. Harnessing the heft of business was an underused key, an X factor, in the struggle for equality. Business and economic levers had to be pulled to create the opportunities, ownership, jobs and assets that catalyze real change.

'Of course I'll come, Tom!' I said. I already had my calendar up on my laptop, ready to rearrange any conflict to fit this in at all costs. 'What's the date and time?'

'That's the thing, Eric, I'm afraid it's tomorrow.'

My heart sank. Checked in, on board my flight to LAX with an important partner awaiting my arrival, I could not delay my trip. Getting off the plane now just wasn't practical. Did I want to be in the room where it happened? You absolutely bet. I relayed my predicament to Tom, who, in true Tom fashion, was totally understanding.

'Don't worry,' he said. 'This is the beginning of something truly remarkable, not the end. Have a safe flight. Let's catch up when you're back in London. I'll fill you in on everything then.'

The call ended and I was filled with a mixture of emotions: disappointment at not being able to attend the meeting, but also something else. It was a feeling that you don't always experience as a Black entrepreneur with gargantuan ambitions to take down hegemony: *hope*.

Just before we were wheels up, I placed a last-minute call to Michael, my spouse, on whose counsel I rely for all decisions large and small. Michael's instincts are usually bang-on. He reassured me that there was no doubt much more in store, and I had to agree.

Even so, as I flew to California I had no idea Tom Ilube would present me with an even bigger opportunity on my return. And as for those emails from the headhunters? I graciously declined the offers. Some I never opened. Without fully grasping the enormity of that moment, I had already embarked on the mission of a lifetime.

Imagine, if you will – and as I did from across the Atlantic – the following scene: *A grey, early summer evening in a house in leafy south-west London. Under way is a secret meeting of top Black industry figures. Clearly, a fire has been lit for much-needed change and the conversation among the assorted group is robust.*

Although I couldn't attend, the way I imagined the meeting was very much how it played out. Tom told me that those in attendance had concluded that, common to all efforts to tackle systemic inequalities in their many forms, pooled resources were critical. This was the most direct way to bring about wholesale change at the pace we desired. In my absence, it was proposed that someone oversee the design of a sustainable funding source to underwrite change. After five years in the UK, I had a reputation for quickly scaling companies and selling them to the benefit of various stakeholders. When the group turned to me to bring an extraordinary concept to life, my desire for challenge and opportunity was fulfilled. We went to work. In a short amount of time, we proposed and established a sustainable model for a global, paradigm-changing movement – one which I believe will result in the world we want to see: an equitable one.

Within months, Impact X Capital Partners LLP was born.

As an investment firm which strategically targets investment and support for Black people and other under-represented founders of businesses, our efforts are focused in the UK and across Europe. We went forward with the mission of 'Funding the undiscovered, creating the extraordinary, impacting the world'. From the get-go, we were not lacking ambition.

Whenever I'm asked how embracing the unexpected applies to most businesses, I like to point out that opportunities often lie hidden in plain sight. They are missed because maybe you weren't paying attention or because you saw an opportunity that seemed too out of reach to do anything about. An incredibly profitable idea could be suggested during a conversation that nobody bothered to see as realistic. For example, there's a great story about how rapper/producer Dr Dre told the legendary record producer Jimmy Iovine that he'd been approached to develop his own line of sneakers. A fanatic for sound quality, Iovine told him to forget sneakers, they should make and sell speakers. Dre thought it over and went for it. He later said that he was motivated by the fact that the cheap earbuds used by most consumers were an affront to his recording artistry. Out of that one conversation, Dre and Iovine collaborated to develop the technology and marketing for the multi-billion-dollar brand of headphones known as Beats, which have disrupted the record industry and changed culture.

Those were the kinds of problem solvers and opportunity seekers who came from under-represented groups that Impact X uncovered in no time at all.

The power of capital

Try thinking like a VC and begin to observe how capital runs not just companies but the world. In a way, that's how I began. It's ironic that I didn't become a VC until 2018, decades into my professional journey, even though, as far back as 1984, at the age of eighteen, I suspected that venture capital could be an important tool for Black empowerment. In fact, a declaration of my interest in becoming a VC one day appeared in Greensboro's *News & Record*, our local newspaper, which at the time regularly featured profiles of high-school seniors. Our academic credentials were shared, and we were asked whom we admired, as well as our future plans. The truth is that at eighteen I had a few professional interests, some of which later materialized and some of which didn't. Given the Q&A format, there wasn't much space to discuss a multi-pronged career strategy. I didn't mention my plan to attend law school and possibly pursue a political career, maybe even an eventual run for Governor of North Carolina. Instead, when pressed to name my future dream job, my answer was definitive: 'Venture capitalist'.

There wouldn't have been much talk at school or at home about the viability of a career as a VC. However, as an avid reader of magazines like *Black Enterprise*, *Fortune* and *Business-Week*, I was hearing more and more about VCs. I liked the sound of investors who provide money (capital) to companies not yet fully developed and generally unattractive to institutional investors, but which have vast potential for high growth. VCs put money and time into these fledgling businesses in exchange for an equity stake in them, and I could see myself doing that.

VCs were not to be confused with the predatory, high-rolling *Wolf of Wall Street* types of this era – whose lawless schemes wound up defrauding investors of millions of dollars of their life savings. In the early 1980s, VCs were an emerging breed of investors. They were adventure-seeking risk takers who provided potent lessons for me. They bet against the status quo by finding companies with revolutionary or disruptive ideas that traditional money sources ignored or didn't value. They bet on

WE DON'T NEED PERMISSION

their own expertise for developing as well as guiding these organizations to hopefully become large-scale, durable, highly profitable companies. VCs looked for companies in places others didn't. Their superpowers, as I saw it, were in creating greater value for all stakeholders and, in ideal circumstances, changing the world in fundamental ways.

The idea of achieving profit *and* purpose struck an early positive chord with me – invest, make money and change the world. The way I saw it, venture capital's early-stage financing of new technologies was already changing the economic landscape via non-traditional pathways. Some recent successes included the launch of fast-growth companies in nascent fields like computers and biotech that folks were just beginning to understand, such as Apple and Genentech in 1980. These organizations would not only become multi-billion-dollar global firms with thousands, if not hundreds of thousands, of employees – at the time of writing, Apple's market cap is over $3 trillion – but their products would transform our lives, all within the span of a generation. In all this good news, unfortunately, there were two striking observations, confirmed to me by the reporting in *Black Enterprise*. The first was that very little of the money flowing from the VCs' coffers was being invested in Black-founded companies. And the second was that very few VCs were Black.

Why was this? Could it be a supply problem (lack of Black entrepreneurship and lack of Black interest in becoming VCs) or a demand problem (lack of funder desire to invest in Black entrepreneurs)? Was it because Black entrepreneurs didn't exist, were incapable of success, didn't have the ambition to innovate and build huge businesses? Or did white investors lack knowledge and/or a network that would provide access to the best companies coming from Black entrepreneurs? Did white investors harbour so much bias that they were incapable of seeing potential from Black sources? Or was capital being withheld?

I didn't get it. Why would VCs disregard an opportunity to make an investment that would change the status quo by questioning what was investable? Then again, VCs were still part of 'the system' – wearing the same blinkers of the age-old white-supremacist economic power structure. Did VCs not value or recognize the investment opportunities represented by Black and other minorities? Worse, I had to wonder: was the rise in the earning power of Black-owned business seen as an existential threat to the controllers of capital – both in the US and the UK, as well as in other economic powerhouses?

When the question of demand flashed through my head, I had to quickly remind myself of the stories about a handful of Black VCs whom I'd been following in publications like *Black Enterprise*. Ed Dugger, CEO of the Boston-based firm UNC Ventures, was already seen as a pioneer of impact investment, and was leading the way both by expanding business opportunities for entrepreneurs of colour and by proving the profitability of investing in Black-owned and/or -controlled companies. Another firm, Syncom Venture Partners in metro Washington, DC, was incubating companies in media and entertainment such as BET (Black Entertainment Television) and Radio One (later named Urban One), a fledgling US company with a woman of colour at the helm. Some VCs were clearly disrupting the field by backing the creators of some of the most successful Black brands in the world.

Why not more of them?

The proof of concept existed. The old system, I could see, was slowly being dismantled. At the same time, I knew that white supremacy was (and remains) insidious. So the resulting lack of demand for Black innovation was predictable. But what I hadn't considered back then was that too often Black entrepreneurs played into the oppressive system by waiting for permission. For many, a two-pronged strategy was being used poorly – first getting access to white money sources and then futilely trying to persuade these VCs to dismantle their white supremacy in order to make an investment. How could this be remedied?

At eighteen, I had few answers to these fundamental questions. What was clear to me, though, was that this was both a problem in need of a solution and a missed investment opportunity. I was also learning that when others don't recognize an issue, challenge or opportunity, it usually means that a market inefficiency – an asymmetry of information – exists. The silver lining, as I'd learned, was that investing on the right side of market inefficiencies creates extraordinary returns on investment. Before the internet, the pages of *Ebony* and *Black Enterprise* were filled with stories of business owners who had created large businesses due to market inefficiencies – in fact, those very magazines were themselves wildly successful market-inefficiency case studies, filling a large gap they'd spotted in the market.

This concept leads back to Step #1: *Embrace the unexpected.* You never know what you can discover flipping through the pages of the magazines you enjoy or scrolling through the social media of Black entrepreneurs in your areas of interest who have become wildly successful as well as impactful. My hunger to learn as much as possible rewarded me with stores of knowledge about how industry leaders, often unexpectedly, learned to harness the power of capital.

That said, the real story of how I was given a foundation in business goes back to my foremothers and fathers, starting with Litey Collins, a free Black in the time of slavery, the first of a long line of entrepreneurs and farmers in my family, and one of the earliest ancestors on my father's side whom I can document. So that's where I'm going to continue next.

2

MONEY IS A TOOL

Step #2: Engage in consistent and continuous acts of disruption

*If you always do what you always did, you will always
get what you always got.*

ATTRIBUTION UNKNOWN

*Personal disruption is the vehicle through which success
and economic growth travel.*

NICKY VERD, AUTHOR OF *DISRUPT YOURSELF OR BE DISRUPTED*

In 1959, Berry Gordy persuaded his family to give him a loan of $800. He wanted to take advantage of a market inefficiency in the corporate and white-run recording industry. The plan was to start an independent label, and he promised to deliver hit records from unknown, unproven Black talent in Detroit. Before very long, his team of artists, writers and producers had upended an industry and Motown music had been dubbed 'the Sound of Young America'.

Berry Gordy has a classic trajectory of an entrepreneur who understood the far-reaching application of Step #2: *Engage in consistent and continuous acts of disruption.*

I'm using the term 'disruption' in its more generic business context here, as a 2013 TechCrunch feature sought to define it. In essence, when a disruptor comes along with a new product, service or technology to serve a market that isn't being addressed, it's known as a 'new-market' disruption. If a disruptor comes along with an improvement to products of its kind already in the marketplace, that is known as 'low-end disruption'. Disruption can also refer to changing entire systems of doing business. Before Berry Gordy disrupted the music industry, the trade magazine *Billboard* charted sales and ranked the hits with two lists – one for pop and one for R&B. Most of the pop artists were assumed to be white and appealed to white audiences, while most of the R&B artists were thought to be Black and appealed to Black fans. Motown blurred the lines.

Gordy told the BBC in January 2019 that he'd wanted to produce music everyone would love – 'Black, white, Jew, gentile . . . '. He also told his A&R people to remember that pop stood for popular, so why not make Black music that was popular? The result was a cultural disruption of massive proportions.

To be disruptive does not necessarily mean to be destructive, as the term is sometimes misunderstood. It is to be extremely innovative in a non-traditional sense. If we look at Berry Gordy, we can see that the playbook for becoming an entrepreneurial disruptor begins by choosing to embrace disruption as a way of life, and doing it without the need for permission.

Not every disruptive venture pans out. Before Motown, Berry Gordy's first business venture was a record store specializing in releases by jazz artists – at a time when customers were only looking for the latest blues records, which he didn't carry. By the time Gordy realized he should probably stock the blues, it was too late and the record store went out of business.

Writing in his 1994 autobiography, *To Be Loved*, Gordy recalls the challenges of getting that first loan to start Motown. After banks turned him away, his last resort was to present his request for a loan to his family's savings club. The rule was that his parents and each of his seven siblings would need to vote unanimously to invest in his ambitious plan. Though his store had failed, he pointed out, he actually had a track record as a songwriter/producer and manager. One of his sisters was a holdout, only agreeing to the loan when he promised to pay it back with interest. He admired her management of the family investment. Gordy vowed to later hire her to help him grow his business. She did all that and more.

In the early 1960s, Gordy came up with the concept of the Motortown Revue – a bus tour with live shows featuring the roster's top artists like Smokey Robinson and the Miracles, Martha Reeves and the Vandellas, The Temptations, The Supremes, Marvin Gaye and Stevie Wonder. Brilliant for record-promoting, the shows succeeded at bringing Black and white fans together under one roof. Yet this was still a time when Black artists were barred from performing in certain segregated venues, and even banned in some Southern cities. After one engagement, shots were fired at the bus. In contrast, on their first trip to the UK, Gordy and his Motown artists were embraced everywhere they went. This turned into a cultural exchange that shook both sides of the Atlantic.

It's common knowledge that The Beatles were heavily influenced by Black/R&B music, and especially by Motown artists and songwriters. The song 'This Boy' is said to have been John Lennon's attempt to write and sing like Smokey Robinson.

Earlier, The Beatles covered Smokey's 'You Really Got A Hold On Me'. And Motown artists covered several Beatles songs, including Stevie Wonder's Grammy-nominated 1970 hit 'We Can Work It Out' – considered by industry historians to be the best Beatles cover ever. (Others, however, would disagree: Paul McCartney, for one, calls Marvin Gaye's cover of 'Yesterday' his favourite.)

Black Enterprise – founded by Earl Graves in 1970 – remains the leading publication covering Black business in the USA and helped to document Motown's meteoric rise. By the time Berry Gordy sold the label in 1988, Motown had been the highest revenue generator on *Black Enterprise*'s top business list for all but five of the years it was an independent company, having altered the recording industry and empowered future generations of Black producers and music moguls – from Prince to Rihanna and from Jay-Z to Missy Elliott.

Lessons learned from Berry Gordy

It's easy to borrow from a lifelong disruptor like Berry Gordy.

Think about Lewis Hamilton, for example. In July 2021 the *Guardian* featured a story about Hamilton's unexpected activism. Formula One's most successful racing-car driver in history, Hamilton is also the only Black star in the sport. The article, written by the journalist, author and Black activist Gary Younge, focused on Hamilton's journey off-track in becoming increasingly vocal about his Black identity and issues of importance to people of colour in the UK. Hamilton had shown solidarity with Black Lives Matter by raising a clenched fist and by taking a knee during pre-race ceremonies to protest racial violence. Then, in the wake of the murder of George Floyd, he went further. Despite a backlash of condemnation in racing circles and threats of violence, he chose to deliberately create waves, using his fame, platform and money to campaign against white supremacy.

Younge, writing about the impact Hamilton has had on fans and on his sport, compared Hamilton's actions to an earth-shaking moment during the 1968 Mexico City Olympics when the American athletes John Carlos and Tommie Smith raised Black Power fists as they stood on the medal podium. Carlos later told Younge that as soon as he gave himself permission to defy the powers that be, his first thought was: 'The shackles have been broken. And they won't ever be able to put shackles on John Carlos again. Because what had been done couldn't be taken back . . . The greatest problem is we are afraid to offend our oppressors.'

When I read the words of John Carlos more than fifty years later, they reverberated for me and helped me better understand the change that takes place when we are willing to disrupt and challenge the status quo. One great thing about dismantling systemic oppression is that it also undoes the benefits that oppressors accrue from the system, the privileges they sometimes recklessly enjoy.

In this way, I learned two critical lessons from Motown's iconic success. First, if others weren't seeing what I was seeing, then something could be done about it. Second, significant investment return was possible with relatively small initial capital infusions.

There are other aspects to Berry Gordy's journey worth underscoring. He was, by all accounts, a successful second act. It's reassuring to know that even if your first venture isn't a hit and you don't become an overnight sensation or make it big straight out of the gate, you are still learning important lessons that will serve you in the long run.

I was not in a hurry to enter my own field of endeavour. That may explain why, even though I expected to become a VC one day, it would still be decades before I would do that for a living. Was my time wasted? Not at all. I was getting better prepared for battle (and it has been a battle), first by completing my university education, then law school and building a network.

I had a lot to learn. Granted, completing higher education is not a prerequisite for disruptive mega-success. University degrees haven't been needed by people such as Lewis Hamilton (#8 on *Forbes*'s list of highest-paid athletes of 2021) or Pat McGrath, considered the most influential make-up artist in the world as well as being the Black female founder of Pat McGrath Labs (valued at $1 billion). Bill Gates and Mark Zuckerberg likewise left university early to get started disrupting on their terms.

Then again, in the Collins family – as in many families of colour in many countries – the desire to give your kids the best education possible was and is seen as one of the most important investments you can make in their future. Part of that intense desire has to do with the many times and ways in which we have been denied access to opportunities and were not given permission to prosper because of a lack of 'pedigree'. But it runs even deeper for many. When you look back at history to when enslaving Black people was legal – or, in some places, not legal but allowed – it was against the law to teach enslaved people to read and write. Educating any enslaved person was punishable by fines and imprisonment, or worse. Literacy was seen as a dreaded gateway to Black empowerment, not to mention to freedom itself. The teaching of financial literacy to enslaved people was no doubt even more threatening to the status quo of white supremacy.

Enter Litey Collins, my entrepreneurial ancestor, first identified in Virginia in the early 1700s. We know this history thanks to the collaborative effort of many of my Collins relatives who decided to research our family tree – having been inspired by Alex Haley's novel *Roots*, published in 1976 and made into an internationally beloved TV mini-series the following year.

Our roots can be traced all the way back to 1724, when the name Will Collins appeared in a court document in Northampton County in Virginia (then still a British colony). Will was most likely an enslaved Black man, but when Litey showed up a short time later in census records he was presumably a free Negro, as he was listed with both first and last names. Customarily, in this period enslaved people were identified only by a first name, as property, no different from a description of a particular horse or cow.

When Litey Collins lived and worked in Northampton County, the existence of Black landowners and business owners was rare. As a farmer and small business owner, Litey was among the disruptive few. He literally built his business from the ground up. The Collins family descendants who stayed in Virginia generally employed the same strategies Litey had begun – farming, landowning and capital accumulation. Many generations stayed in Virginia, leaving only to pursue higher learning but then returning to where they had been raised to grow their businesses and families.

This explains why getting a good education was the gospel coded in my DNA, modelled for me through my parents' and relatives' examples, and reinforced by the communities in which I lived.

Of course, not everyone receives the same encouragement or opportunity. Increasingly, folks struggle to afford the cost of university or find they have to get out into the working world to support themselves and other family members. I have always honoured the sacrifices of the generations who deferred their own ambitions to make sure younger members of the community could afford to complete their education. More and more,

I'm grateful for the premium placed on higher education in my upbringing.

Given all of that, I was alarmed by a BBC report in September 2021 stating that university offers of admission in the UK are less likely for diverse applicants – even for those with top grades. Statistics like these have mobilized activists, thankfully, including my friend and colleague Ric Lewis, Chair of Impact X, whose Black Heart Foundation provides scholarships and funding support for scores of university and advanced-degree students.

The moral of the story is not that the privilege of a great formal education, on its own, guarantees Black business success. Rather, that investment in education and experience should be seen as part of the strategy to accelerate and amplify Black entrepreneurship. We can all agree that in any competitive arena, a person with solid assets such as quality schooling and applicable experiences is at an advantage. Still, an even greater advantage comes with the personal choice to actively apply your accumulated expertise to continually disrupt in small and big ways. Those collected assets increase your commitment to see and do differently. This strengthens your permission to be a self-determiner. And self-determination is a key ingredient to empowerment.

Without self-permission, options for economic advancement are limited. Not only that: without the financial or other means to break open the cages of the systems that restrict you, the possibilities for disruption may be stunted.

To be clear, my version of self-determination doesn't mean the go-it-alone, rugged individualist approach. I'm talking more about self-empowerment that means you get to be your own person. You have the power to set your goals, invest your own resources – including money, of course – but also to leverage the social capital that comes from community support, partners, allies and investors.

You don't have to disrupt all on your own. If our shared history tells us anything, it's that we follow in the footsteps of Black entrepreneurs who overcame overwhelming odds. Those stories matter because they remind us of who we are, what we can accomplish and what remains to be done.

Black business history matters

The fact that people of colour, in the UK, the US and across several continents, do not know our individual, familial or collective histories is regrettable. The fact that we do not know our history as business owners is a great impediment. It is, unfortunately, as the white-supremacist power structure would have it. That's one more argument for the benefits of disrupting early and often in your life – by looking at how those who came before you gave themselves permission to flourish despite all obstacles. In light of widespread right-wing efforts to demonize the teaching of Black history, it's more important than ever to preserve and internalize it.

My business history has its roots in the role slavery played in creating a system that has impacted Black businesses ever since. Black enslavement was never legally embedded in the British Isles either constitutionally (Britain has no constitution) or through case law – as it was, deeply embedded, elsewhere in the British Empire – even if slavery was not outlawed. In Britain enslaving people was not strictly race-based. However, legal tools were aggressively used in the British colonies to erect oppressive and inequitable systems targeting Black people. For centuries British bonding, indenturing and serfdom were legal tools used to ensure that people were the property of, and forced to obey, another. In 1569, during the reign of Queen Elizabeth I, the Cartwright legal case, along with subsequent court cases, reaffirmed that the enslavement of people did not exist under English law. This did not keep enslavement from functioning in Britain. Enslaved people lived in Britain until about 1800. Custom and beliefs about white superiority were very effective in ensuring that Black people had a uniquely oppressed status in Britain. Laws differed in Britain's American colonies, starting in the mid-seventeenth century, and the terrible effects have been fought ever since.

The moment when it happened is revealed in a 1653 court case concerning one Anthony Johnson in Virginia's Northampton County – the same place where, seventy years later, my ancestor Will Collins first showed up in colonial records. Johnson was said to be North America's first known free Negro – as Litey Collins and any Black person not enslaved was then classified. Johnson was also one of the first documented Black people to be a landowner in America.

The social class system imported from England was one of the building blocks of the infrastructure of American white supremacy. This would later influence the type of Black businesses first developed by formerly enslaved people, most of which related to agriculture, craftmanship like blacksmithing and sewing, laundering, food preparation, childcare and housekeeping. Because these businesses entailed jobs that traditionally a white gentleman of means would not do, they were not considered disruptive to the white economic status quo.

No doubt it was reluctance to perform such menial tasks that caused Anthony Johnson, a landed gentleman of colour with a profit-generating farm of more than 250 acres, to depend on the labour of five indentured servants. When one of his servants, also Black, decided to go and work for a neighbour, Johnson sued, claiming the man was indentured to him for life. The court agreed, making the enslavement of people legal (and also allowing free Negros to be owners of enslaved people).

The law made it easier for anyone with an indentured servant to claim ownership of that person and enslave them for life – even with a contract limiting their term of service.

Although the law didn't suddenly equate 'Black' with life-long servitude, it stepped on to that slippery slope conjoining class, status and race. Interestingly, as a non-white free person Anthony Johnson had additional legal rights because he owned land. Status in the colonies followed the English feudal system, with the aristocracy owning land or having been gifted land by the monarchy and the serfs being mere agricultural workers. The Anthony Johnson case is also significant because it reminds us that money can be leveraged for good and for bad.

Over a century after the case of Anthony Johnson, when the US Constitution was being written, landowning was no longer an assurance of equality under the law for non-white citizens. The right to vote was in fact guaranteed to landowners – but only to male landowners, and then only to white male ones. The Promised Land of equality for all American citizens and the right to life, liberty and the pursuit of happiness were still in the distant future.

Conventional wisdom has long asserted that the British were more enlightened when it came to abolishing the enslavement of Black people. The trade of enslaved people was abolished as early as 1807, in the reign of King George III, and in 1833 the holding of slaves was made illegal. That was three decades before Emancipation took place in the US. More credit was given to leaders in the British Parliament with the 1837 decision to have the whole nation shoulder the astronomical cost of abolishing slaveholding in the UK and across most of its colonies and tax-paying territories. In stark terms, that's billions of pounds of debt by today's standards, which was only paid off in 2015.

Some people assume the payments went to freed enslaved people for their years of unpaid labour. Shockingly, the reality is that the money was paid to enslavers to compensate for their loss of property. This story was recently dramatized in *The Whip*, a play by the British Black journalist and playwright Juliet Gilkes Romero. It is also told by Professor David Olusoga, who hosted the BBC documentary *Britain's Forgotten Slave Owners*, which was based on Professor Catherine Hall's research demonstrating how enslavers – from widows to royalty – were compensated for their property losses while ex-enslaved people were allotted no reparations.

Whenever Black history is discussed in the UK, many folks seem surprised to learn, as stated in a special 1981 edition of *History Today*, that 'Black people have been living in Britain since at least Roman times.' The article provided several little-known examples, including the African legionary and joker, 'famous among buffoons', who in AD 210, outside Carlisle, was noted for making fun of Emperor Septimius. 'Blue Men', as Black enslaved people were described by the Irish in AD 862, were brought ashore by Vikings who had conducted raids in North Africa and Spain. And in the early 1500s, records from the Scottish court at Holyrood mention members of what seems to have been a Black community – a number of men, at least two women and a father with a child at court.

It should be equally unsurprising that, for almost as long as Black people have lived in the UK, there have been successful business owners of colour. In 2012 *New African Magazine* published an article entitled 'History of Success for African Entrepreneurs in UK', with examples going back at least two hundred years. Examples include Olaudah Equiano, a leading member of the Sons of Africa abolitionist movement, whose memoir was published in 1789 and was reprinted several times, translated into various foreign languages and even published in the US at a time when enslavement was rife. Then there's George Africanus, who came from Sierra Leone as a three-year-old enslaved boy. After securing his own freedom, he apprenticed at a brass foundry and made his way to Nottingham in 1780, soon establishing his own employment agency. He married, bought property and became 'enormously prosperous'. Made famous by his eponymous Pablo Fanque Circus Royal, founded in 1841, the performer and businessman, born in Norwich, is less well known for being of African descent. Fanque toured for thirty years, built performance venues and was immortalized in 1967 by the Beatles' song 'Being For The Benefit Of Mr Kite'.

Perhaps the most famous example of successful Black immigration to the UK, celebrated in an October 2021 retrospective by www.blackhistory.org.uk, is the story of an eighteenth-century orphan, Charles Ignatius Sancho (1729–80) – born aboard a slave ship – who arrived in England at the age of two, having been sold into enslavement in New Granada, a Spanish colony. Gifted to three sisters, he became a 'servant for life' to them, but at the age of eighteen he ran away to another household. There he continued to work as a butler but was also encouraged for his talents in music, writing and wordsmithing. In time, Sancho left service and spent his next years as a disruptor extraordinaire, first as a shopkeeper, catering to an artistic clientele, all the while making a name for himself as an essayist, playwright, composer, author and publisher, then as an influential abolitionist – a key voice in the movement to abolish the slave trade and outlaw all forms of the enslavement of Black people. A wealthy public figure and estate owner, Sancho was a popular British celebrity who, in 1774, by virtue of being male and a homeowner, became the first known Black British citizen to vote. This was remarkable when you consider the time and the context. Born into an inhuman system where permission was required for every aspect of his life, Sancho permanently removed that yoke, so much so that he managed to disrupt social norms that could have relegated him to minor endeavours.

The lesson history teaches is that the power to disrupt relies on self-permission, especially when the systems around you will not grant permission. You need not be pigeonholed into a predetermined calling. So, when you begin to think like an investor in your own right, investing in yourself and causes you care about, you, like Berry Gordy, may unleash a disruptive force you don't even know you have.

This point was reinforced every which way for me as I was growing up.

My father, my first and most influential role model (and investor), was the brilliant youngest of nine children. A Virginian through and through, Dad descended from that long line of land-working entrepreneurs. He drew from everything he'd learned growing up on the farm to forge a disruptive career for himself in science, education, research and business.

For families like ours, land was leverage, even in leaner periods. On a basic level, your productivity and your financial means endow you with the ability to share your harvest with others. Your money is a tool of empowerment to the rest of the family and wider community. And while sharing and passing on wealth has long been the way with white UK families, it has often been a much tougher proposition for families of colour.

This stark contrast is rooted in the past, yet remains the case today. A government report (ons.gov.uk) in November 2020 noted that, as of 2018, the median wealth in Black families was £34,000, yet it was eight times that much in white ones. The gap can be assumed to have worsened with the pandemic's economic toll on Britain's Black households. One key difference lies in the fact that white families tend to own homes plus inherit wealth, and over time, as we know, wealth begets more wealth. Intergenerational inherited wealth is much less common for Black families. Many seeking to address racial wealth inequality urge efforts to invest in savings to be left as inheritances. There's nothing wrong with that. However, my view is that, as a tool for empowerment, money is better put to use in the form of investments when younger family members most need it – whether it's for buying property or for building businesses of their own. Instead of tucking your hard-earned savings away to pass on after you die, why not get the leveraging started on behalf of your loved ones right now?

My father – who began his teaching career at Tuskegee Institute in Alabama, where my siblings and I were born – had gone to Rutgers University in New Jersey to complete his master's and PhD, which focused on the science of farm crops. My mother's family also prized education and were as business-minded, in their way, as the Collins family members were. My mother's grandmother, influential in the close-knit Black community of the Pennsylvania township where Adeline grew up, had prospered in real estate. My mother's father was a gospel singer, and her grandfather was in law enforcement. For my mother – who received an undergrad degree in music education and later went on to earn her master's in counselling from NYU – the influence of strong Black women was a running theme in her life. But it made her an adventurer who believed that occasional disruptions to everyday routines were opportunities for enrichment. Adeline Davis Collins applied that value to her own life and then to ours.

My parents were the original early VCs of my life. They invested in my ambitious undertakings, in my education and enrichment, my growth and, eventually, my entrepreneurship. When I made decisions that went against the traditional grain, my mother and father would hear me out. Sometimes, when they did invest their money, individually and together, they would offer advice and guidance as hands-on VCs often do.

While you may not have had this kind of guidance given to you, the lesson here is that you can learn to give it to yourself and even to others – to support members of your family, and of course your own children. Part of the joy of being consistently disruptive is giving yourself permission to reinvent the script of your life. As your success follows – and it will – you then can similarly pay it forward.

My mother was a firm believer that everyone had their own style of learning and growing. She honestly would have made a superb CEO of a large corporation and, in some ways, she was CEO of the 'Collins Corporation' entity. When I say that both my parents were akin to VCs who take big risks on investments, I mean my parents' parenting involved risk. They wanted us to have opportunities of our own and fight for others to have the same. Action and hustle were our watchwords.

A decade of protest

When my parents married in 1962 and moved to Alabama, the decision put them at ground zero for the US civil rights movement already raging in the country. As British and American students alike learn at school, the match had been lit in 1955 when Rosa Parks refused to give up her seat on the bus for a white passenger, a disruptive, irrevocable act that led to the Montgomery bus boycott. In June 1963, Governor George Wallace stood in a doorway of the University of Alabama to prevent two Black students from registering. In September that year came the bombing of Birmingham's 16th Street Baptist Church, which killed four little girls, one of whom, no known relation to us, was named Addie Mae Collins.

Two years later, on 7 March 1965, came Bloody Sunday during the March from Selma to Montgomery and the violent assault on marchers – an assembly of more than six hundred that included the late John Lewis, who was nearly killed by a state trooper on the Edmund Pettus Bridge.

During these years, as I would later learn in much greater depth, a civil rights movement in the UK was afoot – almost in parallel to the one in the US – complete with disruptors who used their voices to effect change. One important leader, somewhat forgotten, was Paul Stephenson, who in 1963 (eight years after Rosa Parks refused to give up her seat) led a boycott of the Bristol Omnibus Company (BOC) and their buses. In the UK at the time discrimination was still legal and the BOC, though in need of qualified workers, had refused to hire Black and Asian people. In Bristol, Stephenson employed an evolving playbook and convened supporters of civil rights, members of Black church congregations and organizations to join in the four-month-long boycott. Finally, BOC relented and changed its policy.

The boycott had disrupted the system, using money as a tool. Two years later, the British Parliament passed the Race Relations Act 1965, which banned racial discrimination in public places and made job promotion on the grounds of 'colour, race, or ethnic or national origins' a crime. Three years later, the 1968 Race Relations Act was passed and went further, outlawing acts of discrimination within employment, housing and advertising.

Even with the progress that protest achieved in the UK, the legal gains were not enough to prevent the lasting damage from what became known as the Windrush Scandal. Some of the details would only come to light in 2017, as shocking as they are tragic. The story begins in June 1948 with the arrival of the *Empire Windrush* at Tilbury Docks in Essex. The ship had brought almost a thousand West Indian immigrants to the UK, setting off a state-sanctioned discriminatory policy of persecution of immigrants of colour arriving from Caribbean nations in the British Commonwealth. For the next twenty-five years, hundreds of Black Britons were unjustly denied legal rights, detained for no reason and often deported. The system operated without safeguards, somehow falsely labelling these arrivals 'illegal'. Ironically, these 'illegals' had been invited by the UK government to help with the post-Second-World-War rebuild of the UK. As a result of government persecution, the Windrush generation, after decades of being in the UK, lost the usual access of rights to housing, banking, healthcare, even drivers' licences. Denied proper ID, many faced immigration detention, were deprived of the ability to travel elsewhere, or were eventually sent back to places they hadn't seen since they were children. In 2018 a review was ordered, but much of it became mired in a backlog of cases and disputes. Few of the oppressive policies were subsequently changed.

As a child of the 1960s, not to mention the son of Henry and Adeline, I grew up believing that such injustice – even though it might not personally touch me – was never acceptable. I also grew up in close proximity to leaders who used all the tools available to confront the injustice. Though I have few memories of Tuskegee, the fact that I was born there allowed me a lasting connection to its founder, Booker T. Washington, the author, orator and advisor to several US presidents who disruptively saw Black entrepreneurship as the main avenue towards achieving equality. Tuskegee University, founded in 1881, represented the cradle of Black scholarship, not to mention that it was famous for the Tuskegee airmen whose bravery and sacrifice in the Second World War, flying sorties in Europe and North Africa, was legendary. It was meaningful to me as well that at Tuskegee my father worked in the lab founded by George Washington Carver, a definitive disruptor who needed no permission to upend the status quo. Carver was not just a heroic plant scientist who pioneered crop rotation, but a teacher who showed rural and poor farmers how to bring forth more bountiful harvests without pesticides. In the process he solved the global issue of soil depletion and transformed the reputation of the lowly peanut.

Around the same time that future Motown artists Lionel Richie and the Commodores were students at Tuskegee, my father left academia to work for a Swiss chemical company. That act of disruption took us to the leafy suburbs of New York City for a few years.

It was there, one day, that I first experienced up close how money can be a tool for disruption. Adeline Collins, the disruptor-in-chief in our household, announced to me and my siblings that afternoon, 'Let's go. We have something to do.' She explained that we were going to join forces with a good friend and neighbour to picket our local grocery store. At all of seven years old, I lent my boy soprano voice to our tiny assembled crew as we chanted, 'Don't shop at the A&P! Because they have no Black ENERGY!'

In Alabama, Rosa Parks and the ensuing Montgomery boycott proved that economic pressure could bring down segregation on buses. That's the kind of action it took for the power structure to tilt. Instead of accepting the status quo, Black consumers were increasingly flexing their economic muscles by shopping Black or by withholding money from unsupportive companies. Recall how this strategy was resurrected after the murder of George Floyd. Such was the backdrop for my later efforts, which met with varying degrees of success – from advocating to accelerate Princeton's decision to divest from apartheid South Africa to occupying the Dean's office at Harvard Law School to demand that Black women professors be hired immediately.

These were all acts of disruption, some with high stakes and some not so much. The lesson was always not to turn away from knowing about unpleasantness – whether racial violence, poll taxes, the perils and inequities of being in the racially seg-regated South (commonly called the Jim Crow South), or the inequities that existed in the North as well. It was our respon-sibility to know about the wrongs being done and it was up to us to do something to challenge them. That is, to take purpose-ful action.

Taking action can be as simple as cancelling a subscription to a service provided by a company known for supporting pol-iticians who use hate speech. Or you can go further and launch your own company and disrupt the marketplace. Both options require the use of money as a tool.

The evolution of modern Black-owned business

My decision to follow my brother Bradley to Princeton – I arrived as he entered his last year there – wasn't a departure from tradition for me. The culture shock most of us experience when we leave home for schooling was fortunately eased. I was all the more fortunate to be exposed to students not only of different national, ethnic, religious and cultural backgrounds – plus students who identified as LGBTQ – but also from hugely diverse economic backgrounds. Future First Lady Michelle Obama, who had grown up on the South Side of Chicago with parents who scrimped and saved to pay for her education, was my brother's classmate. There were fellow Black students who would not have been able to attend without full financial assis-tance, as well as other fellow Black students who had trust funds, private jets and families with unparalleled access to power.

Almost everyone warned me about the demanding thesis required of every graduating senior in order to demonstrate mastery of their major field of study. When the time came in early 1988, I didn't have to go looking far for my topic – Black entrepreneurship! If my belief that Black economic empowerment was the missing component needed to disrupt white supremacy, here was my chance to support that very thesis by looking at the ways that Black-owned businesses had evolved in the last half of the twentieth century, both traditionally and disruptively. The three entrepreneurs I studied were John H. Johnson of Johnson Publishing Company, Inc., Michael R. Hollis of Air Atlanta, and Reginald Lewis of Beatrice International Foods. Each case study is a slice of history and provides lessons as relevant today as they were when I first looked at them over thirty years ago.

John H. Johnson (1918–2005) represents the quintessence of the successful, traditional Black entrepreneur. Publishing magazines and books, in addition to owning a syndicated television programme, two radio stations and a cable television contract, Johnson built an empire that dominated the traditional Black-targeted communications industry. The company dwarfed its competitors throughout its eighty-seven-year history (1942–2019), with its main publications earning sales in excess of $180 million per year by the late 1980s. In 1987, *Black Enterprise* ranked Johnson Publishing at number one in its Top 100 Black companies. FYI, another Black business in a traditional sector, music, was number two on the list that year. Guess who? Berry Gordy's Motown.

As an employee of the Black-owned Supreme Life Insurance Company, in 1942 John Johnson had the disruptive idea of publishing a magazine for Black readers that resembled the tone and style of the general-interest monthly *Reader's Digest*, founded in 1922 and so popular that by the 1960s it would have an international readership of 23 million. During the Second World War, the average income for many Black households was on the upswing and growing numbers were investing in insurance policies. Johnson knew that Black policyholders were also readers and might want to subscribe to *Negro Digest*, as he would call it. As many as 1.2 million African Americans served the war effort and Johnson believed that covering their contribution as well as writing about other Black success stories would be widely embraced. When he was turned down for a bank loan, his mother borrowed $500, using her furniture as collateral, and invested in her son's enterprise.

Using a list of names of Supreme Life Insurance Company policyholders, Johnson next created a group of charter subscribers who paid $2 to receive *Negro Digest*. I used a similar Founding Membership model for the initial investors in Impact X (a piece of advice: borrow from the best). Of the 20,000 people Johnson contacted, 3,000 subscriptions were received, a good conversion rate, and Johnson Publishing Company was born. *Negro Digest* lasted nine years, although by the early 1950s when its publication stopped, the major staple of Johnson Publishing – *Ebony* (also launched in 1945) – had become a dominant monthly. *Ebony*, the first glossy magazine targeted at Black America, was also the first periodical to exclusively, glamorously cover Black VIPs – entertainers, celebrities, athletes and public figures from business, politics and even religion. Every story brought the motivational message that the reader too had the ability to achieve the same kind of success.

As reported in 2002, at its height *Ebony* reached a total of 1.8 million annual subscribers with an overall readership of 12 million. In 1951, Johnson Publishing added *Jet* to its communications arsenal. A smaller pocket-book-sized weekly magazine, *Jet* was so named (before there was a digital platform, where it lives today) because John Johnson wanted to reflect the fast-moving speed of information; the shorter articles mirrored readers' shorter attention spans. *Jet* didn't just cover the 'who's who' in Black culture, it also became a model for influencing and driving that culture. The marketing slogan 'If it wasn't in *Jet*, it didn't happen' gave it that buzz-worthy must-read appeal, so much so that it eventually reached nearly 50 per cent of the adult Black population of the US.

In 1957 *Ebony*'s success inspired Johnson to sponsor a nationwide touring fashion show featuring the most beautiful, charismatic Black models – wearing haute couture. The only hitch in its massive appeal was a constant search for cosmetics made for women of all skin tones. And so, in 1973, Johnson launched Fashion Fair Cosmetics, a product line that dominated the Black beauty and glamour market for decades. Its success was amplified thanks to Johnson's choice to freely advertise his brand in his own magazines. Lines like Pat McGrath Labs and Fenty, which rely heavily on fashion, learned a thing or two from the success of Fashion Fair.

While the growth of Johnson's media empire into radio and television was impressive, I wonder how much further the family-run company could have diversified and expanded. Could Johnson Publishing have started a Radio One/Urban One and/or a BET? Could the corporation have gone further, as Motown did, to cross over and disrupt the global mainstream marketplace? Was availability of capital at critical junctures the culprit, and did vision play a part?

Possibly, but if you are contemplating a startup that won't require a lot of money to get off the ground, John Johnson has left you a powerful playbook. Two takeaways will serve you in good stead. First, Johnson Publications showed the world what it means not just to serve an underserved market but to *superserve* it. That's what *Shark Tank* investor Daymond John did when he first launched a hip-hop influenced line of apparel, calling it FUBU, or For Us By Us. He superserved Black hip-hop fans who were already disrupting culture and he got LL COOL J to wear one of his hats while making a Gap commercial, which soon exploded his brand into a global phenomenon. A potent recipe to get you going is to start with a knowledge of your audience, your customers. The second and most important lesson you can take and apply from Johnson is that he did not accept the status quo's depiction of people of colour and told a counter-narrative – on glossy paper in sumptuous, aspirational images.

Johnson and his family-run organization turbocharged a traditional market strategy utilized by entrepreneurs for centuries. It may not be as disruptive to precisely follow an approach that's been tried and proven before. But then again, you can always improve upon what's been done. This was what was Air Atlanta's strategy.

Created in 1984, Air Atlanta, a commuter airline, was the brainchild of Michael Hollis (1954–2012), an Atlanta-based entrepreneur. The carrier was the first Black-owned jet airline in the US. Its birth was prompted by the opportunity which government deregulation of the American airline industry created: competitive pricing and more air routes opened. Using Atlanta's Hartsfield International Airport as its hub, by 1987 Air Atlanta was flying 3,000,000 people annually.

Air Atlanta served the needs of Atlanta's business community not only by providing transportation to and from other centres of business, but also by offering superior services at bargain prices. Perks included private waiting lounges with free drinks and snacks, plus courtesy telephones and newspapers. On the plane, patrons found unusual comfort after passenger spaces were reduced from 125 to 88. Mixed drinks and wine were complimentary. Gourmet meals were served on china during flights. These frills were all provided at economy rates.

Hollis built his success in part thanks to partnering effectively with other airlines, particularly Pan American, Delta and Eastern Airlines. Air Atlanta offered more to customers by cutting wages for employees – not something that endeared the startup to workers, but it was a cost-effective strategy for getting the business going.

Despite its promise, Air Atlanta failed as a business venture. On 3 April 1987 the airline filed for Chapter 11 bankruptcy protection from its creditors, bringing to an end an enterprise that had grown exponentially in a short amount of time.

How had a company that had flown so high fallen so far?

Timing was the big culprit. Air Atlanta was conceived at a point in the early 1980s when deregulation of the industry made launching an air travel business possible. Yet the opportunity also spurred competition like never before. Established airlines fought the market encroachment of small carriers by slashing ticket prices. By the time Air Atlanta even entered the picture, over twelve deregulation-fuelled airlines had filed for bankruptcy protection. The task of making a profit proved impossible for Air Atlanta because of the limited number of routes the airline was permitted to fly – due to restrictions on terminal space – and the amount of passengers that a fleet of just ten aircraft could fly. Hollis had access to those who could open doors for more investment capital to expand his fleet. However, by the time he secured that investment, it was a case of too little, too late.

Timing can wipe out all disadvantages or advantages. Air Atlanta had benefited early on from investments that came at a time when many financial institutions offered 'social responsibility' funds – or token funds set aside for minority concerns. Started under President Lyndon Johnson in the mid-1960s, these funds were expanded over the next decade but by the 1980s had come under attack in conservative circles led by

President Ronald Reagan. In a parallel narrative, in the UK at this time, under Margaret Thatcher, there was also a dismantling of these kinds of social progammes due to a massive scaling-back of public services. Besides being stigmatized as money earmarked for charity – implying money and losses that can be written off – 'responsibility' funding tends to be relatively small and doesn't always attract other investors seeking significant financial returns to add more capital. With token support there's almost an expectation of failure or an assumption that Black entrepreneurs can't deliver more than a token return.

A significant issue for Air Atlanta was that Hollis had never run an airline before. He hadn't practised the art of disruption until he was in flight – literally. In contrast, in 1987, when Reginald Lewis put together a proposal for the acquisition of Beatrice International, he had learned mighty lessons from an earlier deal that had also, in effect, given him a proof of concept. In 1983, Lewis had established the TLC Group – aka The Lewis Company – as a venture capital firm. The following year, Lewis put together a deal to buy the century-old McCall Pattern Company from Esmark, Inc., paying $1 million in equity of his own money and a $24 million loan from First Boston Corporation.

Already this was a non-traditional, risky deal. Lewis had to quickly refurbish an old company in a creaky sector that mainly made sewing patterns – at a time when the market for such products was in steep decline. Now that more women were entering the workforce, fewer had time for or interest in sewing their own clothing or home soft furnishings. Ignoring the naysayers, Lewis homed in on the positive attributes of the company – a significant brand franchise, strong management and a healthy cash flow. He immediately remade McCall by developing a new product line of home knit patterns, and then,

WE DON'T NEED PERMISSION

timing being everything, entered the Asian market by exporting patterns to China. He then went completely non-traditional by branching into greeting cards, using McCall's vast distribution network. Earnings soared to a historical high of $14 million. Now he had a calling card – the fact that he had just led McCall to some of the best fiscal years in its hundred-year history.

Lewis then began looking for a much more ambitious deal. Once he set his sights on Beatrice International, finding the right investor or partners was daunting. But, in July 1987, Lewis made a deal with a British company, the John Crowther Group, for them to buy McCall for $63 million in cash, in addition to absorbing $32 million in debt in the acquisition. Meaning that Crowther purchased McCall for more than $90 million and that TLC made a $90 million return on a $1 million investment.

A short time later, Lewis was interviewed about the McCall sale by the journalist Alfred Edmond, Jr, who recalled the conversation in a 2012 article in *Black Enterprise*. Edmond remembered asking the most important question of his thirty-year career when he looked at Lewis and said, in effect, 'Well, what do you plan to do next?'

For a beat, Lewis just stared at him. Was it disbelief that Edmond had the nerve to ask that question? Or was he impressed? Lewis clarified, acknowledging that the sale of McCall was not the biggest thing he was ever going to do. No other reporter had bothered to ask him about his next venture. Edmond interpreted that response to mean that if Lewis was white, the McCall sale would be seen as just the start of bigger things to come. But as a Black businessman, his coup with one big deal was seen in mainstream circles as the height of his potential success – the 'pinnacle of his achievement – or rather, over-achievement'. Edmond knew from his own observations as a Black business journalist that Lewis at forty-four years old was never going to rest on his laurels. What was next, then?

Lewis refused to show his cards, though he did say that what he had up his sleeve was going to be ten times bigger than the McCall sale.

Give yourself permission to borrow from Reginald Lewis – for all those times you may have been underestimated or expected to have reached the limits of your aspiration and abilities. His declaration is the definition of disruption. You have that same capacity in you.

In the summer of 1987, TLC was cash-rich as Lewis prepared to enter an agreement to make the biggest leveraged buyout of an overseas operation in history. Would Beatrice, a conglomerate headquartered in Chicago, sell to him? The firm manufactured snacks, beverages and other food and household items, and comprised sixty-four companies in thirty-one countries, including making ice cream in Italy and crisps in Ireland. In 1986, Beatrice reported $2.5 billion in sales.

After some close calls, TLC's bid was accepted. The final price was $985 million. This price was well below the premium of the firm, but because of debt Beatrice International needed capital quickly. They'd found it difficult to run a 'far-flung' company – something I would come to know intimately later on in my role as a corporate executive in charge of divisions in distant, even remote locations.

However, Lewis's plan was not to run the sixty-four-part firm. Almost instantly, he sold three divisions of Beatrice for $430 million but he retained Beatrice's European core because it accounted for the majority of sales. Many US investment firms sat up and took notice, apparently unaware that Europe held unique, promising potential. In another example of underestimation, the prospect of a global conglomerate headed by a Black business mogul and enriched by its European division was shocking.

Lewis financed his deal in four parts – with the last part

coming from Michael Milken and his firm Drexel Burnham Lambert, which sold high-yield or junk bonds. This was the highest risk taken in light of subsequent legal troubles for Milken and Drexel, stemming from allegations of insider trading. Yet Milken rightly bet on Lewis and brought in the capital needed to finish the deal.

With the phenomenal success of the Beatrice deal, Reggie Lewis became the first US Black billionaire and disrupted the entire global investment industry. In telling his story, my hope is that you dare yourself to be as disruptive as any of the Black entrepreneurs we've discussed – and remember that you don't need permission!

At the time of writing, at the start of 2022, it's incomprehensible that there are still no Black companies in either the FTSE 100 or the Fortune 500. When there are, Reggie Lewis will get the credit for paving the way. He succeeded at changing the stakes for entrepreneurs and investors alike. Though, tragically, he died in 1993 at the age of fifty from brain cancer, Lewis must have known that by enabling Beatrice to almost break into the Fortune 500, he had laid down the gauntlet for future Black entrepreneurs. In 1996, Beatrice was valued at $2 billion and ranked 512 on the Fortune 1000. I wonder what Reggie's next venture would have been and what new milestone he would have set? But I also wonder why there aren't more Reggies.

One of the byproducts of his successes is the Reginald F. Lewis Foundation, whose goal is 'to be a force for economic and social justice in the US and beyond, particularly for African American youth. Since 1987, the Foundation is committed to redressing the consequences and legacy of institutional discrimination by investing in youth and moving America towards a state where opportunity comes more equally.' It is a worthy goal for all founders willing to learn to use money to disrupt the status quo. Without question, Reginald Lewis changed how I thought about what I could do non-traditionally, and how far I could go. That is his other legacy, and it's at the heart of the next chapter.

3

WHAT'S IN A NAME?
WHY AMAZON AND NOT THAMES

Step #3: Let go of small – think bigger, think global and prepare for pitfalls

Judgement hinders imagination.

*

An open mind is not an empty one.

PROFESSOR ROGER FISHER, AUTHOR OF *GETTING TO YES: NEGOTIATING AGREEMENT WITHOUT GIVING IN*

The moment my first class started at Harvard Law School I knew I'd made a mistake. Why I had chosen to study law was a question that dogged me that first semester as I plodded through required coursework. I stuck it out, but it wasn't until midway through the second semester that I fully corrected that mistake by adapting my goals. Correcting my course took something of a mindset shift. At first, I questioned my game plan. Had I been thinking too ambitiously? Or not expansively enough?

No question about it. I had limited my imagination and had thought more about how impressive a law degree would be and less about the reality of practising law. The time had come to let go of living up to the expectations of others and to expand my imagination to see alternative ways to put this opportunity to use. Opening up my mind required me to understand Step #3: *Let go of small – think bigger, think global and prepare for pitfalls.*

There are a multitude of ways this step can work for you. Once you've given yourself permission to take on the status quo, you can use this principle as a measure of how far you can see your endeavour taking you and others, and as a test for how committed you are. It's a reminder that bumps in the road can be met with the power of a declaration to exceed expectations in new and innovative ways.

My first act in letting go of small thinking came with the realization that I could make the most of studying law by focusing on the various legal constraints and protections that either hindered or helped the emergence of Black entrepreneurs. The more I looked at my role models who had used their law degrees to open doors that would have stayed shut otherwise, the more I could see the value of my old plan but newly adapted. For example, before founding TLC as an investment firm, Reginald Lewis – who in 1965 was the only person in the then 148-year history of Harvard Law School to be admitted before he even applied – had structured historic deals to encourage more minority-owned businesses. Vernon Jordan, a graduate of Howard University School of Law, started as a powerhouse attorney and civil rights leader, then became a key political advisor, and a leading businessperson who raised millions for investment in Black businesses. Debra L. Lee, CEO of BET and a fierce proponent of diverse representation on corporate boards, started her career in the private sector practising law after receiving both a JD from Harvard Law School and a master's in Public Policy from Harvard's John F. Kennedy School of Government.

Whenever you hit a snag in your plans, or run into an unforeseen business pitfall, it's easy to be thrown off course. The challenge is to not let the setback or roadblock force you to give up or dampen your determination. As you recalibrate your plan, prepare for pitfalls the next time. But don't downsize your aspirations. Instead, push yourself to think bigger and differently about your goals. In my example, I decided to shift my already ambitious goal of wanting to build a local or national network of Black businesses to imagining that one day I would create a global network. How? That's what I had to learn.

Remember when you were a kid and people asked you what you wanted to be when you grew up? Like me, you may recall excitedly relaying all the things you would become. I recently heard Arnold Donald, the President and CEO of Carnival Corporation, talk about how he dreamed of becoming an astronaut and several other careers simultaneously. When we are young, anything seems possible because we haven't yet been taught to tamp down dreams and goals. I can't think of any children who imagine they will be only minimally successful one day. Most of the young kids I recall had almost unlimited imaginations. Something happens as we get older, however, and we stop thinking so expansively. We are afraid to set our sights higher or further than we believe our reach to be. Frequently, we scale back and reckon we should just attempt disruption on a personal local level, as a test of the terrain. Some people may wrongly think they are simply facing reality.

Ask yourself: why only change the status quo in my immediate vicinity? It's not just those close around us who stifle change. If our aim is Black economic power on a large enough scale to create sustained societal change, the simple starting place would be to let go of the constraints of thinking small. Too often, unfortunately, we limit ourselves by setting out to achieve 'realistic' goals – as defined by our world view at the time and by where we see ourselves in its hierarchy. If your goals are along the lines of 'I want to change my life, my family, my community, my city, my country,' that's a great start. The next question to ask yourself, to expand your vision even further, is: how might impacting change on all those levels lead to Black empowerment? By asking questions about impact, you challenge yourself to become a visionary. Not just someone who envisions a better way, but someone who also sees their own path towards achieving it.

Let's be clear. There is nothing wrong with Black founders and business owners in marginalized communities choosing to be pragmatic – particularly when seeking investment from others. The problem with being dogmatically realistic is that it limits your imagination, your vision and potentially your disruptive impacts. True, when you go small in how you see the potential scale of your disruptive enterprise you may limit risk, avoid a loss, possibly break even, or go on to achieve a decent return on your investment. You might gain local notoriety, even domestic adoration. On the other hand, disrupting power structures as globally entrenched and as monstrously widespread as white supremacy requires a commitment to entrepreneurial undertakings that are likewise global and behemoth-sized – high-risk, yes, but with high rewards of untold proportions. *Think big*.

The tricky part in all this is in the way we think about what *is* or *is not* possible. As an Entrepreneur.com piece by Michael Mamas published in 2016 put it, 'The fastest way to expand your possibilities is to see past the limitations you imagine are holding you back but really aren't.'

When making this point to founders who prefer an incremental approach to building their companies, I invariably hear the objection that the most iconic, disruptive and dominant organizations had to start small. 'After all,' this argument goes, 'even Jeff Bezos started Amazon in his garage.' 'Yes,' I typically counter, 'but if he hadn't been thinking big and thinking globally, he would have named his company Thames, not Amazon.'

The promise of your business name

The name you choose to label your company can clearly be indicative of how big and how global you are thinking. What's in a name? Quite a bit! In business, according to Adam Fridman in an August 2015 article on Inc.com, a startup name is as important as the actual function of your company and can 'make or break' your entire enterprise. Branding your venture begins with a name. It's the first thing investors and consumers see. A brand name can also tell a story about what your enterprise does and what your company values are.

Actually, as the story goes – as noted in 2019 by *Business Insider* – in July 1994, when Bezos founded his startup, he had first settled on the name Cadabra. As in the magical phrase 'Abracadabra!'. A lawyer for the nascent firm argued that not only was the reference too obscure, but that if the person taking calls in the garage office didn't enunciate clearly, the name of the company sounded like 'Cadaver'. Not so inviting.

More details about how the name was finally chosen were revealed in an October 2021 piece in the *Washington Post* by Travis Andrews and Roxanne Roberts titled 'The Love Affair Between Jeff Bezos and Star Trek'. It seems that at one point

Bezos wanted to name his new business www.makeitso.com, in tribute to the stock phrase of Captain Jean-Luc Picard – played by the actor Patrick Stewart. 'Make it so' is a standard British Navy go-ahead command that's been around for centuries. Certainly, by the early 1990s, as the dot.com startup boom exploded, www.makeitso.com did seem to capture the can-do, explore-new-worlds, entrepreneurial spirit of the times. In hindsight, such a brand name might have perfectly hinted at the galactic scale of Bezos's ambitions, as evidenced in his actual exploration of space of the 2020s.

Bezos majored in computer science and electrical engineering at Princeton, and we overlapped. He had an active presence on campus. He vanished from my radar for a decade after heading off to climb the ladder in the field of finance. Nothing especially disruptive stands out in Bezos's storyline until 1994, when his trajectory suddenly changed while he was in the process of researching opportunities in new business sectors for D. E. Shaw, a non-traditional Wall Street firm known as a pioneer in computational finance. Many who were paying attention at the time concluded that there was untapped potential for selling goods and services on the emerging global communication network newly minted as the internet. Bezos saw its potential in dramatic terms. In a speech called 'We Are What We Choose', which he gave in 2010 at Princeton, he recalled seeing data for internet-user traffic growing in a short period of time at an unheard of rate of 2,300 per cent per year, and a new scale of thinking followed: 'I'd never seen or heard of anything that grew that fast, and the idea of building an online bookstore with millions of titles . . . was very exciting to me.'

This must have marked a strong shift of world view for Jeff Bezos. From then on, he seems to have operated as if there were no limits to how far he could go to sell not just books, but later movies, music and eventually almost every consumer product in the known galaxy. In fact, it was his vision for an 'Everything Store' that he laid out to get his first significant investment from his parents.

My point here is that even before Bezos had sold one book, his vision was to disrupt an entire age-old delivery system. He was going to do that not as the first online bookseller (there were a couple of others at the time) but by thinking massively, and by being the one-stop shop for millions of consumers to locate the book they wanted and have it delivered on a global scale unattainable by any bricks-and-mortar store or chain.

In his 2013 Bezos biography, *The Everything Store*, author Brad Stone writes that in late October of 1994,

> ... Bezos pored through the A section of the dictionary and had an epiphany when he reached the word *Amazon*. Earth's largest river; Earth's largest bookstore. He walked into the garage one morning and informed his colleagues of the company's new name. He gave the impression that he didn't care to hear anyone's opinion on it ... 'This is not only the largest river in the world, it's many times larger than the next bigger river. It blows all other rivers away.'

Similarly, in 1998, after two Stanford grad students, Larry Page and Sergey Brin, had decided to call their search engine 'Backrub' because of how it used backlinks to sift through information, they realized they needed to think bigger. As recounted in a *Business Insider* article in October 2015 by Nathan McAlone, during a brainstorming session another grad student, Sean Anderson, suggested they borrow the outsized maths term 'googolplex', and Page shortened it to googol (which is one followed by 100 zeros). They then managed to misspell that word when registering it. This could have been a naming pitfall, but it turned out to be genius.

Google is the ultimate name for ubiquity. It has changed how billions of users plough instantly through information and has transformed how we search and digest that information, as well as how advertisers reach consumers. Google has become a reflex, an action, and both a noun and a verb, and, of course, a trillion-dollar behemoth that has grown many tentacles – just as Amazon has developed numerous tributaries.

An organization's name – whether aspirational or utilitarian – may not be the only factor that ultimately determines entrepreneurial success. Yet a name can certainly hint at greatness to come, even during the incubation stage. Take the name of 'Acorn' used by the UK-founded tech firm that since the 1970s has quietly been the cornerstone that made Cambridge into Britain's Silicon Valley equivalent. In a June 2020 *Business Weekly* UK issue by Tony Quested, the company's evolution and massive ambition in the founders' vision was described with a hat tip to the common phrase 'from tiny acorns mighty oaks grow'. Even so, when Acorn developed its 1981 personal-use computer, the BBC Micro, the most ambitious number of units they imagined selling was 12,000; in fact they sold 1.5 million, many of them for use in schools.

Acorn co-founder Andy Hopper, interviewed in October 2009 by Nick Heath for ZDNet.com, acknowledged that they'd had no idea at the start that they would grow as mightily as they did. So much so that, after becoming a pioneer in computer and software design, Acorn evolved, morphed and then sub-divided to become the behemoth ARM Ltd. The new acronym, which comes from Advanced RISC Machine, refers to the actual technology utilized in processors and semiconductors. At the time of a negotiated sale in September 2020 to the American graphics company Nvidia, ARM was valued at £31.2

billion ($40 billion) and its technology had long since been embedded in most smartphones around the world and numerous other household smart devices. Although the plan to combine the two global tech giants failed, ARM's predicted IPO will be the stuff of legend and ARM remains headquartered in Cambridge – serving as an anchor of the UK's increasingly influential tech hub.

This ripple effect, or 'flywheel of opportunity' as I think of it, is a reminder of what is possible for under-represented founders. We can see in these examples how thinking bigger and on a global scale is an ever-evolving process. Which is why the step of letting go of small includes preparation for pitfalls and shortfalls. When you prepare for the possibility that you may need to adapt your original plans, pitfalls can be proving grounds that lead to opportunity, sometimes even becoming happy accidents. Think of Google's misspelling, a lawyer questioning Bezos about Cadabra, or Cambridge computer scientists managing to exceed even their wildest aspirations by going from Acorn to tech domination.

Thinking big and thinking global is a powerful way to begin any entrepreneurial journey. Without a focus on all that can go right, as opposed to what could go wrong, you may lose momentum over the course of time as you turn your business idea into reality. You can also gird yourself and prepare for a pitfall or two. Being a problem solver is one hallmark of an entrepreneur, and there is nothing wrong with using your imagination to think big and to be solution-driven as you encounter obstacles. Plus, doing so means you go forward with an awareness of how initial ideas and plans may be too limited or limiting. The power play is that you make room for opportunities to grow your vision, your connections and your reach.

Turning problems into possibilities

How visionaries solve problems, confront obstacles and put big ideas into action has been a source of fascination throughout my life. That goes hand in hand with a desire to understand the barriers to opportunity for Black entrepreneurs, other minorities and women, particularly in the rapidly evolving technology field. The story is often the same across many sectors – few founders, board members or top-level execs are Black. Yet there have always been globally minded entrepreneurs who defy the odds and find a way to break through.

David Steward is a prime example of a Black entrepreneur who thought expansively from the start – going so far as to declare the business he founded in 1990 in St Louis, Missouri to be worthy of the name World Wide Technology (WWT). That was audacious, to say the least, given the fact that his background was in sales and marketing, and that his first two firms were regional in scope, focusing mainly on being technology suppliers to transportation companies. Yet he could see a multitude of possibilities to come from the tech arena and found a reasonable entry point – in the reselling of computers, printers and phone/fax equipment.

In April 2021, *Forbes* reported David Steward as the second-wealthiest Black American billionaire ($3.7 billion) – behind private equity financier Robert F. Smith ($6 billion) and ahead of Oprah Winfrey ($2.7 billion) – with Steward earning a ranking of 807 among all billionaires around the world. As for the top Black firms in the US, *Black Enterprise* ranked WWT at number one, writing in 2020 that the global IT company, headquartered in Missouri, served public and private businesses and an array of their technology needs. By then David Steward's company was well established as the largest Black-owned business, generating an annual revenue of $13 billion, with a workforce of over 6,000 employees and more than twenty facilities across multiple continents that provided around 4 million square feet of warehousing as well as business integration. Steward's company name set the course from the start.

The extraordinary success of WWT reveals Steward's basic practicality which, I would argue, is something that comes relatively easily to Black, minority and immigrant business owners – out of necessity. The idea to repurpose technology for resale had to spring from a mind that refused to see resources like office equipment going to waste. Add to that the ability to modernize and make the leap from analogue to digital. When you combine common-sense pragmatism with the flexibility to see new trends and take on new core competencies, you seize upon another form of thinking bigger. By no coincidence, it turns out that David Steward's son – David Steward II – has cultivated his own brand of disruptive, imaginative, big thinking. He is also the founder of Lion Forge, an animation production company with which Impact X Studios partners. He and his team prioritize diverse content as well as content creators who have been under-represented in the graphic novel and animation worlds.

While these stories prove the power of continually expanding your vision, of thinking big, calling your business Amazon rather than Thames is of course not a surefire recipe for success on a global scale. In *The Everything Store* Brad Stone writes that Bezos knew there would be pitfalls and even warned his parents that there was a good chance they'd lose money on their investment. A June 2021 *Business Insider* piece detailed a couple of major missteps by Bezos and team. A recent effort to launch a multi-player game system, Crucible, took years and millions and failed to launch. A collaboration with partners to create a global healthcare organization went south before the business came together. An Amazon competitor to Instagram was a flop. Amazon Restaurants, a prepared-food delivery business, lasted two years in the US and in London, but didn't catch on. Amazon Tickets, intended to compete with other concert-booking outlets, rolled out only in the UK with plans to expand to the US, but the live-performance-venue ticketing business was not a good match for Amazon and it closed within eighteen months. A foray into hotel-booking only lasted three months. Amazon Wallet was a dud. The costliest failure was an effort to develop a mobile phone, the Amazon Fire, which could barely be given away for free.

Reporting in *Vox* in 2017, Timothy B. Lee reveals the deal that saved Amazon from extinction early in its history when revenues had yet to exceed debt. Bezos was warned by an advisor that the company should have a 'stronger cash position' in case suppliers of goods being sold wanted payment faster than the company could afford. Bezos moved rapidly, putting together an innovative deal that helped Amazon stay afloat and survive the bursting of the dot.com bubble in 2000 that was especially merciless to e-commerce companies. Remember the popular UK companies like Pet.com, Boo.com, Friends Reunited or Jewishnet.co.uk?

The causes of the popping of the dot.com bubble were numerous, from good ideas being far ahead of current technology and infrastructure potential, to too much capital needing a place to invest and finding too many mediocre companies to fund – a supply-and-demand miscalculation which meant there were many businesses attempting to monetize and profit from the consumption habits of a limited number of users. This left most companies to compete for life or death over a small pie. What those that survived and later thrived figured out is that what you really had to learn to do was to bake a bigger pie.

Getting to yes

When you begin to challenge yourself to let go of small and allow your imagination to entertain possibilities that you'd never considered before, you'll discover that you are doing more than teaching yourself to aim higher with a new business. You are also learning new ways to be imaginative in how you build and run your business, how you collaborate with others, how you interact with co-founders, funders, suppliers and employees, and how you beat the odds that are realities for entrepreneurs who come from marginalized backgrounds.

The major lesson I learned, not long after arriving in Cambridge, Massachusetts and attending several weeks of law school classes at Harvard, was that I was being offered opportunities that would provide me with knowledge I could put to use however I chose. Or not. For instance, I was immediately put on notice that there was extraordinary brainpower and ambition among my fellow first-year law students. There was an atmosphere of collaboration and competition I found invigorating. That first year I met the young Barack Obama – who in 1990 would become the first Black president of the *Harvard Law Review*. Years later, after being elected the first Black president of the US, Barack appointed me to a role working on the Council for Underserved Communities in the Small Business Administration. That first year, I struck up lasting relationships with many fellow law students who remain in my life to this day – as friends, colleagues or both. Build your networks, wherever you find them.

A takeaway from this experience is an awareness that it's never too late to learn how to think bigger. When you see peers imagining possibilities you've never thought of yourself, why not learn from them? In that initial phase when I'd decided law school wasn't for me, I had to use my imagination to be solution-driven. One constant irritant was that, as much as I liked my professors and my fellow law students, a lot of the instruction was based on the Socratic method. That is, verbally sparring with a professor over a series of questions to help the class nail concepts. Personally, I love a robust argument, but I found the verbal back and forth very counterproductive from a learning perspective. I started seeking an alternative that might suit me better. I even looked into leaving law school and getting my MBA, or at least a joint degree, only to have my applications to business school rejected because 'Eric, we're looking for top candidates who have at least two to three years of business experience.'

Business experience, for anyone wanting to attend Harvard Business School, was code for working in an investment bank, a consulting firm or some other highly competitive and selective programme that regularly tapped pools of ambitious young people to run the world. Then and there I could have abandoned the law ship to take the time and gain the requisite experience. That's when I 'flipped the script' and decided – *Why not turn my time at law school into my own version of business school?* I didn't need permission for that.

Thinking bigger allows for shifts in perspective. When you find out that you don't love the path you're on, flipping the script helps turn the narrative around to your own liking. I started to hoover up as much information as I could about all sorts of successful business structures and strategies. I looked for the 'origin stories' of entrepreneurs of colour, how they conceived their businesses, how they built companies, the twists and turns of their careers, and the critical decisions and impediments to success. Until this point, the Black business playbooks I'd been studying were built mostly on self-reliance and grit to create local, state, regional and national businesses.

Now my exposure was broadening my curiosity to learn how businesses operated across borders.

For anyone who hits a wall after enrolling in a rigorous academic programme or accepting a job, I recommend putting your bigger thinking to the task of seeing what you might gain from sticking with it. Lots of people drop out because they question whether the cost and time will be worth it. Yet some of those same dropouts later regret their decision when they discover that certain credentials and certifications increase their competitiveness, therefore opening more opportunities. We hear frequently of the billionaire founders who chose not to get their degrees. That said, a 2018 study by the UK's AdView found that only one in eight of the most successful entrepreneurs dropped out. In the highest growth sectors, nearly 50 per cent of founders had graduate-level degrees.

The opportunity of my law school's access to other Harvard University academic departments and professional schools was one I wasn't going to waste. Such access meant my context for empowerment – the framework – changed. So, in a departure from looking mainly at socio-economic influences in Black business growth (or lack thereof), I now had the opportunity to study the multitude of laws and governmental policies enriching or limiting all forms of commerce (tax laws, competition legislation, monetary policy, education financing). The specifics were interesting enough, but not overly compelling. Yet in the context of Black entrepreneurship, I was gripped. That exploration, in turn, led to in-depth study of international law and business and gave me answers as to how not just US history but global history had fed systemic white supremacy, legitimizing inequities that further marginalized communities of colour everywhere.

It is easy to bemoan the fact that the system has long been rigged against businesses founded by people of colour. So what do you do about it? Think back to Henry and Adeline – map out a plan and then start your business without asking for permission. It's also worthwhile to ask what empowering influences successful under-represented entrepreneurs have harnessed to overcome oppressive systems.

Let's highlight resources and user-friendly strategies entrepreneurs should bear in mind:

- *Successful entrepreneurs are able to rise above lowered expectations from outside and within.* You'll also want to prepare yourself for pushback from folks who view you as an interloper, competitors and naysayers, even among your own family and friends. Historically, different cultural groups feel differently about whether entrepreneurship is acceptable or what kind of business 'people like you' should pursue. Within every society, certain norms and values exist which determine what is 'acceptable' behaviour and what is not. For example, childcare businesses were for decades considered appropriate for women entrepreneurs to grow. Throughout the British Commonwealth, various cooking businesses were considered appropriate for Black women and men. All over the world, sport and music are traditionally businesses in which Black people are expected to excel but not to run. It's your choice to be as traditional or non-traditional as you wish. You don't need permission.
- *Social mobility can both enable and hinder business building –* the degree of opportunity that exists within a society allowing individuals to change their status matters. On the one hand, marginalization can limit opportunities in the marketplace. On the other, marginalization can

create built-in or captive buyers within a group. This explains how segregation, for all its ills, produced self-sufficiency. Black businesses can target Black consumers and achieve good success. Yet if you are thinking bigger, the broader your customer base, the bigger and more enduring the success.

- *Businesses and business owners need some security to prosper.* Questions you'll want to answer will determine your own need for security. Does the rule of law protect me and my business? Can I handle the risk? Can I deal with setbacks, pitfalls and even failure? Does the current political, social and economic climate favour my startup? People are averse to beginning enterprises that involve huge uncertainty, right? But, paradoxically, when there is too much security there is no incentive to pursue entrepreneurship as a means to economic or social gains. Much to my fascination, it turns out that entrepreneurs emerge in an environment which is neither too secure nor too insecure.

- *Economic factors always matter.* Capital is the lifeblood of every business. We're also talking about the availability of labour, employees and raw materials, appropriate supply chains, the level of technology available and required, and the ability to find and exploit markets to support your business. While you think ambitiously, you may also want to look at resources needed for compliance issues such as licensing requirements and taxes.

Some successful Black entrepreneurship has also been shaped by certain ideologies that promote traditional beliefs in doing good, doing God's work, practising thrift or being a good citizen. Personality traits common to these Black business owners include an intense desire to do well, an ability to set definite and realistic goals, to defer gratification, a willingness to take risks, and a tendency to see self-induced changes as possible. Those traits are aligned with using your imagination as to how best you can harness resources and create alliances with other Black entrepreneurs.

These traits may also explain how certain places that may seem unlikely have become hotbeds for multiple industries dominated by Black founders. A prime example is Durham, North Carolina, where Black-owned businesses in the insurance and financial industries have boomed. Instead of Rockefellers and Carnegies, we have Spauldings and Merricks.

Knowing the commonality of these traits and noting examples of success was empowering for me, absolutely. But as long as white supremacy continued to reign, opportunity remained limited.

My inclination was to begin to imagine – boldly, broadly and ambitiously – possible solutions. No one had to give or deny me permission to do that, nor did I have to leave law school to put my imagination to use. Still, something was missing. What I needed was a highly sharpened set of tools for problem-solving and solution execution most often learned on the playing field of actual, lived experience, not in the classroom. But there are exceptions, and one of them was right there at Harvard Law School in the form of a class on negotiation, mediation and conflict resolution that taught me how to think big in solving business challenges and harnessing an open-minded, solution-driven imagination. These tools would change my life forever.

The class – taught by law professors Roger Fisher and Bruce Patton – was not part of the required curriculum. Many of my peers thought the negotiation seminar was a soft-skills course. For me, it became the cornerstone of thinking big and thinking global. The late Roger Fisher was already the renowned author of *Getting to Yes: Negotiating Agreement Without Giving In* – required reading at policy programmes, business schools and some law schools, as well as a perennially popular business book for general readers. Together, Professors Fisher and Patton had co-founded the Harvard Negotiation Project and Institute in 1979 with a mission 'to improve the theory and practice of conflict resolution and negotiation by working on real-world conflict intervention, theory building, education and training, and writing and disseminating new ideas'.

When Roger Fisher passed away in 2012 at the age of ninety, Bruce Patton explained his teaching philosophy in an obituary in the daily college newspaper, *The Harvard Crimson*. Professor Fisher had wanted to build a toolkit for 'analyzing and diagnosing' why situations failed different parties, and how it might be possible to use that toolkit to find some common ground. These tools needed real-life testing, as with any hard science. That required practice; it required experience.

Roger Fisher had distilled a novel way of thinking about conflicts and solutions that arose at individual, group, commercial, governmental and societal levels. And with everything I learned from the main principles of *Getting to Yes*, my world view was altered forever. His experiences in the Second World War, working on the Marshall Plan to help rebuild Europe, and later as a lawyer and law professor, helped form the foundation of his approach. He built upon that start with successful outcomes that included negotiating Middle East treaties at Camp David, building peace in Central America, and bringing to an end the Western Hemisphere's longest-running war, between Ecuador and Peru. Roger Fisher had been a participant at so many critical junctures of history – the 1980 resolution of the Iranian hostage crisis, helping to warm the Cold War between the US and the Soviet Union and, famously, being part of the negotiations and constitutional process that led to the end of apartheid in South Africa.

It was not lost on me that I had a rare opportunity to ingest these principles directly from the source and apply them in my future business life. Knowing that Roger Fisher's section of the class would have more competition for space, I chose to take the path less travelled and sign up for Bruce Patton's. Pragmatism secured my place and immediately opened a door to a relationship with an important mentor who recognized my competitive drive and fanned its flames.

For anyone in any kind of business, there are few skills more useful than the ability to negotiate effectively – as opposed to reaching agreements in the same way you'd approach a pub fight. Diplomacy requires an open mind. Successful deal-making can be boiled down to three of the most important lessons I took away from *Getting to Yes*, ones that you can easily apply to your own business toolbox and your entrepreneurship goals:

1. Listening is more important than talking. A good question is as powerful as a great speech.
2. Common ground is an excellent foundation for durable solutions to conflicting interests.
3. The best way to change another person's mind is by using fair and objective criteria to challenge their own biases.

These strategies take time to adopt. Any of us who grew up in settings where we were marginalized know all too well the feeling of not being heard, of being dismissed when we had answers to share, or of being disregarded. However, when you set that baggage down for a minute, it's possible to open your mind to the possibility that if you listen to

WE DON'T NEED PERMISSION

someone else, you might find a place of mutual interest on which a deal can be built. If you ask a good question, the other person may reveal something you haven't heard before. Everyone wants to be treated fairly and is more likely to be persuaded to change their mind when faced with rationales that emphasize fair treatment. If you present your proposals using fair and reasonable arguments, and demonstrate that you care about reaching a point of agreement that benefits you both, you are cooking.

This is where the pie-slice metaphor comes in. Instead of having an argument about who gets the bigger piece of pie, you can think grandly and come up with ways to cook a better, bigger pie. This understanding is at the heart of my thesis that Black business is good for equity, for communities of colour and for the global economy. We are not fighting over a sliver of the same small pie, we are baking pies that don't even exist yet. And who doesn't like pie?

Getting to Yes thinking doesn't happen overnight. When I began in Bruce Patton's class, we were assigned cases and had to negotiate actual outcomes – which required preparation, researching fact patterns, negotiating with fellow students and then presenting the case conclusions in class. Being extremely competitive, I went into each negotiation feverish to win – to attain the best terms, the least compromise, the most money – and not necessarily to use the negotiations to build working relationships with my classmates, who seemed much more relationship-driven than I was at the time. If I did well, that was on me, I decided, and if not, that was on me too.

It took me a while to question my assumptions enough to even consider that, while winning is great, when you win at the expense of others you can create a challenging environment for future work. In business that can be a huge liability, especially if you have strained trust. Luckily for me, I demonstrated ability and didn't overstrain trust, so was invited to become a teaching assistant for the next year's class and asked to lead summer seminars in *Getting to Yes* for global business executives and high-level government leaders. Clearly, my decision to stay in law school was paying off, both as I had hoped and in unexpected ways.

At those times when you've decided to stick with an earlier plan, you may not always get a ringing endorsement right away as to whether you've made the right choice. When you find yourself second-guessing your decisions, objectively evaluate the merits of the opportunity and weigh out whatever still makes you uneasy. At the same time, don't waste too much energy looking back. Focus more on charting where you want to go and less on where you've been.

By the time I was getting ready to graduate, I'd come back round to thinking that maybe I should give the practice of law a chance. Then again, embracing the unexpected (Step #1, as you recall), other possibilities were now on my horizon.

Putting hustle and action to the test

In the decades to come, Atlanta, Georgia would become ground zero for Black VCs, a hub for Black business and innovation, with success stories like Calendly, the cloud-based scheduling app that became an Atlanta-based unicorn in January 2021, as reported by UrbanGeekz, the online publication for Black innovation. But in 1989, when I secured a summer internship at a top law firm in Atlanta between my first and second year of law school, there was little evidence of that movement. At the time, there were few Black partners at most of Atlanta's top ten law firms. My saving grace at the firm where I was employed that summer was their one Black partner – Ted Lackland. An extraordinary commercial lawyer and litigator, Ted had a master's degree from Howard

University and JD from Columbia Law School. He'd worked in NYC at what's known as a 'white-shoe' firm – in the UK, the 'Magic Circle' – the name for a handful of the world's most prestigious multinational law firms, to which entry is particularly competitive. Made up almost entirely of White-Anglo-Saxon-Protestant attorneys who had attended the most elite boarding schools, universities and law schools, these sorts of firms rarely hire lawyers of colour, or other minorities for that matter. Ted encouraged me to have experiences, evaluate multiple possibilities and try out as many things as I could before choosing where to hang my hat. Sage advice for anyone considering good or not-so-great options in life.

In his practice, Ted worked with a number of Atlanta's entrepreneurs – from the nascent (who paid nothing) to the huge (who paid full rates). After getting to know Ted further, I got to talking with him and told him about my interest in the use of capital for Black empowerment.

'So,' he asked, drawing me out, 'you're interested in venture capital.'

How did he know?

From then on, Ted invited me to shadow him and work alongside him, where I put the Collins family values – hustle and action – to the test. I soon realized that we are too often taught that a mentor comes along to help us discover our strengths out of the generosity of their spirit. Actually, I believe that a mentor shouldn't be expected to be a benevolent guide who gives wise counsel in return for nothing. I think that when you seek mentorship you should be able to offer something in return. With Ted Lackland, the opportunity to learn was not to be taken for granted. I went to meetings with him, produced memos related to clients' commercial issues, and generated drafts of formal documents when needed. When I returned to law school that Fall, it was with a deepening respect for the real-world application of the fundamentals of negotiation and mediation, as well as the practical application of risk capital to Black businesses.

During my third year, I saw this evidenced even more when I was introduced to the work of Conflict Management Inc. (CMI), the strategy consulting firm co-founded in Cambridge, Massachusetts in 1984 by Roger Fisher and some of his students, including Bruce Patton. CMI was a hybrid of think tank and a for-profit/non-profit organization that catered to the C-suite of private and public companies as well as public and not-for-profit institutions – all operating within national and international boundaries.

Being in the CMI orbit was a heady experience. Getting to take a peek behind the curtain, I saw very clearly how negotiation theories were being applied practically to complex problems in multiple sectors. I learned that in heated political and commercial disputes there are means of making conversations more effective, of trying to establish an equation leading to an outcome whereby – contrary to cynical views of deal-making – everyone could go away having achieved all their most critical ends. As consultants and facilitators, CMI designed processes that ensured durable solutions built on the mutual interests of different parties.

Coincidentally, the best VCs live by a similar creed: that if the interests of most stakeholders (from founders to funders) are not aligned and addressed, then the shared goal of creating a hugely successful company becomes much more difficult. This is a creed you should consider for your endeavours. It's strikingly different from opposing parties sitting down and battling over 'I want this' and 'You want that'. CMI strategy consultants helped make bigger and better pies. They had the job of getting their clients to think more broadly and more imaginatively by putting together a process for different parties

WE DON'T NEED PERMISSION

to come to the table and move forward with a solution that embraced mutual interests.

I realized that the key to the most successful conflict resolution efforts is the power of imagination. Removing judgement and having an open mind can change outcomes overnight. The CMI strategy consultants I met were like engineers untangling intractable problems through the power of creative thinking. That observation made it easier for me, when I finally made up my mind, to forgo a job offer at a top New York firm where I'd interned. Eventually, when I received a job offer from CMI, I went for it – making one of my many disruptive moves to come.

All along, I'd gone back and forth about whether I should go right into action as a founder and invest in my own ideas or stick with a law career. The position at CMI was a third way, and it was going to give me unparalleled access to how organizations are run at the highest level and allow me to rub shoulders with the folks doing so.

My new career had me spending 70 per cent of my time travelling around the world and back, all the while advising and ministering to organizations of every purpose, shape and size. At the age of twenty-five, I quickly expanded my world view.

Wherever you are in your entrepreneurial journey, my guess is that you know a bit about putting yourself on the line with hard work, hustle and action. When you let go of small thinking and stoke your imagination to see bigger possibilities, you also begin to strategize what your next move might be even when fully engaged in what you're doing at the moment.

If you feel that you are not where you'd ultimately like to hang your professional hat, try to attune your vision to bigger things ahead while still seeing your current situation as a valuable stepping stone. Can you think bigger, think global and continue to grow even after pitfalls?

But having a vision will only get you so far. Without the ability to execute that vision well and put it into tangible steps – which may require tweaking – your big idea can't get off the ground.

Thinking big, it wasn't long before I began to see the outline of a grander scheme than being an in-demand strategy consultant for the rest of my career. Keeping an open mind, I saw my work at CMI as an opportunity to develop the skills to lead a large Fortune 500 company, or even to run my own company. CMI seemed to offer the ideal training ground for doing that.

That's when I had a memorable conversation with Irma Tyler-Wood, a brilliant legal and problem-solving mind, who had started as an educator, came through Harvard Law and the Negotiation Workshop, then to a large Washington, DC law firm before finally becoming CMI's only Black partner and one of the most in-demand consultants in the field.

When you are open to guidance, without expecting a mentor to hover over you and do the hard work of decision-making for you, often the right mentor steps forward. That is, if you've demonstrated your own initiative, hustle and open-mindedness. Irma reached out to me and was very direct. She said, in so many words, 'Eric, you can be whatever you want, you have the drive and the will. If you want me to help, I can help. If you want to do this on your own, you can do it on your own.' She saw that there were promising possibilities for me. And she also saw that, along with my assets, I could get in my own way, undervaluing working relationships by stepping on my colleagues' toes, being somewhat competitive by nature and thereby leaving hard feelings among my teammates. I could see where I wanted to be and I wanted to get there with speed, but I didn't quite have the tools to do so without a lot of collateral damage. Irma could help with that.

When I said, 'I'd love to have your advice, thank you,' she

was honest. Without her candour, I wouldn't have made it through the organization.

My word of advice on this point is to not let constructive criticism get to you. Even if it's difficult to hear, sometimes it can make all the difference. Irma helped me adjust my approaches to communication and relationship-building, and that's how I made it not only to senior associate but eventually to partner. Irma agreed that it was always important to give myself permission to excel, making no apologies for ambition or talent. Yet it was also important, she pointed out, to understand that I would have detractors who would use excuses – 'He's a kid, he doesn't grasp the culture' or 'He's from the South' or 'He's Black' or 'He's a horse's ass', or whatever it was. Irma's advice was to not let their bias and their need to point out 'You are not one of us' get to me. It's the sort of bias that can stop you in your tracks.

'What do I do?' I asked.

Her advice was fourfold. First, she said, master your domain and be unequivocally excellent. Second, *listen*. That is priceless for anyone who aspires to run any kind of organization. By listening you can observe all that you need to know to be successful in your interactions. Her third piece of advice was always to discuss the undiscussable. My Southern upbringing made that a tough one. It's something that I've noticed isn't easy here in England, where so much is implied euphemistically rather than addressed head-on.

Address it head-on.

In business, Irma insisted, a failure to put everything on the table and up for discussion can be fatal to all interests. Her fourth piece of advice helped me to define my sense of purpose from then on: 'Remember,' Irma would say, 'you also work for the underdog.'

In the classic match-up of David versus Goliath, our clients were often those with money and power who could afford our expertise for growing and running their organizations. We had to superserve our Goliath clients. In almost all our work there was a David, i.e. stakeholders with a lesser voice. We were also there to work for the betterment of the underdog, David, or the stakeholders who didn't have the resources of access to power or advocacy. After all, if David's interests were not met, any solutions Goliath thought they had were not guaranteed. Finally Irma helped me see that even as a third party to a situation, there would be times when going down with the ship but fighting to the death was the right action, but that didn't have to apply to every situation.

That was a direct, personal message of Black empowerment to me.

From a business-class seat, I saw the world. My experiences were mind-expanding, fascinating, exciting. And yet still discouraging. At a time of so much technological progress, the lack of opportunities for people of colour was maddening, not to mention that white supremacy existed in some form almost everywhere. Even in some of the African nations, remnants of colonial white rule remained. I rarely saw Black decision makers in any organization that I advised. There were innumerable times I entered a room to launch a project to find people shocked when I walked through the door; it was visible on their faces. The explicit and hidden headwinds I faced leading interventions were often enervating. At their most benign, I might get the reaction: 'Eric, you aren't what we expected,' and sometimes, more corrosively, I'd hear: 'Eric, there is no value you can add and we don't want you.' It's a reaction you will have encountered as a Black person, as a woman or as a minority. How you respond to it is crucial.

The experience of having your legitimacy questioned can be exhausting. I have found that the best way to respond is to answer through the actions you take to reach and surpass goals. Instead of allowing someone else to determine what you are capable of doing, just go and do it. And while you are at it, once again, think big, think global. The risk you take in reaching far is failure. Or you might just succeed beyond your own wildest expectations. And theirs. And there are occasions on which to take Irma's advice and put on the table the direct discussion of undiscussables in order to address a pressing problem.

By the way, not all entrepreneurial risks are created equal, and some risks aren't worth it. Many of them, as you are about to see, aren't all guesswork. In any event, when you are ready to put your thinking into action, it can be the adventure of a lifetime – like exploring the Amazon. This is where the power of your ideas meets the cauldron of experience and becomes real. Or not.

4

FACTS WORK BETTER THAN MYTHS

Step #4: Take risks and use data to mitigate the downside

*The pawn can only move one space forward,
it's still the same moves . . . until you start to change
the rules of the game, then there can be a significant
impact on new agents coming into the industry.*

FUNK BUTCHER, AKA KWAME SAFO

One business stereotype you hear often is that to be a successful entrepreneur you have to be a daring risk taker willing to throw caution to the wind and go for broke with a good idea, product or service. That's actually a myth. In fact, a *Forbes* analysis by Chris Carosa in August 2020 corrected that assumption. The data shows that 90 per cent of the startups that fail are the result of taking risks based on thinking all you need is a good idea and lots of investment. It turns out that one critical difference is that truly successful entrepreneurs have learned how to take *calculated* risks. There's nothing wrong with being risk-averse, Carosa tells us, unless it holds you back from starting a business in the first place. Your success will be determined by whether you are able to 'manage risk properly'.

What does that mean exactly? Well, if we can categorize this point under a heading of 'things I wish I'd known back then that I know now', it means that even though risk is inherent with most business enterprises, there are resources and actions that will help you improve your chances of success and decrease the toll taken by failure. The action that can serve you well is employed with Step #4 – *Take risks and use data to mitigate the downside*. Let's say you are trying to decide whether or not to embark on a particular venture. The risk involved requires you to calculate what you might gain and what you might lose. Not just money but time, reputation, opportunity, influence and experience.

The importance of using data for crucial decisions should be a no-brainer. Yet all too often when we're faced with those decisions, we forget the truth of this chapter's title – Facts Work Better Than Myths. This is especially illuminating for entrepreneurs of colour because we know the negative effects of myths that have been used against us for centuries. Even today, many of those myths prevail – for example, about how creative we are in the arts rather than how worthwhile an investment our startups might be to others. So we need to command facts to counter bias in its many forms.

My first real entrepreneurial venture that involved considerable risk happened in the 1990s, when in the midst of a career as a consultant I rather unexpectedly became a first-time independent film producer. It was one of those experiences from which I learned a lot, and fast. And which also helped to inform my decision twenty-five years later, in the spring of 2020, to accept an invitation to appear in the front of the camera.

After much deliberation, there were a few reasons I said 'yes' to the opportunity to host Channel 4's *The Money Maker*. The four-part series was based on the format of the American TV show *The Profit*. In similar fashion, I was asked to select four standout but struggling small businesses or startups, choose to invest my own money in them (or not), put in place a transformational plan, and then work closely with those entrepreneurs and their teams to make all of us real money.

This entailed a good deal of risk for me, not just because it was my financial investment on the line but because of the compressed period of time required for helping the featured organizations transform and deliver exceptional returns. The other concern was that this was a real departure from my work in venture capital as CEO of Impact X, and also strayed from our focus on Black and under-represented founders in the UK and Europe, whose companies had already gained traction and were ready for the necessary capital to become as enormous and ubiquitous as such European-born entities as World Remit (now Zepz, the cross-border mobile payments unicorn founded by Black entrepreneur Ismail Ahmed), Spotify or Wise.

Still, the offer was compelling. It had the potential to be both disruptive and popular. It was a chance to shine a spotlight on the UK's undiscovered gems and small business owners of all backgrounds – who, after more than a decade of austerity programmes and recent Covid-19 lockdowns, were hurting badly. If I could share tools that I'd learned to use in my entrepreneurial journey and consulting life, I believed that we could encourage entrepreneurship and do a lot of good while making money. More than anything, my producer Nick Parnes's convincing argument was: 'Eric, after so many have called for greater visibility and positive representation of Black people in media and entertainment, how can you say no?'

He had a point.

And there was plenty of data to back it up.

Facts get you further

A piece in Deadline Hollywood, an online news site for the entertainment industry, in January 2021 reinforced a maddening reality. Rather than making strides for greater diversity on television, even after the racial reckoning that took place in the wake of George Floyd's murder, the reverse had occurred. A report from the Creative Diversity Network had looked at answers from 36,503 entertainment industry insiders in the UK over a period of about a year up until summer 2020. Representation went down for professionals of colour on screen as well as behind the scenes – which took the numbers from 12.3 per cent in 2019 to 11.8 per cent in 2020; this corresponds to the recent finding that people of colour are down to 13 per cent of the UK workforce.

The facts spoke for themselves and were painfully amplified by a study released in August 2021 about racism in the UK's entertainment industry. Commissioned by the Racial Diversity Group, a project of the Personal Managers' Association, the report was conducted in part by the Sir Lenny Henry Centre for Media Diversity. Of Jamaican descent, Lenny, my colleague and founding member of Impact X, provided the foreword, noting: 'Every time we see a great actor like Thandie [sic] Newton, Idris Elba or David Harewood leave these shores to find opportunities denied to them in the UK, it is a painful reminder of why casting is so important.'

Daniel Kaluuya, the first Black British actor to win an Academy Award (2021 Best Supporting Actor for *Judas and the Black Messiah*), had burst on to the global scene with his starring roles in the award-winning *Black Panther*, *Widows* and *Get Out*. He told Jonathan Dean of the *Sunday Times* in a 2020 interview that in the UK he had suffered no lack of audition opportunities. He'd often come very close but then wouldn't get the parts. He had only one conclusion: the colour of his skin.

Another award-winning Black British actor, producer and director, David Oyelowo, who gained global acclaim for his portrayal of Dr King in the 2014 movie *Selma*, told *Variety* in 2015 that in England he felt systemic bias in his industry. Oyelowo recalled feeling pushed out of the UK because of the glass ceiling he could feel himself hitting time and again. Fellow actors at his level were making the leap from theatre and TV to leading roles in film, while he was not. Oyelowo could feel that the industry operated on the myth that Black actors weren't real movie stars, or that they didn't believe he could be a leading man like James McAvoy or Benedict Cumberbatch.

Another example comes from Idris Elba, who has spoken in Parliament and led petition drives for measures to stem discrimination in film and television casting and beyond. He has said on more than one occasion that his success has not negated his experience of racism, personally or professionally. In an interview with Ellie Phillips in the highly conservative *Daily Mail Online* in June 2020, Elba said that asking him if he has ever encountered white supremacy in its different forms or been treated as inferior, because he is Black, is the same as asking him if he has ever breathed.

These personal accounts align with the facts. Yet myths and private theories about causes and remedies can cloud the issues. Some argue that progress must be happening by virtue of the existence of directors who have been appointed to champion the cause of diversity and inclusion. This myth suggests that because people are *talking* about good goals, results are being achieved. Not necessarily so. The other myth is that progress is being made and that opportunity is spread evenly, especially among all under-represented entertainment industry members. The existence of Idris Elba as a major star proves that the best will make it even in a hard industry like entertainment. The false belief is that a level playing field already exists. The facts show that progress has not been experienced equally within the Black, Asian and other communities of colour.

A case in point cropped up in response to a comment made in early 2021 by a director of diversity for the BBC about the gritty crime drama *Luther* and how the lead character had been written. In fact, the series creator/writer had conceived of the driven, haunted character of PCI John Luther without pre-scribing his ethnicity or background – which led very deliberately to casting with a colour-blind approach. As reported in Indie-wire, BBC diversity chief Miranda Wayland, speaking off the cuff at an entertainment industry conference, didn't see this as a win, because when the series premiered – although everyone loved the character – there were some unforeseen issues. Luther didn't have any Black friends. Some of his lifestyle choices didn't feel convincing. Wayland's concern was that the charac-ter and the storytelling lacked authenticity. While her comments rightfully touched a nerve about the need for audiences to see themselves authentically represented by on-screen characters, there wasn't a consensus view. Elba didn't respond to the com-ments directly. Instead, with a post on social media, he suggested that this was not a fight worth having; his focus was only on moving forward.

All of these facts are of interest, and they need to be used to inform what happens next. They certainly supported my own decision to move in front of the camera.

As you make informed decisions of your own, involving risk, it may be helpful to remember that your success – whatever your field – provides data from which you and others can bene-fit. This gives us a whole other take on the value of data-driven decisions not just in building and running our careers and our own companies, but in leading behemoth-sized corporations. After all, when you have billions of dollars at stake, you'd better rely on solid facts, not myths, in order to steer the operation.

Netflix, which launched in 1997, did not get to where it is today because its management were taking cues from what all the experts were telling them about upcoming trends. They weren't going to guess what they *thought* you wanted to buy but were going to discover and sell you precisely what you wanted to buy. Netflix made huge moves and massive investments of capital after gathering detailed information from customers' user habits. They adapted rapidly to changing preferences in technology. They worked with the facts, with data. Reed Hastings, co-founder of Netflix, has said in different settings: 'If the Starbucks secret is a smile when you get your latte . . . ours is that the Web site adapts to the individual's taste.'

Behemoths like Alibaba, Google and Amazon likewise are data sponges, continually adapting to changing facts as they arise. They continually absorb consumer cues to gain insights that allow them to mine present trends and predict future trends, avoiding falling for myths or folklore about the desires of consumers.

Another way to understand why facts get you further than myths is to recall that in the 1990s, again, one myth in the venture capital world was that billions of consumers were lining up to spend money on the internet, which led to excessive capital being dumped into dot.com startups. The facts, had anyone been paying attention to the data being generated by usage, told a much more modest story. In a 4 December 2018 Ideas.TED. com piece, internet historian Brian McCullough noted that there were only 400 million users across the entire internet at the time the dot.com bubble burst in 2000. Twenty-odd years later we have an estimated 4.9 billion users. That's hugely more potential viewers and consumers.

This vast overestimation of user numbers and usage behaviour was disastrous for the global economy, which lost trillions. Timing can be your saviour or your undoing. True, you can't always control timing, but having multiple datasets – including consumer trends as well as economic conditions – can help you better manage risk. Perhaps you had a disruptive, big business idea but it failed to take off because you were ahead of the curve. The takeaway, as many survivors of the dot.com era learned, is that riding the wave is often preferable to being ahead of the curve. If you are ahead of the curve, hopefully you can adapt to changes in the currents so you can ride the wave when it finally catches up with you. In doing so, the running theme here is to rely on the facts to keep you from a wipeout.

The need for representation

One of the best arguments for investing in under-represented founders, regardless of the trends, comes from research into the advantages of startups owned and run by diverse entrepreneurs. Reported by Jeff Green in *Bloomberg Business* in February 2020, a study from the Kauffman Fellows Research Center, written alongside MaC Venture Capital in Los Angeles, examined data starting in the 2001 wake of the dot.com bust all the way to 2018. They looked at the facts from 260,000 founders and 20,000-plus businesses. Despite encountering more barriers to funding when they first launch their businesses, ethnically diverse teams deliver a 30 per cent premium at exit or sale over their non-diverse peers. The same applies to outperforming at later-stage investment series and when the company goes public. This is all the more impressive considering that white founders represent 79 per cent of all fund-seeking startups – versus 16 per cent Asian and 5 per cent Black and Latinx combined.

One explanation for the overperformance of minority-run startups comes from the school of having to come up the hard way, often using resources more efficiently, and gaining early traction for their businesses from sheer hustle and action. The other factor helping startups that don't attract early investment is that they more readily bring together diverse teams who have differing viewpoints. We tend to think that teams made up of similarly minded folks get to solutions faster and are more productive. That's another myth compared to what the data says, as put forth by *Harvard Business Review* in 2016 – that diversity leads to more discomfort *and* better performance.

Even with all this encouraging data, VCs and other investors – on both sides of the Atlantic – share biases and see investment in non-white first-time entrepreneurs and women, white and non-white, as risky. It's doubly hard to approach those risk-averse investors with funding requests for entertainment productions. The myth, for decades, has been that investing in entertainment vehicles will boost your ego or feed your vanity but won't make you any money.

In a 2016 LinkedIn piece, Carla Morales, a producer of colour, recalls just how difficult it was for years to get investors to back theatrical, film and TV productions. Then she connected with a top agent (to the likes of Tyler Perry, Beyoncé, Jay-Z and Sean 'Puffy' Combs) who never had any trouble finding investors. The agent explained that this was because entertainment projects rarely die on the vine as so many well-funded tech startups do. Countering conventional wisdom, the agent had a track record proving that not only do most entertainment and media ventures stand a good chance of getting made, but that they can actually deliver the fastest 'legitimate' money you can make.

Realizing this, if you've ever been told to 'dream on' when imagining yourself in the entertainment field, I say – go for it!

The conversation about the need for greater representation in all forms of entertainment and media, particularly in film and TV, goes back to the earliest days of 'talking pictures'. It's mind-boggling to observe that between 1929 (the first year for the Oscar Awards) and 1996, there were only six Black recipients of Academy Awards for Best and Supporting Actors and Actresses. For those sixty-seven years, not one Best Actress Academy Award went to a Black woman and only one Academy Award for Best Actor was given to a Black actor – Sidney Poitier for *Lilies of the Field* (1963). Three Black males were recipients of Academy Awards for Best Supporting Actor: Louis Gossett, Jr (*An Officer and a Gentleman*, 1982), Denzel Washington (*Glory*, 1989) and Cuba Gooding, Jr (*Jerry Maguire*, 1996). Academy Awards for Best Supporting Actress went to only two Black women: Hattie McDaniel (*Gone with the Wind*, 1939) and Whoopi Goldberg (*Ghost*, 1990).

In the post-1990s – the years after I had my first foray into producing – the number of Black Best Actor wins increased. Breaking the drought was Denzel Washington for *Training Day* (2001), Jamie Foxx for *Ray* (2004) and Forest Whitaker for *The Last King of Scotland* (2006). Supporting Actor wins were achieved by Morgan Freeman for *Million Dollar Baby* (2004), Mahershala Ali for *Moonlight* (2016) and for *Green Book* (2018), and Daniel Kaluuya for *Judas and the Black Messiah* (2020). Representation of women of colour in Best Supporting roles rose too in the twenty-first century, with wins going to Jennifer Hudson for *Dreamgirls* (2006), Mo'Nique for *Precious* (2009), Octavia Spencer for *The Help* (2011), Lupita Nyong'o for *12 Years a Slave* (2013), Viola Davis for *Fences* (2016) and Regina King for *If Beale Street Could Talk* (2018). Only one Black woman has ever won the Academy Award for Best Actress: Halle Berry, for *Monster's Ball* (2001).

The facts are fascinating, so let's press on with them. They're eye-opening.

The story has been no better in the UK. A 2018 analysis of the BAFTAs dating back to the late 1960s – from diversity group Pearn Kandola – was similarly disheartening. Out of all the categories for entertainment industry awards, 94 per cent of the winners were white. A flagrant concern was that men of colour who had won in the Best Actor in a Leading Role category had invariably been cast as characters that could only have been played by them: Sir Ben Kingsley in *Gandhi* (1982), Jamie Foxx in *Ray* (2004), Forest Whitaker in *The Last King of Scotland* (2006) and Chiwetel Ejiofor in *12 Years a Slave* (2013). Add to that Rami Malek in *Bohemian Rhapsody* (2018).

No Black woman has won Best Actress in a Leading Role at the BAFTAs.

Actors of colour have won an equally small number of Best Supporting Actor awards. Samuel L. Jackson won for *Pulp Fiction* (1994), Barkhad Abdi for playing a Somalian pirate in *Captain Phillips* (2013), Dev Patel for *Lion* (2016), Mahershala Ali for *Green Book* (2018) and Daniel Kaluuya won his first BAFTA for *Judas and the Black Messiah* (2021).

Actresses of colour who have won for supporting roles are Thandiwe Newton for *Crash* (2005), Jennifer Hudson for *Dreamgirls* (2006), Mo'Nique for *Precious* (2009), Octavia Spencer for *The Help* (2011) and Viola Davis for *Fences* (2016).

In 2020 the nominations for 2019 films had zero nominations for actors of colour, prompting an outcry of 'BAFTAS So White'. The following year, nominations were definitely up and so too were the number of diverse presenters. Four women of colour were in contention for Best Actress in a Leading Role – Bukky Bakray in *Rocks*, Radha Blank in *The Forty-Year-Old Version*, Alfre Woodard in *Clemency* and Wunmi Mosaku in *His House*. Yet it was white American actress Frances McDormand in *Nomadland* who won the award.

What's my point here?

There is no question that the BAFTAs and the Academy Awards have a long way to go when it comes to representation, as does the entire entertainment industry. If there is any bright spot on the horizon it is the fact that many producers and VCs, like me and my colleagues, have begun to look past the myths and at the facts of why there has never been a better time than now to invest in more content from Black film-makers that creates more opportunities for diverse representation on screen and behind it.

In the mid-1990s I was given a crash course in independent film production and, more importantly, in risk management. This was my first real chance to risk wisely and use data to mitigate downside. It was also an instance of learning to put together the earlier steps we've covered – embracing the unexpected, disrupting constantly and using money as a tool, thinking big and thinking global while preparing for pitfalls.

At the time I'd been at CMI for a few years as a strategy consultant. In those days, I was often the only Black person on the team brought in to work with C-suite executives in various-sized companies in all kinds of industries. Being that one person of colour in the room may be familiar to you. It's something you learn to take in your stride, although deep down the feeling weighs on you. So, back at my office, I would mull over strategies to try to drive better representation in these different industries and organizations that happened to be my clients. One of those sectors, entertainment, seemed to hold promise. Before I leaped to conclusions, however, I began to gather facts.

Owning the game

This was a time of considerable growth enjoyed by cable broadcasters such as MTV, Nickelodeon, VH-1, and E! Entertainment Television. In a changing landscape, opportunities for under-represented content creators already existed. For instance, in 1991 the film *Daughters of the Dust*, one of the first commercial indie films directed by an African American woman, Julie Dash, had been released to much acclaim. We were still a long way from the Promised Land of equity in entertainment (and still are), but media was starting to become more inclusive. You could see that Oprah Winfrey was conquering daytime television and becoming a cottage industry in her own right, while Black movie stars had begun to claim leading roles – not just getting cast in the part of sidekick.

With a string of 1980s smash hits – *48 Hours*, *Trading Places*, *Beverly Hills Cop*, *Coming to America* and more – Eddie Murphy had again disproven the myth that a Black star couldn't carry a film to box-office success (Sidney Poitier was the original when he was the #1 box office draw of 1968). Samuel L. Jackson had made his movie debut in the 1980s as well, going from a smaller role in *Ragtime* (1981) to the Spike Lee-directed groundbreaking *Do the Right Thing* (1989), and eventually distinguishing himself as the number-one live-action movie star whose films cumulatively have made the most money at the box office. As of 2021 the total gross for all Jackson's movies is more than $27 billion. During the 1980s, Denzel Washington had challenged another Hollywood myth, that TV stars can't carry the big screen, when he leaped from the small screen of the hospital television drama *St Elsewhere* to deliver one stellar performance after another in feature films like *A Soldier's Story*, *Cry Freedom* and *Glory*.

In the 1980s, there was a similarly rich harvest of Black British films, many of them highly acclaimed for being disruptive in their storytelling and social commentary about the challenges for people of colour trying to survive in the UK. With diverse subject matter, these films also proved that Black Brits have diverse experiences. During a time when the Thatcher government propelled the myth that struggles for people of colour did not exist in the UK, other stories were being told by gritty films such as *Babylon* (1980), *Burning an Illusion* (1981), *The Passion of Remembrance* (1983) and *Playing Away* (1986).

In publishing, journalism, television and most media in the UK, a handful of Black pioneers were making inroads towards greater Black representation. Nothing had happened easily. In the late 1960s, many years before Black presenters Trevor McDonald and Moira Stuart became known for breaking the colour bar in TV news, Barbara Blake Hannah regularly appeared on Thames Television as one of three on-camera reporters. Most newspapers had publicized her appointment but, as she told the *Guardian* in January 2021, the *Daily Express* held out. They even stipulated, Blake Hannah claims, that no stories of people of colour could appear on the front page. Her reporting was top-notch, but after nine months in the job her contract was not renewed because, she was informed, there had been a deluge of letters and calls from viewers who objected to seeing a Black person on their TV 'delivering serious stories'; they were palatable, she was led to understand, only if they were in the field of entertainment.

If anyone needed proof that white supremacy was alive and kicking in the UK, this was it. Now that it was a known entity, broadcast companies could choose to take a stand, which they did in 1973 when Trevor McDonald made his debut on ITN and in 1981 when Moira Stuart joined the BBC. Black viewers held their collective breath, but both McDonald and Stuart were ultimately embraced, for the most part, and have been since.

At the same time, Margaret Busby was changing perceptions around the world as she built an iconic publishing enterprise in London. Born in Ghana and educated in Britain, Busby launched her publishing company in the late 1960s, while only in her twenties. In an October 2020 profile of her in the *Guardian*, she recalled the groundswell of activity that happened not long after she became the youngest publisher in the UK, as well as the only Black British female publisher.

The first book published by Allison & Busby, which she co-founded with Clive Allison, came from an introduction to the African American author Sam Greenlee, a former serviceman who had completed a novel that had been rejected by forty US publishers. Busby was enthralled by the fictional story of the first Black man recruited by the CIA for a visible role that made the spy agency look good but was no job at all. Busby loved the subversive twist of the thriller and decided to take Greenlee under her wing. When the *Observer* declined to publish an excerpt from Greenlee's novel, *The Spook Who Sat by the Door* – because they weren't used to excerpting fiction – Busby told them they were 'wrong' and upended the myth that only non-fiction was fit to print in journalistic pages. They couldn't argue and ran the excerpt. Greenlee's book went on to be an international phenomenon, was translated into multiple languages and made into a film that was so provocative in its portrayal of institutionalized racism that the powers that be worried it would start a race war. The FBI shut the film down.

Busby was relentless in bringing under-represented authors to the fore and in providing a platform for voices that needed to be heard. Among the many groundbreaking writers she championed were C. L. R. James, H. Rap Brown, James Ellroy and Hunter S. Thompson.

In the 1980s, Busby used her voice to advocate for greater representation in print and in media by joining GAP (Greater Access to Publishing). She recognized that representation lets others see their own possibilities. If you don't see someone of colour in your industry, you assume that it's exclusively white and possibly conclude that you don't belong.

That is not a myth, it is borne out by facts.

What Margaret Busby, Oprah Winfrey and others were

learning was that the only way to truly change the game was to own the game. And that was starting to happen, though more in the US than in the UK. By the 1990s the US was starting to see the rising influence of such corporations as BET and Radio One – two Black-owned/run media companies I'd been following for years that had benefited from the early investment pioneering of DC-based VC Syncom Venture Partners. Both are powerful examples of the ways in which Black entrepreneurs risk wisely while adapting to meet the interests of their consumers.

In 1980, BET was founded by Robert Johnson, no relation to John H. Johnson of Johnson Publishing, although he began by following a similarly traditional model of identifying an underserved demographic – African American viewers – and choosing to superserve consumers who had been taken for granted in the pre-cable universe. His background included working for a pay-TV subscription channel which had allowed him to understand the cable business at a time of technological and business model revolution. In 1991, BET went public and became the second Black-owned corporation (after Johnson Products) to be traded on the New York Stock Exchange. In 1998, the company went private again (after buying back 35 per cent of its stock for $300 million, at double the value of the shares). The risk was tremendous and at the same time wise. Johnson and his partners knew their audience – even then, they had the data. Plus, it was just in time to be ready to seek possible suitors for the sale of their global media company, which had almost no direct competition.

The expansive and non-traditional component of BET came about because all along Robert Johnson was going for Amazon scale, not Thames. He understood that because BET was ubiquitously available as part of almost every basic cable plan, he could monetize in three ways: through paid advertising

WE DON'T NEED PERMISSION

from growing the numbers of brands seeking to reach consumers of colour; through a share of basic cable subscription fees; and by negotiating international distribution fees. In 2001, BET reached 62.4 million homes. That number would climb to over 88 million by 2015. In turn, the momentum skyrocketed the channel's valuation enough for its phenomenal sale to Viacom in 2001 for $3 billion – which officially made Robert Johnson the first Black American male billionaire and his wife Sheila, a BET co-founder, the first Black female billionaire.

The story of Cathy Hughes and Radio One/Urban One, the largest Black-owned and -operated, multimedia/broadcast conglomerate in the US – is the best example of how data was used to risk wisely. Gaining her first skills in Nebraska selling radio ads for a local AM radio station – which she eventually bought – Hughes refined the art of gathering data on how many listeners the station reached, what kind of music the audience wanted, and communicating that data to advertisers. She refined that skill after going to DC to teach at Howard University, where she became head of radio sales for the university's station. In one year she famously brought in twelve times the annual ad revenue. By 1980, as the first woman Vice-President and General Manager of a radio station in DC, Cathy had instituted and popularized a format that was being called the 'Quiet Storm', a commercial, smooth, jazzy R&B categorized as Adult Contemporary. The music was not jazz, but was relaxing to listeners. It went on to be adopted by 480 stations nationwide. Not one to be limited – a model of thinking big – Hughes then turned to talk radio that focused on Black issues of the day. Over the next two decades, Radio One came to dominate the urban radio market with a diverse portfolio of more than sixty stations that played everything from hip-hop, R&B and gospel to talk radio formats. In 1999, Cathy Hughes became the first African American woman to chair a publicly held corporation.

I was fortunate to get to know Cathy during President Obama's first term, when she led the administration's council for creating greater access to opportunities for under-represented individuals and groups, working in conjunction with the Small Business Administration. I had a chance to see Cathy as a leader in action and understood better how she had infiltrated the mostly all-boys' club of media ownership – including radio, TV and digital.

Cathy was always by far the most well-to-do person in the room, yet she was completely down to earth, very inclusive and consensus-oriented. She was a great listener and extremely interested in what other people had to say. Her collaborative manner must have been disarming in the years she was building Radio One and negotiating terms. She had been a single mother in those early years, and I imagined she hadn't forgotten the challenges. As a result, Cathy genuinely wanted her success to create opportunities for others who were in the same tough straits in which she had been. She could not have been more passionate about encouraging representation of Black leadership in all aspects of business.

The other piece of tell-tale data not to be ignored in the 1990s was that mainstream advertisers were finally paying attention to the power of Black viewership and consumer patterns. Content had to keep pace. So, after decades of family-friendly sitcoms about Beulah, Julia, the Sanfords, the Evans family, the Jeffersons and the Huxtables, this was when TV programmers began to realize that, yes, there was a hunger to see more diverse portrayals of Black experiences – from the irreverent sketch comedy *In Living Color* to Will Smith moving from the inner city to the mansion of his well-heeled relatives in *The Fresh Prince of Bel-Air*.

In the UK a similar pattern existed, starting with 1956's *A Man from the Sun*, starring Cyril Grant, as a counter to the completely racist *The Black and White Minstrel Show* (1958–78). Those shows gave way to *The Fosters* (which mirrored the US's *Good Times*), along with *Empire Road*, *Mixed Blessings*, *The Lenny Henry Show* and *Desmond's*. Eventually, the biting social commentary of the sketch comedy show *The Real McCoy* came to be must-see television.

By the 1990s, though we were nowhere near having doors swing wide open so we could be invited in, the entertainment world recognized that content featuring people of colour was worth considering. So it was in that atmosphere that I took a chance to try my hand at producing.

Two questions. Could I make a quick decision to veer off-piste? And could I handle the risk?

When you think about how you might manage an opportunity that seems to fall into your lap but may well throw you off the path you've been on, your lifeline can be a ready-made process for risk assessment. You may well have your own way of figuring out pros and cons, the weighing up we necessarily do in order to reach what feels like the right decision. If you do, great. If not, you can always borrow from mine. The key, again, is to gather facts, not myths, to help you choose whether to say yay or nay to the possibility being offered.

They call it 'show business' for a reason

When a call came to me at my CMI office from Monica Harris, a law school friend, I could tell from her tone that this was more than a social conversation. Quickly she got to the point. *The Promised Land* was the name of a movie that she had written and wanted to direct. At first, I thought she wanted my feedback.

'That's terrific,' I said, or something supportive along those lines.

Monica described the story to me – about a Black female lawyer, Sydney Banks, who, in seeking the 'Promised Land' of success at her firm, is drawn into a tale of deception she has to unravel before things spiral out of control and she gets taken out by criminal forces. Think Tom Cruise in *The Client* meets Mario Van Peebles in *New Jack City*. There was no question in my mind that if Monica set her mind to getting a movie made, she would do it. A savvy, larger-than-life presence, Monica's intellect and drive combined to make her unstoppable – an overwhelming persuader and a natural leader.

Monica was that one first-year law student who had a summer job locked in before any of the rest of us. She also wrote for the *Harvard Law Review* and, on top of that, used to recruit her friends to help when she made short movies in her 'spare time'.

My first thought was that if Monica had a script she wanted to get made, there wasn't much to stop her. I said as much. Before I commented further, she said, 'I want you to make it with me.'

Her idea was to put together a production company, raise the money ourselves, and get it done in five months with a team of our other close friends. My brain immediately went into risk-assessment mode as I tried to quantify three aspects that would offer me facts before I said yes. That is – Risk, Exposure and Reward.

When you consider a venture, it makes sense to look first at what you are *risking*. How much money? Time? Reputation? As in my case, are you going to jeopardize other jobs, relationships, opportunities and investments by throwing yourself into this potential? In other words, what do you have to lose?

The next question is to ask what your exposure to that loss

might be. This is where having facts rather than myths is so important. What you are asking, really, is what is the likelihood of your making returns and what protections might you have if you do go forward. If you are walking along a cliff, a very risky thing to do, your exposure wouldn't be severe if there were some kind of guard rails. No guard rails? The facts tell us that no matter how exciting and promising this opportunity might be, you may be far too exposed to risk it all on a business proposition.

The calculation of the reward is an assessment that tells you what you have to gain. If you can see that there's a lot of money to be made, backed up by data, that will mitigate the possibility you might lose your investment. Better yet, if you can see rewards that include gaining experience in a new arena, the possibility of earning a calling card that can advance you to the next opportunity, or – being honest with yourself – the potential to learn even if you fail, that's a solid reward.

My mind raced as I thought of all the logistics and the ridiculous risk of taking months off from my job at a firm where I was finally on track to become a senior associate, then partner. Five months could set me back or derail my career. But my exposure wasn't severe. The facts told me that if you were ever going to produce a small-budget independent Black movie, this was the time. There was a demand. Not to mention we had something that was mostly missing in the marketplace – a Black female-driven feature. In my head, I was operating under a slight myth that I was going to produce this movie and then become the next Black big-budget producer of the adrenaline-packed action movies that were all the rage at the time. Of course, I had a lot to learn – including the core principles of Step #4: how to risk wisely and use data to mitigate the downside.

There is one other measure that I use that is less about data and more about future-gazing. Whenever you are making a decision that will be disruptive in risky ways, try imagining yourself in the future if you were to stay on the same trajectory you are currently on. In that scenario, would you look back at the risk you passed up and regret it? If so, that is valuable information to give yourself. Mitigating downside if you don't do well will allow you to go forward without regret.

Before we got off the phone, I said, 'Okay, let's do it.'

The conversation had lasted all of ten minutes.

Once I read Monica's screenplay I knew that my rapid risk assessment was on point. Monica had taken the commercially viable thriller genre, thrown in some sly humor, borrowed elements of a hit movie of recent years – *Working Girl* starring Melanie Griffith and Harrison Ford – given it the twist of a Black female lead and set it in the back-stabbing world of a law office.

Next came the call to my parents to let them know of my decision. Law school, consulting and now film-making. How do you justify that? Adeline and Henry were quiet on the other end of the phone as I presented my case. When I told them that we weren't trying to 'sell' a movie to Hollywood but rather we were going to produce it ourselves, thus attempting to rewrite some of the rules that kept outsiders from breaking in, neither of them could hold back their enthusiasm. In true parent-VC style, they offered and then committed to becoming investors. They believed in me, of course, but I think they recognized that new doors were opening in the entertainment industry and, like me, they were excited by it.

Universal and Paramount takeaways

Bringing a movie from concept to reality was a process that was messy, sometimes ad hoc, yet also straightforward. Show business is a contact sport that doesn't require impressive university degrees. In Hollywood neither I nor my two partners – writer/director Monica Harris and Shemin Proctor, a fellow Harvard Law grad – had any kind of real calling card. Shemin was the furthest along in her career, being in line to become a managing partner in a top legal firm, already highly respected for her work in energy, gas and oil. Yet none of us had street cred for having produced anything before. In other words, we didn't know how to play the game.

What we did have was a great idea, strong networks and a clear understanding of the facts: there was appetite for a film like this. We created a detailed budget for the film (preproduction through post-production) and agreed on raising a total of $300,000, starting with our own family and friends, and then reaching out to friends and colleagues of family and friends. We weren't relying on one money stream, which was in our favour. Yet we certainly had to hustle. The best analogy I can offer is that this was kind of like a potluck. We created a support system of investors and everyone brought something to the feast. I was reminded of the kind of rent parties folks would throw – with good food, music playing and dancing. Everyone would pitch in whatever they could to help someone make their rent or open the doors of their business.

The takeaway here is that the hustle to raise money doesn't have to be the same slog as if you're trying to get a loan from a bank. When you gather the data, you discover that lots of start-ups combine teams and allies of the willing and able. When you pitch in together, pool resources, you share the risk together.

For Monica, this was more than a one-off effort. She saw this film as her ticket to making her name in the entertainment industry, and from the start I wasn't far behind her. I was all-in. It was my first truly entrepreneurial endeavour, and I experienced the oft-reported adrenaline rush of ownership which made the grind all the more meaningful. Not wanting a penny spent on anything extraneous, I lived the proverbial Hollywood rags story by relocating to Los Angeles and actually sleeping in my friend Joe Voyticky's car, with the occasional luxury of a spare couch, shower and washing machine. That alone convinced me that the struggle myths were true; I found out early on that the actual day-to-day business of film and TV production was far from glamorous. There is a lot of 'hurry up and wait' – securing permits, preparing locations, getting shots set up, correcting lighting and sound, doing take after take, delivering film to the processing lab. Every day of shooting was like making a new meal around a campfire without getting to taste the finished product. Every day was also a race against the clock, since each day cost real money for salaries, rentals and food.

The key was a belief in the project, the team we assembled and a detailed production and sales plan that drew in investors. In this way, we countered the myth that we couldn't compete with big-budget studio movies by presenting factually based arguments for why and how we'd take advantage of growing opportunities to sell movies to cable, premium channels and video stores. We used our law and business expertise to set up two companies – Sweaty Palm Productions (because we were always nervous) and Gravy Train Pictures – which were built to last. Pooling all of our resources was the charm that gave us a running jump into the work. Combining networks expanded our reach. When we searched around to cast the lead, we could barely get on the phone with any of the top agents. Then, through kismet, one of us knew someone who connected us to Reuben Cannon, one of Hollywood's first Black casting direc-tors, whose extensive credits included *The Color Purple* in 1985. Reuben is Hollywood royalty and he loved our intention to pri-oritize hiring Black talent – for cast and crew.

In 2018, more than twenty years later, the fully realized version of these principles came to life with Marvel's *Black Panther* – which grossed $1.3 billion, the second-highest box office for the year, the biggest-grossing film ever by a Black director (Ryan Coogler), the second-highest box office opening ever, the ninth-highest-grossing film of all time. With a script by Coogler and Joe Robert Cole, leading roles played almost entirely by Black stars, and strong female characters, it finally put to rest the old myth that predominantly Black and under-represented teams couldn't conquer the global box office.

In our own scaled-down effort, we set out to 'be the change we wanted to see' and hired over two dozen women and men of colour who had acumen in various aspects of the industry to work in some capacity on our movie. When you are struggling to combat bias based on the myth that under-represented folks aren't as qualified as the over-represented (usually white males), it can be all the more empowering to you when you look for a chance to share the opportunity with others. When you choose to become a door-opener, watch how that effort multiplies and pays dividends for you as well.

We tuned out the scepticism and mythology suggested by anyone who didn't believe that (on our budget) we'd get the best candidates who were in the minority in the industry. We proved otherwise. We were aided immensely by the data and resources contributed by Reuben Cannon, including his track record of excellence that convinced Lela Rochon to play the lead in our movie. That was a game-changer. With Lela on board, the quality of the remaining cast took a big step up.

Another prevailing myth of that era was that indie films had trouble getting distribution. It was partly true, but there was new data coming through that told us there was a growing audience for smaller 'straight-to-video' thrillers and mysteries, as well as darkly humorous content like ours. Straight-to-video was like making a film for Netflix today and bypassing the theatrical release. In fact, our category of 'dramedy' was perfectly suited for this evolving world. The expanding universe of cable and premium channels offered an alternative form of distribution. The hitch was that, in order to appeal to those buyers, you had to market your movie at international film festivals. Happily, we found a sales agent and made it into the Venice Film Festival. But then, in a maybe not-so-wise risk, we decided to pull *Legal Deceit* (the renamed film – *The Promised Land* was taken) from that festival to qualify for Cannes. Sadly, we weren't accepted at Cannes.

This experience gave me an invaluable lesson about risk. This was a classic moment of having a 'bird in the hand' and not appreciating it. Getting into the Venice Film Festival was a bird in the hand! But we decided to risk it so we could get into Cannes. We were inexperienced and didn't have the data that would have told us the advantages of movies like ours getting distribution deals at Venice. We went with the myth that Cannes was the be-all and end-all for making it. The bird-in-the-hand reminder can be applied in many situations. If you don't have the data, do your due diligence and go find as many facts as you can.

All was not lost in our case, however. Because of contacts made from all of these efforts, we scored deals with HBO and Cinemax, then with Blockbuster and a couple of other video rental outlets. The remainder of our distribution channels were secured with foreign territories, airlines and luxury cruise ships.

All told we did well, earning our calling card and repaying most of the capital everyone had invested. We would have liked to have returned a profit but didn't. And from that I learned another potent lesson about how to view your personal Return on Investment (ROI). In addition to profit, what you also get in return on every investment is valuable data that can be put to use for an even greater return in a later venture.

What really worked for us was proving the doubters wrong. For every entrepreneur, my message is to lessen the volume on the unsupportive sideliners and their myths. Amplify your facts and let the facts speak for themselves. Your job should also be to look at the shortcomings – or what didn't work – and act like Sherlock Holmes or Luther so that further data can be gathered.

For most business startups, the takeaway as far as risk goes is that a great idea with pooled resources and combined networks can get the difficult done and sometimes attract attention from sectors you never suspected. It will still be hard work, but an aligned team can get better results faster.

Keeping the team together is another issue. That's a big lesson.

To no one's surprise, not long after our two months of production roughing it for a common cause in Southern California, we disbanded. We knew from the beginning that Shemin Proctor was drawn to making a movie as a friend – to be of help – but wasn't interested in a career change. Monica, ready to make that change, soon went to work for Dick Wolf Productions of *Law & Order* fame. She later started her own company.

In my journey as an entrepreneur, I took away a new appreciation for how important it is to choose the right partners in any endeavour. The reality, not a myth – which you may have experienced with your own partnerships – is that when you go into business with your friends, there is a risk that either the business or the friendship might suffer, or both. It is wise to choose carefully with whom you work, for what goals, and for what period of time. Your best rule of thumb when setting up a partnership is to create an agreed-upon process before there are any disagreements about direction.

Our project should have had more impact, as measured in getting better reviews, becoming a cult classic or making more money, I felt. The byproduct would have been more clout, individually if not together, along with providing a roadmap others could follow, in turn empowering lots more Black producers to employ more people of colour behind the scenes and on screen. This was to be a recurring revelation – we could have done more to change the game. That being said, after my return to work at CMI I was able to parlay lessons learned and the changing facts of the cable TV industry to become that much more relevant to clients like HBO, MTV, and E! Entertainment Television. Without my first film venture, that would not have been possible.

Don't forget that your journey to being a wise risk taker is an ongoing process. What you learn from one undertaking can be put to use powerfully on the next one. When you take a hard look at what worked and what didn't, you may even solve a problem that can be monetized as a business unto itself. Which is what happened to me in my next venture.

dot.com

Between 1998 and 2001, the journey I took with speedsolve, my tech startup, taught me a tough lesson about what mitigating downside means. The idea crystallized as the result of not being able to resolve technical snafus on the job while making the movie. The creative industries are, well, creative. There may not be robust systems in place for when deliveries are delayed or the wrong equipment shows up. Things go wrong. The cost of a delayed production can snowball. Tempers flare. My tech startup idea, just in time for me to ride the dot.com wave and nail down the capital to make it happen, was to create a mechanism to alleviate those kinds of problems in record time.

I'm often asked how you know when you've got a winning,

investable idea. In this instance, the idea made sense because I'd already done the groundwork. All my expertise from *Getting to Yes* was about imparting systematized solutions, all based on principles that worked. speedsolve was about sharing those principles in other business conflict settings and, much like an engine that printed money, the startup had the potential to be very profitable. From there, I thought, if we've already created workflows and processes and worksheets that we use with people 'in real life', why not do the same thing digitally? With the help of data-mining information and archiving methodology, I was sure we could develop a user-friendly interface. The word-of-mouth would be phenomenal.

In classic problem-solving mode, I compiled an inventory of issues often raised in conflict-resolution settings and saw how the steps for alleviating those problems were similar. Monetizing this product was a no-brainer. As a strategy consultant, I was paid well to custom-design a solution and facilitate on behalf of clients. However, not everyone with a customer complaint and not every business with routine, hassle-filled paperwork could afford the money or time to have a hands-on consultant. What they could afford was an automated problem-solving system invented for the global marketplace that put power into the hands of users to report, track, monitor and resolve their consumer complaints.

Imagine the late 1990s. There were no apps, there were no ubiquitous laptops and smartphones. In the web-based world of 1990s dot.com technology, speedsolve offered an automated customer relationship management system for the most common complaints that users would self-select, and it usually resolved their issues. From there, if that didn't work, there was an escalation process that would still keep users in digital mode that had a high rate of resolving everything speedily. When those steps didn't work either, the user could speak live to a customer service agent and receive, in essence, hands-on mediation over the phone; in rare cases my startup offered services to connect users with binding arbitration. Based on the data simulations, we could accurately predict that 99 per cent of complaints would be resolved without hands-on mediation. Less than 1 per cent would require any human intervention.

In building speedsolve, I found out why it's so tough to choose the right data when you manage risk. There appear to be an infinite number of facts for every situation, so selecting which ones you need becomes a challenge of identifying 'signal versus noise'. When a fact comes through clearly from your research, that's a signal. Noise is basically distortion. You may learn that all facts are not created equal.

My data came from reviewing numerous studies about consumer experiences from transactions and business conducted online. Complaints included issues of fraud, products not delivered, errors in amounts billed or not credited, wrong items, incorrect charges and damage. The clear-cut signal in the data said that 99 per cent of the problems had digital solutions.

During the dot.com boom years, the myth was that Silicon Valley VCs couldn't invest enough money fast enough. To get speedsolve off the ground I had been prepared to speak to hundreds of third-party funders and be rejected, even when the data was able to help me determine that I'd found a hugely scalable idea that applied in an ascendant market and in a fast growth space. Luckily, I didn't fall for that myth and wasn't shocked by the fact that after hundreds of emails, calls and meetings I received no investment.

Another myth was that this revolutionary ascendent market could only go up even more as technology and e-commerce increased.

Wrong.

Refusing to be discouraged, I reminded myself that there

was a huge amount of capital available in the world, a lot of excitement about new ideas, and a flow of facts about the gestation of new disruptive companies on a daily basis. You may wonder why I did not go back to the same set of friends and family that had funded the film. The fact is that not all investors are right for all enterprises. Investors have their own interests and objectives. Aligning your shared interests is what makes for the best outcomes in risky ventures.

There were valued advisors who were supporting me, but who were slow to bring in the investment needed to move along and get the product ready for launch. At a critical juncture, the anticipated infusion of cash fell through and I had to consider alternative plans. In that moment, the dot.com bubble burst and speedsolve was speedily dissolved.

Timing was wrong and I missed the wave. Wipeout.

The facts and time have proven that electronic customer relationship management is a huge and profitable sector. CRM is ubiquitous and one of the biggest software sectors in the world, expected to generate over $80 billion by 2025. I was just a bit too early. Because the market has evolved, if I started speedsolve today I would have to think long and hard about consumer behaviour. Resolving a minor or even major complaint is easier than ever for digital customers. Current default practice is to send it back free of charge or get an instant credit if you are dissatisfied. Would speedsolve still be disruptive? Probably not.

Over the years, I have heard every successful entrepreneur under the sun declare that nothing creates success like failure. I'm not sure that's a fact. Then again, I also got the memo that failure isn't fatal.

Was I going to give up? Of course not.

This wasn't solely about me, I realized, but about the bigger goals of empowering Black entrepreneurs in all sectors. I was bruised, for sure. But not quite broken. Mostly, I was ready to come back with more experience under my belt that would allow me to ultimately change the game.

The biggest factual takeaway – which can be applied liberally – is about the aspect of risk that you can't control. Timing. Timing is a double-edged sword, first offering opportunities you might never have been given but then taking them away when the economic pendulum you don't control swings the other way.

How do you get control? It has to be earned, and I'll tell you how.

5

EVERYTHING DESERVES A GOOD TURNAROUND

Step #5: Put your money where your mouth is and make your resources matter

Impossible is just a big word thrown around by small men who find it easier to live in the world they've been given than to explore the power they have to change it. Impossible is not a fact. It's an opinion. Impossible is not a declaration. It's a dare. Impossible is potential. Impossible is temporary. Impossible is nothing.

MUHAMMAD ALI

Where you are is not who you are.

URSULA BURNS, BUSINESSWOMAN, ENTREPRENEUR, VC

In 1987, in a lengthy *Harvard Business Review* article, John O. Whitney told of the special skills required for turning around an ailing company and suggested that those same turnaround abilities could be used to revive an ailing economy. But that wasn't all. Whitney also observed that, in a highly competitive world, for every enterprise the fundamental tools you need to succeed are the same ones required for the turnaround of a business on the brink. In other words, when you are in need of a turnaround – which can be loosely defined as the financial recovery of a poorly performing company, economy, or indeed an individual – you may weather the storm better if you've already sharpened the main skills required.

Not every turnaround succeeds, but when it does it revitalizes a company's fortunes and secures its future. No practice is as vital to a good turnaround as the skill you develop with Step #5 – *Put your money where your mouth is and make your resources matter*. This step can give you control by getting you to focus on your value, even in times of crisis, and on possible silver linings of timing you might not instantly recognize.

For example, by the summer of 2021 a consensus among leading economic analysts was that there was a silver lining in the midst of the global pandemic's tsunami of devastation: a startup boom the likes of which had not been seen in decades. In April 2021 *Forbes* reported the findings first released in the *Financial Times* that, as of July 2020, the US had seen a record number of applications for starting a new business – 551,657. That was a 95 per cent increase from the same period a year earlier. In September 2020, Japan's new business registrations were at 10,000, 14 per cent above the figure for September 2019. In the UK, the last two months of 2020 saw an increase of 30 per cent for registered companies. The double-digit rise in the number of startups from June 2020 to April 2021 was said to be in response to demands from consumers in the 'logistics, delivery and IT industries'. Online trading in the UK had further driven the startup boom for most of 2020.

In the wake of economic upheaval, entrepreneurship has

WE DON'T NEED PERMISSION

long been a tried-and-tested strategy for surviving financial disaster. And, as we saw earlier, Black people have learned in the past to turn racism on its head by being self-sufficient, in turn creating entrepreneurial opportunities. All of which is not to downplay another set of data points that showed the disproportionate number of communities of colour brutally hit by Covid-19.

Even before the pandemic, Black and under-represented business owners in the UK and the US knew the regular struggle of barely keeping their doors open. That made survival less likely during any kind of difficult economic headwinds. In the US, between February and April 2020 Black business ownership fell by 40 per cent, 'the largest drop across any ethnic group', as *Forbes* reported in early 2021. Part of the problem in both the UK and the US was to do with the types of Black-owned businesses most affected – especially sole traders whose work is based on personal contact such as shops, restaurants, fitness trainers and gym owners, hair care and other types of beauty salons. Along with the toll taken on all businesses by mandated closures, according to a *Forbes* piece by Kemberley Washington in June 2021, many Black businesses had to incur the familiar barriers to financial relief – from the challenges of securing private loans and investments to onerous requirements for government approval to get assistance more easily procured by white business owners.

The other issue, applicable in the UK as well, was that, historically, Black families have faced and continue to face a growing racial wealth gap. Wealth, according to *Forbes*, is defined by the assets amassed over time. That includes savings, retirement funds and property, from which you deduct any debt, for example credit cards and a mortgage. *Forbes* notes that 'Institutionalized racism has put the Black community far behind its white counterparts when it comes to accumulating such wealth.'

When I checked how things stood in terms of Black wealth in 2020, I was appalled yet not shocked that there were only four Black individuals in the UK's Rich List (which records a total of 1,000 of the UK's wealthiest people). One was Lewis Hamilton, two were tech founders, and one was a retiree from the financial services arena. And of the several super-rich billionaires on the list, none were Black. Then, in May 2021, news broke in numerous outlets that our first British Black billionaire, Strive Masiyiwa, had made the list. Originally from Zimbabwe, Masiyiwa had made his fortune as a telecom industry founder and had amassed wealth of £1.087 billion. In the midst of the ravages of Covid-19 sweeping the African continent, Strive Masiyiwa was putting his money where his mouth was by seeking solutions for providing vaccines to the more than 1.3 billion Africans at risk.

In the US, the numbers for African Americans among the ultra-wealthy have been somewhat better in recent years, but barriers remain for people of colour – both in terms of the acquisition of wealth, power, influence and opportunity, and in terms of access to credit and capital. Those same barriers were evident in the UK's *Colour of Power* report that in 2018 showed little improvement over the previous year in the number of key roles held by Black Britons, confirming that – from the arts to the military to politics, from bureaucrats to services to business to sports management, from the North to the South – little power is little power and always will have little power if nothing happens to change the dynamics resulting in the slow progress in the first place.

However, the possibility for major change in the UK as well as in the US suddenly made itself known amid the Covid-19 pandemic with the blasting-off of a startup boom and the highest-ever amount of venture capital invested in companies in the first half of 2021. In the US Crunchbase stated that the amount was $300 billion. In the UK, KPMG reported the sum to be £11.8 billion, while Tech Nation put the number at £13.5 billion. Adding to that potential was an unprecedented $50 billion of pledges to confront white supremacy – pledges made in the boardrooms and C-suites of the global corporate ruling powers in response to the murder of George Floyd, which had set off a global uprising.

A lengthy special analysis from the *Washington Post* published in mid-2021 recalled how companies from Wall Street to Silicon Valley rallied behind the Black Lives Matter movement and repeated the slogan. Jamie Dimon, CEO of JPMorgan Chase, took a knee with his employees. McDonald's embraced George Floyd – and others like him who had been murdered at the hands of police brutality – as 'one of us'. The commitments made, the rhetoric and optics offered, were seductive. Clearly, corporations had received the memo that empowering, enriching and elevating Black businesses could positively change the world. Still, the jury was going to stay out until further notice as to whether meaningful action would follow lofty promises. Would these corporate spenders abide by their stated values and put their money where their mouths were? Would they really use all their resources like they meant it? And would they give Black and other under-represented entrepreneurs the support and the opportunities to specialize, grow and soar? Or would these potential silver linings ultimately deliver only for people who were already privileged and connected?

The best way to achieve the turnaround we want is to remain vigilant. It is our collective responsibility to ensure that the keepers of the coffers do the right thing by following through on what they say they are going to do. When we expect the individuals and institutions making commitments to have the courage of their convictions, we are not asking for permission. We are empowering ourselves, our allies, public servants and the media, along with investors, to make sure that everyone puts real money where their mouths are.

A turnaround that can empower and significantly lift Black businesses worldwide will benefit all of us.

Opportunity in crisis

There are hopeful lessons to be recalled from past turnarounds – like the ones we saw after the wreckage left by the dot.com bust and also in the wake of the 2008 global financial meltdown, where resilient and innovative founders were willing to take what they'd learned and commit to a complete reinvention. Rightmove and eHarmony started in 2000, the year the dot.com bubble burst. Startups that were launched in the crush of the 2008–9 global recession include Airbnb, Groupon, Uber and WhatsApp. Those founders understood that nothing is impossible, even – or especially – in times of crisis.

Other smaller to mid-sized businesses were similarly born during bleak periods. In some cases, many were not starting from scratch but able to adapt or dramatically repurpose themselves. Sometimes this is called a pivot. I'd seen and experienced first-hand how a hard pivot and a major reset can come in the form of a top-to-bottom turnaround.

Among the secrets of turnaround, particularly after a cycle of boom to bust to boom again, is the importance of a period of reflection. The truth is that it's hard to move forward with new gusto when you don't know the full story of what took you down to the bottom in the first place. Once you reflect, once you've spent time working out what went wrong, you are poised to seize the moment, set your goals and use the power-play of Step #5 and put your money where your mouth is and make your resources matter.

Here's the thing about this step. One of the fastest routes to empowerment for Black people is to begin – much as my mother urged us to do when we protested unfair hiring practices at the local grocery store – by putting our money where our mouths are *in all phases of our spending*. It's a reminder to hire Black contractors if you're building a house, to patronize Black-owned businesses and engage under-represented professionals (accountants, lawyers, doctors and investment advisors) as much as possible. *Putting your money where your mouth is* means contributing to candidates who share your values and who will take active stands against policies that oppress people of colour. Shockingly, in the US 8 per cent of the African American vote went to Donald Trump, and in the UK general election of 2019, 20 per cent of voters of colour went for Boris Johnson and his Conservative Party, despite a track record of racist, xenophobic and homophobic remarks and policies.

When we invest, it's vital that we don't add capital to companies that have discriminatory practices or that fund the fringe groups who are openly or subversively chipping away at our rights in multiple ways around the world. I marvel, and despair, at how people weigh their needs and rationalize that class or financial interests supersede issues of race.

On the business front, making your resources matter is a reminder to take strong positions in leveraging your own success and your networks to hire, promote and elevate more Black employees, especially more women of colour – which we'll come back to in Step #8. Of course, it's also a call to all Black leaders in organizations, unions and professional alliances to prioritize policies that address inequities wherever they exist. It's what we do as VCs at Impact X, urging others to join us.

When crisis throws you, your company or the entire economy into peril, the situation forces you to pinch pennies. When you have very little in terms of cash flow, you must consciously and deliberately marshal your resources every which way. During the Covid-19 lockdown, the founder of a restaurant supply business asked my advice about his decision to move to a bigger and more prestigious office address and attract more customers. That's not a terrible move during periods of growth. But it made no sense to spend all that money and time to expand to a bigger office when most employees were working remotely, customers were doing transactions online and foot traffic was minimal. In crisis, the last thing you want to do is to splash out by taking on permanent expenses you don't really need.

Learning to *be deliberate* in planning how you will use the smallest and/or the most ample of resources should be a staple in your recipe for success. It's common-sense guidance and just a smart way to focus your energies on the part you can play in your own Black empowerment on the micro and macro levels. When we give ourselves permission to align values with actions, growing wealth, power and influence, if we are deliberate we get a nice byproduct – less time wasted on things which don't matter.

Knowing what matters helped to ground me in the time after the dot.com bubble burst. There was a moment when I came close to imagining that the shelving of speedsolve was the worst thing that had ever happened to me. It wasn't. It was an opportunity to learn the truth of that saying – *What doesn't kill you makes you stronger.* In fact, in time I came up with a saying of my own – *Cherish the bust.*

When you can begin to process the information – however gruesome it is to confront – you can gain from it. You can acquire an advantage you would never be given otherwise. Cherish the bust can be your daily entrepreneurial mantra. It's yet another way of not needing permission.

Sometimes you have to depart from your intended path to discover these and other secrets of turnaround.

History matters

Don't get me wrong. I didn't love the period of self-reflection required of me in the aftermath of the dot.com bust. Looking back at my own history wasn't something I did out of habit. For the most part I am extremely forward-focused, always ready for the next venture. But history matters. In the same way that you need to amass and analyse data to move forward, so you need to look at what has gone to assess what might happen next. I was encouraged to take the time to recap where I'd been by my partner, Michael, who, as a historian, often offered a perspective I would have missed. A look back was what was needed.

I very much recommend this sort of process as an exercise for anyone feeling derailed or stuck, especially if caused by circumstances beyond your control, even when you feel overwhelmed. Look at your own decision-making and observe that there are lessons to be learned, and maybe there's even a grand design in it. That gives you a chance to seize some control that can begin your personal, if not business, life turnaround. Throughout my twenties and thirties, for example, even when it looked like I was taking surprising detours off the prescribed path, I could see that every step taken was helping me to put down a foundation for my eventual future as an entrepreneurial VC.

In everything I did, I was building a story, and a future. And you will also see that all the lessons you have learned can similarly be put to good use later on. Glance back now and look closely at the future you have been building. Ask yourself – is this the story you want to continue to tell?

In my tenure as a strategy consultant for CMI, I had been on the frontlines of negotiations and mergers, downsizing and turnarounds – that word again – of major corporations. A brief hiatus to produce *Legal Deceit* gave me a headlong plunge into entrepreneurship. I then advanced further as a strategy consultant after becoming a managing partner in Thought-Bridge, a firm I co-founded with my mentor/peer partners when we spun out from CMI in 1996. There, we built a good business. But when I left to launch speedsolve in 1999, I knew that I had reached my 'sell-by' date.

Knowing that it is time to move on happens in different ways for various folks. I was spending a tremendous amount of time thinking privately and talking to my partners about ways to make a consulting firm more like a fast-growth dot.com company. I was spending less and less time focused on client engagements and business development. My time was up.

The kindest thing for yourself and others is to have an explicit conversation, decide what to do, and do it. That is not what I did. In hindsight I would have done it differently. But by the time I started to treat any hesitation towards my ideas from my partners as a personal impediment, I knew it was time to leave. If this sounds at all familiar to you, the takeaway may not surprise you. It's an old one but a good one. That fact is that when you leave a venture, by choice or default, try not to burn bridges. The most empowering thing you can do for yourself is to assume responsibility and then rise to the challenge.

At the height of the dot.com boom, I fully expected to be running my own company for at least the next five years – at which point I would orchestrate a meaningful exit strategy. Instead we lasted three years, still longer than most who jumped in at the height. Understanding what happened required looking at the context.

A matter-of-fact distillation of what happened later appeared in Brian McCullough's book *How the Internet Happened: From Netscape to the iPhone*, in which he delivered a post-mortem about what was effectively a numbers game. In 2000 there were 400 million people online, and even fewer spending money online. However, within a decade there would be 2 billion internet users. While there were only 17 million websites in 2000, ten years later there were about 200 million. This was not a fad or a gold rush, as sceptics warned after the bust. The dot.com era taught the world habits that 'ingrained themselves into the rhythms of everyday life. The dot-coms from that time, the training wheels for the internet, taught us to live online.'

By January 2021 there were 4.66 billion internet users and in June 2021 the number of website addresses was 1.86 billion. But that was little comfort to me back in 2001 when I had to figure out my personal turnaround. For a while, when I ran into friends and colleagues, I'd hear 'Your timing was bad, you were just ahead of your time.' And the truth was that within six or seven years of things falling apart, almost every remaining company in e-commerce used some form of technology to optimize customer service. But the recipe for speedsolve's demise not only comprised poor timing. It also had to do with my own naivety and unwillingness to be creative on investment terms that ended up pushing the main funder out. It meant speedsolve wasn't able to launch its product more quickly in the marketplace and embed it within companies before the bust.

This was the lesson I should have learned from our *Legal Deceit* foray into film festivals, when we ignored the fact that we had a bird in the hand and passed up the opportunity of the Venice Film Festival. Sometimes you have to learn a lesson twice.

When I was given an investment offer at speedsolve but didn't like the structure of the deal, I once again didn't appreciate a bird in the hand. We were so close, right at the start line, with the momentum getting us ready to launch a promising enterprise and I quibbled, believing I'd have other options. Had

I been putting my money where my mouth is, allocating my resources better, I would have followed my own expertise from *Getting to Yes* – evaluated the likelihood of other options, calculated the time value of money, then accepted the terms of the negotiation with minimal tweaks. Instead I equivocated and that, along with the end of 'easy money' in the dot.com boom, spelled the end of my venture.

Time to regroup and retrench. In short, it was time for hustle and action in my turnaround. I found that the key to making peace with the bust was to stay open to ideas and once again rekindle the fires for thinking big.

Lemons into lemonade

When there's nothing left to lose, Janis Joplin sang, you're finally free. That's what it's like to hit rock bottom. You may know that feeling too.

I hit the pavement: paying to attend conferences, knocking on literal doors, emailing and calling everyone I could, searching all of my associations, no matter how far away. Marshalling my resources, I leaned on past connections, in multiple networks, and expended more money than I could afford, getting myself, for instance, to a distant trade fair with a pricy entrance fee.

Your turnaround, when you are between gigs, may require you to swallow some pride. In that moment, believe that there are folks who are putting their money where their mouths are and may need you as much as you need a great opportunity.

But you have to kick into gear.

Once I did, three possibilities materialized. One of them took me out to Hollywood working at a film studio putting together documentation for TV and film projects. Another was an opening in the strategy department of a media company.

Those two were mildly interesting and I would have taken either as money was tight. When money's tight, you tend to do a little less thinking and simply buckle down. The third possibility, thanks to a friend of a friend I ran into at that distant trade fair, was a potential role at Time Warner, a job that would have been in the co-COO's office. This sounded *very* interesting.

When doors aren't opening, double down and force them open.

In the movie *The Pursuit of Happyness* there's a scene that offers a practical method for getting at least a foot in the door. The character played by Will Smith is the real-life Chris Gardner – who went from homeless single father to become the founder of one of the world's most successful Black-owned institutional investment firms. In the scene, a re-enactment of a moment that changed his life, Gardner approaches a stranger who has just stepped out of his red Ferrari and asks him two questions: 1) What do you do? And 2) How do you do that? The fellow was a stockbroker, took Gardner to a trading floor, and suggested that he look into a low-paying internship offered by some local financial firms. Gardner still heard the word no a lot, but was finally given a shot. The rest, as they say, is history – including the promise Gardner made one day to open doors for people without access or connections. At his Chicago firm he started his own internship programme for high-school students. For years, Chris put his money where his mouth was by providing full four-year scholarships to university for interns who committed to a year of after-school hours and kept their grades up.

This story is also a reminder that you are not out there in the cold alone. I will always be grateful to the friend who introduced me to the opportunity at Time Warner.

The co-COO at that moment was Dick Parsons – an

African American captain of industry who served on the board of Time Warner and who had overseen the merger of America Online (better known as AOL) with the media conglomerate. A chance to work alongside, interface with and learn from Dick Parsons? Yes, please. Dick presided over all the content businesses for Time Warner. At the time he was helping Warner Bros adapt the Harry Potter series and accelerate its DC Universe. He was helping reshape the magazine business with titles like *Time* and *Life*. And he was doubling down on the cable network portfolio that included HBO and CNN. Finally, he was at the helm of a changing music landscape in the form of Warner Music. Huge brands, all. I was sold.

However, I didn't impress Dick's gatekeepers, especially when I flubbed typical consulting evaluation scenarios. I watched the opportunity evaporate. The opportunity loss stung even more when Parsons was later named as the successor to the departing CEO. For a while I wondered what my career might have been had I been hitched to Dick's star. If you pause to feel your disappointment when one opportunity doesn't pan out, that's healthy. But once it's settled, there's no point in wasting time on what might have been. Instead, look at what's coming next. Appreciate what folks in your community are doing to turn lemons into lemonade.

You can turn a negative into a positive, or at least find consolation. That's what happened when I didn't get to work for Dick Parsons. Instead, I was brought in as a negotiation specialist – that was, after all, where at least some of my skills lay – and then assigned to the mobile unit at AOL.

In the 1990s the AOL service was the way most first-time consumers of home computers gained access to the internet. Hot as AOL was, I wasn't assigned to their core product divisions that managed the delivery of online services to consumers. Apparently, I would be a good fit for the team that supported the mobile group's deal-making. I could have viewed this as a serious demotion. In such instances, when your business goes bust and you have to go out and conform to the status quo of a working situation, or when you face a setback that gives you little control, it can be truly demoralizing. In these situations, the best way to navigate your way back to the lane you'd rather be in is to get in the flow of traffic and watch for openings to move ahead at a faster pace. Try, if you can, to imagine that you can learn something new from whatever is being thrown at you.

I could have felt resentful. Previously, as an entrepreneur and my own boss, I'd been a co-founder and managing partner of a consulting firm, an executive producer, and a founder of a tech startup. Now I was hanging on to the lowest rung of the proverbial executive ladder. But I was cashed out and I needed this job. What's more, I was looking for a turnaround, something new and a fresh start.

Faking it until I made it, I went forward, grudgingly I'll admit, and attempted to put a hopeful face on the situation. Not surprisingly, I performed miserably in the 'paper-pushing' role for which I was hired. So much for faking it. Nobody was impressed. Once it became clear that I was not working out in this spot, I was reassigned to oversee a backwater company that at the time nobody cared about.

If I could have given myself a pep talk then, I would have said what I say to Black and under-represented founders every day – *Do not close a door that's been opened to you until you find out what is behind that door.* Before jumping to conclusions based on everyone else's report, look behind that door and find out for yourself. I'm not sure where I'd be today had I not lasted long enough to look behind this last door.

Initially, when I flew out to Seattle to inspect the backwater company, I felt as if I'd been shipped off to Siberia. On the contrary, that little software technology firm, Tegic, turned out to be the best thing that could have happened to me at the time. Tegic needed a turnaround and so did I. We were made for each other. This was also the first time that I would be able to see on a larger scale the control that comes from putting your money where your mouth is and making your resources matter.

The opportunity to grow with a company, even if it's not your own, can be a gift that will empower you. The key is to appreciate it.

Earn a calling card as well as an income

Tegic was an overlooked, underleveraged diamond in the rough. The company was already quietly doing deals all over the world for licensing and embedding a technology into mobile phones that had been developed for people with physical limitations. The software predicted what words and phrases users wanted to say, which made communicating easier and faster. Phone manufacturers and mobile networks had started adapting the same technology to help drive usage of their very profitable text-messaging businesses. At the time, texts were big business and paid for per message or as bundled packages. This was many years before Instagram and Snapchat. Along with airtime, texting generated substantial revenues for mobile networks. Anything that encouraged users to spend more time texting was golden. Tegic had the best predictive text software, a good business model and an experienced sales team. This technology is ubiquitous now, of course, but in 2002 this was cutting-edge.

As if someone had spun a globe then plonked me randomly down in an unassuming set of offices on Lake Union in Seattle, I stepped into an exciting, disruptive, developing arena. Of course, though unexpected by me, it wasn't by chance.

The fact that I was a good fit is a reminder that opportunities are not handed out like hors d'oeuvres at parties. They are most often a culmination of various skill sets acquired over many years, especially when you have a track record of working incrementally towards business goals of any scale. Your track record in getting the job done, wherever it has been, is your USP – unique selling proposition.

In short, don't bank on overnight fortune or fairy-tale trips to the ball. Bank on yourself. If you don't have a USP, employ every and any opportunity to earn one.

Tegic was among the leaders of the pack in embedding mobile software, at the forefront of what became apps and applied artificial intelligence, which then became the gold standard, and one of the biggest technology revolutions in the world.

My turnaround began when I grasped this potential.

Here was yet again a disconnect between myth and the facts. The myth at the time was that this small company could not be a major contributor to AOL Time Warner's bottom line. The bold fact that the Tegic team helped me see from the start was that 75 per cent of mobile phones were shipping around the world with Tegic software pre-installed and prominently branded as T9. Handset manufactures like Nokia and Samsung were paying Tegic quarterly licensing fees under long-term contracts for the right to embed our software and display our logo. Users were increasingly demanding the software by name.

Users also wanted more texting languages, slang and even emoticons to enhance their experience. Naysayers thought of Tegic as a tiny innovation that belonged on the scrapheap, but it had never been more relevant. My goal became to change the way that the deals were structured to make them more profitable and Tegic's narrative more investable.

I was in my element right away. Pulling my own team together, I began to put 'my' money (the budget I was given for staffing support) where my mouth was in terms of advancing more people of colour and women in Tegic's US office and around the world. My overarching responsibility was to increase revenues, improve terms and outcomes, and if I needed a contract specialist to assist me or a project or product manager to improve sales pitches, I brought in the best and brightest, who were – it hardly needs to be said – often women and from diverse backgrounds. A key lesson for me was to surround myself with the best people, and I got to it.

A 2020 report from the UK's Tech Nation pointed out the need for greater numbers of women in tech. While 49 per cent of the general workforce are women, in the tech workforce overall 81 per cent are men and only 19 per cent women; at the director level, 77 per cent are men and 23 per cent women. This compares to the fact that in the general workplace, directors are made up of 71 per cent men and 29 per cent women.

www.diversityintech.co.uk estimates that 19 per cent of folks in tech are men and women of colour, a positive contrast to the 12 per cent in the general workforce. However, those people of colour are concentrated in sales, marketing, people function, finance and IT. They are not in engineering.

What this tells us is that there is opportunity to be had in the technology field. With the right USP and track record, a background in tech helps you along the path – whether with job security working for established companies or as a founder in your own right.

As I built the diverse team around me that I wanted to see, the pace of work kicked up several notches. Now I was back on the road – or, more accurately, up in the air – up to 70 per cent of my time. As an operating executive in charge of offices in many different countries I was zipping around time zones constantly. Exhilarating and exhausting in equal measure. AOL Time Warner had tentacles and counterparts that were dotted around the globe, while also expanding to places where the corporation wasn't yet ensconced. I learned how to have in-person meetings on three different continents in two days. One of the destinations where we were building up an outpost was in the UK. The more time I spent there working, the more I hoped to explore the countryside at some point. But there never seemed to be enough hours in the week.

In the past I'd been hired to advise executives as to the best strategies for optimal outcomes. I was now an executive responsible for implementing those strategies and making sure that all the moving parts of our operation were firing on all cylinders. That kind of coordination would never have been possible had it not been for a handful of particularly brilliant colleagues, a reminder to use resources, particularly human resources, like you mean it.

Two people, diverse in their own way, stood out.

The first, Lisa Nathan Rode, who'd advanced quickly to become head of Tegic's product management, was then a rarity as a woman (white) in tech. In every field, especially in hostile environments where they haven't been welcomed, women bring vital perspectives that come from having keen foresight and insights, eyes and ears for detail, depth of experience, and they aren't afraid to speak up, as team members or as whistle-blowers. At eBay, Meg Whitman was a pioneer for other women to earn their calling cards in tech. In the UK, Jackie Wright, Chief Digital Officer of Microsoft worldwide, advocates constantly for other women to join her ranks.

Lisa impressed me right away. In her view, having looked at the numbers, we were underperforming. Bluntly, she explained, 'I think our product is underpriced.'

She was right. After reviewing all our existing contracts, I was amazed. Her willingness to challenge with 'We could do better' was a game-changer.

Lisa was also a champion of other women in key roles at Tegic. Interestingly, in these years, even though many leading corporations 'talked the talk' of diversity, not all put policies into place to incentivize pay equity alongside diverse hiring. In fact, there were naysayers who pushed back against findings that showed diversity was beneficial to better work environments, as well as to company earnings. The foes of workplace inclusion regarded promoting 'diversity as either nonconsequential to business success or actually detrimental by creating conflict, undermining cohesion'. Others counter that old-school way of thinking by citing studies that make stronger cases for gender and racial diversity.

Such findings were included in a later report from Catalyst, a research organization focused on gender parity in the workplace. Released in 2004, the study on the impact of gender diversity and corporate financial performance pointed out that financial performance was higher when there was a higher representation of women on teams. Companies with more women leaders had a 35 per cent higher Return on Equity than ones with fewer women leaders; they also had a 34 per cent higher Total Return to Shareholders than teams with fewer women. Across five different industries, higher Return on Investment was evident in companies with the highest women's representation.

This is not simply recent thinking, then. People have been working hard on it for years, but with added impetus of late. Twenty years ago, with Dick Parsons at the helm of AOL Time Warner, putting a face and a voice to diversity as a priority, I was given a lot of leeway in hiring. In 2003, Parsons raised the bar for the media and entertainment industry, pointing out that even though diverse hiring was improving for many companies, generally minorities were not being promoted often enough to decision-making positions. In a speech on the topic to the US's National Association for Multi-Ethnicity in Communications, he made the case for why cable subscribers would be more effectively served by assembling teams that reflected diverse communities of viewers and users. Parsons made a powerful point, saying: 'We tailor our programming to the communities we serve, but unless the community is reflected in your employee base, you're not going to be completely sensitive to all of their needs and be as successful as you could be.' It's as simple as that. But while some industries and companies and individuals have been banging the drum for decades, others have only just heard it. Diversity is good for business.

My second key colleague was Scott Kim, already an employee at Tegic when I arrived. One of the lessons I knew about diversity but had never fully embraced until arriving at Tegic is that you maximize the strength of a diverse team by helping to identify the individual strengths of each player. The prime teacher of that for me was Scott. He may be one of the few people I know who is absolutely multicultural – able to seamlessly code-switch among the cultures in which he interacts. He initially oversaw part of product management critical to our growth, eventually joining the sales team to head the Korea office and in time heading the entire revenue organization. He could code-switch like nobody else and walk into any room with authority.

Most of the time I held my own in unfamiliar settings, given the reality that I was often the only American, and certainly African American, in the room. Some people dealt with my 'otherness' better than others. But I remember being surprised that no one in any meetings in the more remote settings of Asia or Europe ever seemed surprised when I walked in. My assumption was that few folks had dealt with a business leader who looked like me or came from my background; yet nobody blinked an eye. Only years later did Scott confess that, when setting up meetings, the word would go out – 'There's going to be a big Black American coming to your office . . . '.

The lesson at the time began with the realization that the world was not as progressive and inclusive as I had imagined, but there are effective strategies to manage. Being the outlier in the room can be awkward. But it's necessary to get past the feeling that it's up to you to democratize other cultures. It can be helpful not to make it personal and to imagine what other people are thinking, what their expectations are – to sit in their shoes, and not in your own head. Doing business with people gives you common ground and common goals, and the more you focus on the substance of that, the more you will thrive.

Initially, the Tegic team set target goals of strengthening a particular contract with, say, Samsung. Every contract renewal became not an opportunity to increase price but to deepen Tegic's working relationships with customers – and a diverse team meant we were connecting with a more diverse customer base. Scott Kim was the execution specialist who delivered on the strategy.

The eye-opener for me was that sometimes a company's turnaround is not a reinvention or a jolting reset. Sometimes it's a matter of optimizing what's already there but is being undervalued. The same is true for us as individuals. Your turn-around can be as subtle as the pride and confidence that comes from taking small but determined steps to change your prospects for a better future. Your turnaround is when you realize that you've got resources that have a value in the marketplace and you have a plan to put your money where your mouth is.

My turnaround involved an appreciation of the grand design that had brought me this far. I'd been helping other corporations in an advisory capacity from the sidelines. Now I was actually leading a technology business – with the same values that I would have used if it was my own. As long as I was delivering results, my changing slate of bosses at AOL head-quarters didn't seem to interfere or pay much attention to how it was being done. How it was being done, and by whom, mattered mostly to me.

This was liberating and empowering. When you earn a little success by putting your priorities into action and then deliver results, that can be your USP. When you show that you don't overspend or undervalue company resources or investments, you'll be trusted.

Working on my terms, suddenly a contract that had been bringing in $1 million a year jumped up to $5 million the next year and doubled after two years. Ten million dollars for one contract? Tegic rapidly became the upstart that could. More importantly, perhaps, my own turnaround – from a mismatch with the corporate behemoth to a needed division head – empowered me.

I had not rushed to judgement but had stuck it out at first to see the jewel in the rough that this opportunity was. I'd advise you always to do the same.

At Tegic we just kept raising the bar, even as our parent AOL was experiencing something new: business contraction. Folks were going to their cable companies to get high-speed internet and signing in with Yahoo and eventually Gmail accounts. The world was changing in ways to which AOL was finding it hard to adapt. Tegic was bucking the trend. Over five years, revenue grew to fifteen times where we began.

Tegic was to become my proof of concept, my USP, for the kinds of companies I wanted to build later – technology-driven, global in scope and, crucially, diverse throughout. Your USP can be achieved by taking on challenges nobody else is anxious to handle. Remember that under-represented entrepreneurs and disruptors have found opportunity in places others ignore. If you spot the opportunity, even if it's not working for someone else, seize it. If nothing else your turnaround will be that you stopped waiting for permission.

Turnaround in the UK

Recently I read a book written in 1952 by Roi Ottley entitled *No Green Pastures: The Negro in Europe Today*. A review described the book, on the author's travels as a journalist and government attaché, as being about the problems faced by Black people in Western countries (mainly Europe) outside the US. It noted that England, in particular, had a history of racism but 'loses perspective on her own very real issues while criticizing the United States'.

Has the UK engineered a turnaround?

During the early battering of so many Black and other families of colour by the pandemic and resulting economic troubles, I thought often of that recognition in *No Green Pastures* of the challenges associated with being of colour. To me, the attitude towards Black people and other marginalized groups hadn't changed much over the decades, and yet still many otherwise well-informed individuals would continue to say, *Oh, we don't have the problems of white supremacy the US has.*

In the UK, by the time of the pandemic, there had been well over a decade of austerity measures exacting a terrible toll on the majority of citizens, aggravating an already 'entrenched racial inequality in the UK' – as observed in a 2019 UN report. Spending had been pared to the bone on everything from housing, education and jobs to medical and mental health care, services for the young and elderly. Cutting many forms of welfare – including basic food assistance for the hungry and homeless – had been sold as character-building. In its coverage of two highly critical UN reports, the *Guardian* commented on how a poverty expert pointed to nineteenth-century

WE DON'T NEED PERMISSION

workhouses as being similar to contemporary Conservative welfare policies. Unless an end was put to austerity, the expert said, the poorest people in the UK would be subjected to lives that are 'solitary, poor, nasty, brutish, and short'.

Many have called the 1990s the lost decade for much of Great Britain. Even in the years of the first decade of the 2000s, with some progressive programmes under the Labour government and more moderate party leaders, the improvements were quickly reversed once the Conservatives returned to power, a reinforcement of the lesson that political channels do not always lead to sustainable change.

And yet I can see the emergence of a turnaround in the growing numbers of Black-owned businesses, in more diverse governing boards of major corporations (please note this is almost exclusively white women); in the meaningful increase when it comes to hiring marginalized and under-represented professionals (please note this hiring is almost exclusively at the entry level); and particularly in the wave of women of colour who are moving up to C-suites (please note this is almost exclusively in the US, although Sharon White, Chair of the John Lewis Partnership, Vivian Hunt, former managing partner at McKinsey, and Karen Blackett, CEO of Group M and Chancellor of the University of Portsmouth, are UK exceptions).

Empowerment invariably happens when you decide to orchestrate your own turnaround, put your money where your mouth is and make your resources count. You don't have to wait for the boom days to thrive. Take what you've got, lemons and all, and turn it into sweet tea. Do it with others and make a pitcher while you are at it.

If a career or a business can be turned around, so too can an evil embedded system that is literally killing us. Capital is the key, along with the lessons that come next.

6

SUPERHEROES DON'T
NEED PERMISSION

Step #6: Leverage what you know

Never waste the opportunity of a good crisis.

MACHIAVELLI

*My forebears refused to cut the sugar cane for plantation owners,
and I am recognizably a product of that background.*

**DIANE ABBOTT, FIRST BLACK WOMAN ELECTED TO THE UK
PARLIAMENT, 1987**

Long before my VC days began, I had already identified a key
attribute to seek in any founder when deciding whether to
invest or not. The big question for me usually comes down to
whether an entrepreneur is a seasoned veteran drawing on personal experience in creating a business or if they are a 'tourist'
speculating on disruption by borrowing or appropriating

experiences from locals. There are other considerations, no question. Still, I'm especially drawn to founders who show high potential to upend the marketplace by leveraging their own lived experience – a capacity I know gives you and your enterprise a competitive edge.

This isn't expertise gained just from training or from educational and professional degrees. I'm talking right now about deep knowledge and wells of experience. Knowledge attained over many business cycles, including crises, is golden. So too are the innovations and solutions you've mustered when they were needed urgently. When business solutions are infused with passion, purpose, personal insights, outright mission and a bit of panic, that's usually a clue that your ideas might be disruptive. It's also a sign that you may possess the entrepreneur's superpower: being relentless as they seek optimal results. All the other metrics might check out impressively. But it is leveraged knowledge tied to relentlessness that sets you apart from your competition.

Which brings us to Step #6 – *Leverage what you know.*

I'm calling this attribute a superpower because I believe disruptive founders are modern-day superheroes. More to the point, throughout history, Black and other oppressed people who have taken on systems of oppression are indeed superheroes by any measure. That's why I bet on entrepreneurs of colour who are overcoming the odds to get where they want to be and are tirelessly leveraging what they know – *watch out, here we come*, they're saying.

Leverage experience, curiosity and passion

The UK's Pat McGrath, of Pat McGrath Labs, is a superhero three times over, at least. She's Black, a woman, and a disruptive, self-made entrepreneur whose company (now based mostly in the US) received its estimated valuation of $1 billion in July 2018. She is now Dame Pat McGrath, having been given the DBE by the Queen in the 2021 New Year Honours list, and is considered the most influential make-up artist in the worlds of fashion and beauty today.

Her nickname, 'Mother', refers to her nurturing persona, as well as to her countless make-up innovations, which she began to create in her early days as a make-up artist for fashion shows and photographic shoots. In a classic take on leveraging what she knew, before Pat was ever interested in make-up as a career she learned fundamentals about beauty and style from her Jamaican single mother, a first-generation immigrant, and from recipes devised at home. Not able to find many cosmetic lines that worked for brown skin, her mum repurposed whatever darker foundation she could find at the shops and then added in her own pigments and tints. Her mother's love of texture and fashion innovation inspired the use of extra fabric and notions that would later become a calling card for Pat's own bold creations for make-up and hair, which famously incorporate feathers, sequins, petals, pearls and glitter for consumers of all colours. Pat leveraged what her mother had used in styling the body, brought that knowledge to the face and wove it dramatically into her designs. Pat also leveraged what she has described as her mother's rejection of racist views. As she told *Allure* magazine in January 2021, Pat saw her mother celebrating the beauty of her own colour and focusing on all the beautiful Black people represented in culture.

Born and raised in Northampton, where she attended college and studied art, Pat McGrath never trained formally to do make-up, though she had been playing with lashes and bold colours from a young age. She has often shrugged off the prescribed tools of the trade and instead applies make-up with her hands, rather than brushes. After making a name for herself at major fashion shows and photo shoots, creating dramatic looks for top fashion designers at every design hub in the world, Pat became the Beauty Editor-at-Large for British *Vogue*.

When the Pat McGrath Labs brand was established in 2006, Pat and her team clearly leveraged what she knew – cosmetics that made the wearer feel bold, confident and beautiful – and translated those elements to packaging, branding and marketing language. Still, Pat prioritized product value, telling Lisa Niven-Phillips of the *Guardian* in 2019 that no matter how high-profile the influencers behind the brand, no matter how appealing the presentation, nothing matters without formulas that work. Consumers, in her experience, care most about quality.

Who better to make sure that formulas work for women of every age and background than a nurturing make-up artist who comes with multi-generational knowledge about her craft and has had her hands in that make-up for decades?

It could be argued that not all wildly successful entrepreneurs can boast of a lived experience from which to draw. Did Jeff Bezos have a significant lived experience or special connection to book- and record-selling when he decided to build an online store? Apparently not.

However, one of the areas of fascination he was able to leverage, according to a 1999 Chip Bayers *Wired* interview, was how to turn any kind of mundane activity into an adventure. The example used was of a full-scale operation he ran not long after founding Amazon while on vacation. He, his brother and father, on walkie-talkies, headed into a convenience store as their mother sat behind the wheel. What looked like a military covert operation was a game Bezos created to see how fast he and his team could get in and out of the store. The idea that consumers should have a good experience while they shop – without spending long hours and having to be talked into buying what they didn't want – was clearly important in creating the online experience of making speedy purchases on Amazon. It's likely, in this sense, that he was drawing from a lifelong enjoyment of innovation and adventure-planning. You can imagine that what-if/aha moment before he started his company when he thought – *Hmmm, what if you could skip a run to the bookstore or the music or video stores, and have your selections come to you?*

It follows logically that when Bezos did the research and discovered there were 3 million active book titles, that was the strongest case for building an online business – because no bricks-and-mortar store could be built to contain that many choices. The other way in which entrepreneurs like Bezos apply the step of leveraging knowledge is that they build teams with diverse lived experiences – like a hive mind – which is a potent recipe for innovation. In other words, you leverage what you know and what the members of your hive know.

Deep knowledge of your core business can be gained by something I once heard a colleague say: 'sticking to your knitting'. Once you do, then, if you're Amazon, you can become the 'Everything Store'. In June 2021 – with Amazon valued as a $2 trillion company, and Jeff Bezos achieving a net worth of $182 billion, give or take – the newsflash was that the gross value of all things sold on Amazon over the preceding year came to $610 billion and, for the first time, surpassed Walmart's $566 billion in total sales during that time. This victory, explained by Shira Ovide in an 'On Tech' newsletter, was a case of a company leveraging deep knowledge. Amazon's domination, she said, stemmed from its ability to understand consumer habits, prioritize convenience and systemize the movement of merchandise from location to location.

Similar to the point I made about the use of data in

decision-making, it is often more effective to leverage what you know versus what your imagination proposes as a great idea.

Let's say you've come up with a solution to make flying more appealing by getting rid of first-class cabins and expanding business class. Your knowledge comes from air travel you've experienced possibly a handful of times a year. Your challenge will be to profitably operate your flights. You may have no knowledge of building an aviation company or any knowledge of the intricacies of the airline sector, such as the target profit margins on fare classes, the costs of customer acquisition by fare class, the relative revenue contributions of freight versus passengers, the cycles of business-passenger demand, or the impacts of jet fuel costs. That is not a recipe for a good bet for the investors you'll need. Remember Air Atlanta?

In February 2000, David Neeleman, a former employee of Southwest Airlines, leveraged his knowledge of the airline business to launch New Air with a 'fleet' of one Airbus and one route between New York's JFK and Florida's Fort Lauderdale. With lower, more competitive costs for tickets, he added back some of the frills that the competitor, Southwest, didn't have – reserved seating, roomier leather chairs, TV screen monitors at each seat. Thanks to the improved flying experience, within a year the renamed airline, JetBlue, had added multiple destinations and aircraft. A total of 1 million passengers helped to give JetBlue $100 million in revenue in its first year. Unlike most major airlines that lost vast sums of money when air travel slowed after the attacks of 9/11, JetBlue's in-flight attention to detail provided a sense of comfort and security, along with affordability, and the company was able to make a profit even in those challenging years.

What if Air Atlanta had had a David Neeleman, a disruptor in air travel who had already created a low-frills, low-cost alternative to major commercial airlines?

Richard Branson used his disruptive knowledge to parlay expertise from the marketing of Virgin Records to his 1980s foray into the airline business. Virgin Airlines imported rock 'n' roll cool all the way to the airport ticket counter – complete with a red carpet for passengers waiting in the queue. Virgin's own brand history on its website says it best:

> Using the same skill we'd developed promoting the likes of Culture Club and Simple Minds, we set out to inspire the public to fly with us . . . We hired happy people with lively personalities to be our cabin crew. And we didn't charge the earth. We gave people a choice. A bright red, fun, friendly, fabulous choice that made travel attainable for everyone. Back then, our personality was cheeky and over the top. We were a tiny airline up against much bigger players. We needed to use quite radical language to get attention. We were the airline that loudly proclaimed 'BA doesn't give a shiatsu' to promote our onboard massages. 'Play with yourself' was the way we chose to advertise the first ever seatback games. Not exactly subtle, but it got us noticed.

As the story goes, Branson's lived experience for needing to disrupt the industry in the first place was having suffered the slings and arrows of a flight being cancelled while he was on his way to the Virgin Islands for a romantic rendezvous. He turned the crisis into a mission to create Virgin Atlantic as an airline that would be known as the carrier you'd choose to fly if you wanted an adventure. His mantra of 'Screw it, let's do it' was fully leveraged into the self-avowed cheeky marketing that has worked to this day.

There are various shades of knowledge-leveraging that go on at all levels of commerce. Knowledge is not always gained without pain, as I learned after the sale of Tegic to

Nuance – which I helped facilitate. In leading the transition, I experienced what founders and C-suite executives face when you are part of an exit and, for example, have to decide who stays and who goes. When that time comes for you – whether you are deciding who will go, or your future is in the hands of others – no matter how indispensable you think yourself to be, you don't always control the outcomes.

You bring your full self to work – lived experience and all – but sometimes the business simply no longer requires you. That's a fact of life. When it was my job to scale down the team it was a gut-wrenching process. It's never enough to say 'This is business and not personal,' even when that is, frankly, very much the case.

I've learned that you stand a better chance of being one of the retained crew, if that's what you want, by cultivating knowledge that makes you an asset your employer can't risk losing. Better yet, if you are known for bringing a particular skill to the table, that will serve you no matter where you land.

Watch and learn

With advances in technology, most of us are living some form of waking up to a 'Brave New World'. In the mid- to late 2000s, as the speech-to-text and predictive text capabilities became more and more commonplace, the advances of artificial intelligence (AI) were almost creepy. You could type the word 'Can' and the software recommendations appeared for you – 'Can we speak?' This was a massive advance in technology which was designed to help minds like Stephen Hawking's communicate easily, free up time and do all kinds of good in the world. Still, keeping up with the technology meant leveraging what you didn't always really know, and that could be sobering. With the acquisition of Tegic, Nuance became the leading provider of technology for speech, imaging and keypad solutions for businesses and consumers worldwide. With the other acquisitions Nuance had made, there were several core businesses under one roof, so to speak, with technology that included dictation products, voice-activated web-search engines, the latest navigation systems, and conversion of documents into PDFs. There was even a Healthcare division that used AI for improving communication in medical settings.

Moving from one parent company to another after splitting up the team can make for an atmosphere of upheaval. Transitions are rarely plain sailing. As a strategy consultant, I'd seen what happens in mergers and acquisitions when the folks who built one club were asked to join a new club; those experiences had taught me the age-old truth of 'to the victor go the spoils'. I also realized something new – that sometimes, after you build a club, you don't really care to join a new one. For founders and directors of Black-owned businesses, this feeling might be especially acute. After all, when underrepresented entrepreneurs build a company, you may forget what comes after achieving the shared goals of becoming worthy of an acquisition or merger. When you've leveraged all that you and your team members know, your sweat and your brainpower, and created something you love together, it's difficult to see it morph into something else, according to someone else's vision.

When Berry Gordy sold Motown Records in 1988, it had become too hard for independent labels to survive in an era dominated by corporations. He believed he was selling the label and its roster so that it could last when he turned it over to the capable hands of MCA, later taken over by Universal/Capitol Records, while he held on to part of his most valuable asset – the publishing arm of Motown, Jobete. Gordy then focused on writing and producing *Motown: The Musical*, along with books, articles and screenplays, nurturing music and acting careers and taking on other enterprises that allowed him to leverage what he knew. In 2019, multiple outlets reported that Gordy, nearing the age of ninety, had announced his retirement.

Reginald Lewis didn't stop for a moment when the time came to sell McCall, the company that TLC had turned around. He focused on putting together his next big deal, Beatrice, and leveraged everything he had learned.

Achieving exits for your own company or for the company that employs you is one of the most powerful ways that Black business can leverage our collective knowledge to truly change the world – because exits release capital to be used elsewhere. For that reason, I had to learn to make the best of a transition that was a mixed bag of good and bad experiences.

The lesson you have a choice to learn comes from asking yourself how you will take the knowledge you gain and put it to use in your next endeavour. As you ascend a ladder, as a founder or with responsibilities that point you to the C-suite, if you are part of a transition process you will be served by acknowledging that you are going to be working for people who may not know you. When you find yourself a stranger in a strange land, learn what you can from the discomfort. You will have that much more knowledge to leverage later if you do.

Working for Nuance was unlike anything I'd done before or would again, mainly because of the iconoclastic CEO, Paul Ricci, whom I'd gotten to know during the rigorous negotiation process for the acquisition of Tegic. When you have the opportunity to observe someone at the top of their game, take it. On the one hand, he was a textbook example of someone who leveraged what he knew. He combined the knowledge he'd culled from his time at Xerox as a corporate vice-president with a healthy balance sheet to build a disruptive, diversified company. On the other hand, there is no textbook for building an organization that is being patched together, built, grown and run at the same time that it is being assembled. Somehow Ricci not only made it work but built a formidable technology business.

The opportunity to learn from a tech colonizer and multi-billion-dollar disruptor was incomparable. I witnessed a type of bold ambition that I had rarely seen up close, and which I was keen to emulate. I was given access to deal-making processes that differed markedly from my default – the winner takes it all. Nor had I seen unbridled permissiveness of that kind, not in such close proximity. When you worked for Nuance you had carte blanche – as in the use of the 'white card' – to build a strong team and try new ideas. It was a kind of entitlement that worked for Paul because he was in the driver's seat. He leveraged what he knew and, wow, he knew success.

Entitlement can be a powerful thing as long as you don't forget to leverage the experiences that fuelled you from the start. Jay-Z was an entrepreneur from the word go. He leverages his lived experience for creative purposes and in business. He is smart, he receives inbound opportunities, and, as an ambassador of Black entrepreneurship, Jay-Z offers a playbook for how to make money and change culture while you are sleeping. After years of hip-hop couture being all about baggy jeans and oversized athletic jerseys, Jay-Z shifted the style of a movement by putting out the word that suits and ties, or at least button-down shirts, might be a nice change of pace for the boardroom.

Let's not forget that as entrepreneurs we are the ones who foot the bills. That's responsibility and it's power. Paul Ricci was open to opportunities as long as you could make a case for the investment. Or if there was a deal to pull off, the capital was there for the asking. That kind of autonomy can make for heady stuff. As a VC I have leveraged much of what I learned at Nuance.

There is something to be said about a level of swagger that says to the world – 'Make me an offer.' Paul was also a case study in demonstrating how to litigate to get what you want. The experience confirmed for me that nothing is impossible when you leverage the power of capital and knowledge together to *make things happen.* That can be intoxicating because disruption is fed by an entrepreneurial desire to make things happen. But there's a flipside – the fact that disruption without careful consideration and deep knowledge can make things happen that aren't for the better.

Depending on where you are in your business, you may be questioning how you might have a chance to get to observe someone like my former boss in action. My suggestion is to start to put out feelers for a local entrepreneur who will give you five minutes of her or his time to answer two questions – *How have you learned to leverage what you know? What happened when you weren't able to leverage what you knew?*

Nuance continued to grow while I was there and continued to grow after I had gone. So much so that in 2021 Microsoft paid $19.7 billion to acquire Nuance's most prized divisions. The full lesson was eye-opening. However, you can only wonder how Nuance will integrate into Microsoft, the colossus so famous for ingesting other companies. It's fascinating to see that the acquirer can become the acquired.

In every underdog-versus-the-giant contest, the kind we all know and love, remember that you are not always David, not always Goliath. The superhero play in the grand scheme of things is for a seller to always think like a buyer and a buyer to always think like a seller. In other words, how will the buyer's future be enhanced through this sale and likewise, in addition to capital, how does the sale secure the seller's future?

I was pleased to have contributed to Nuance's growth, but

there was a ceiling to my own growth within the empire's structure and in late 2009 an option to cut my contract short was exercised. That's a polite way of saying that I was let go. It wasn't personal, although no one likes to be blindsided. The fact is that I had become too expensive and had exceeded my usefulness.

Getting fired was a first for me, but now I had lived experience on which to draw that could only improve my knowledge base in terms of hiring and firing others. You put that kind of experience into your wheelhouse and move forward. What's more, I had real-world experience as to how it feels when a company you helped build is sold and you go from being a surrogate parent, so to speak, to being a short-term nanny. Ultimately, I moved on armed with equity and other parting rewards to cushion the blow.

I was now an evangelist for the effectiveness of using what you know to be disruptive. The question that had begun to burn deep down was what it was that I most wanted to disrupt. It's a question that I put to young founders all the time. It's a question to ask yourself as you create the recipe for your own disruptive success: *How will I use my assets to effect change?*

You may not answer the question right off. You may still need to gain knowledge and lived experience to hone your superpowers. You may need to change yourself – or expand your list of leverageable ingredients and experiential knowledge – before you can change the world. Quite possibly, you are still gathering up your tools. Or you are still gaining knowledge about the industries, systems and conditions of the world you'd like to disrupt.

Back then, I had the sense that my direction would be dictated not so much by gaining knowledge that I could leverage further but by a desire to know what I did not know. Back in 2009, the destruction that happens when growth is pursued without a well of knowledge and careful consideration was a lesson that the world was having to learn.

Leverage lessons from loss and hardship

In 2012, a study from the University of Warwick concluded that if your aim is to be a business winner, it's important to learn from 'losers' too. Reported by Anna Blackaby on futurity.org, the study's thesis was that if we only borrow how-to lessons from the most successful people or corporations, we won't be able to reproduce the element of luck or privilege those examples may have enjoyed. The study also said that most of us regular folk are more likely to apply lessons in our own lives or businesses when we borrow from examples of entrepreneurs who only came second, or who had the right recipe but didn't bring it to fruition. Many founders have had big aha moments of inspiration by saying – *Hmmm, what went wrong? How could I do it right?*

Similarly, leaders in industry and in government should endeavour to command knowledge that comes from looking not just at successful solutions but also at the ones that failed. The questions to ask next are – *What can we learn from this failure? How does this hardship impact people's lives? What action can we take so we don't let this happen again?*

When economic disasters strike, just as when corporations go under or when social initiatives don't work, there is much knowledge to be gained from finding out why. Whenever we think that these are merely episodes that don't affect us, we should think again. When the stock market plummets, the hurt can be felt by everyone, even folks who have no investments.

For instance, during the global financial meltdown of 2008–9, which effectively cost millions of people their jobs – along with their homes, their savings and more – few sectors of the economy went unharmed. We saw that this is what happens when controllers of capital use complex financial instruments such as derivatives with unintended consequences. Bank failures, housing shortages and credit crises collided at the same time. Many people around the world hadn't yet recovered from the aftermath of the 2000–2001 dot.com bust and the 9/11 terrorist attacks. In the US, in order to stabilize the economy and promote lending, the Federal Reserve lowered interest rates to unprecedented levels while also lowering taxes on businesses and the wealthy. The result was a massive real estate and financial market boom. Along with that came a historically high amount of personal debt.

With the start of economic gyrations and the real estate market crash of 2007, the Great Recession arrived. By 2008, we learned what 'too big to fail' meant for long-established banks around the world. And we learned the cost of having to float billions of bailout pounds and dollars and all other monetary units when a global economy is in freefall. The fall of the dominos took down many huge businesses on both sides of the Atlantic. And plenty of small ones too.

In the UK a million jobs were lost, and a disproportionate percentage of those were among communities of colour. A 2015 report from the Immigration Advice Service, written by Paul Fisher and Alita Nandi, published by the Joseph Rowntree Foundation, stated that after the 2008 crash, the Britons most likely to be in persistent poverty were Pakistani and Bangladeshi groups; the second two minorities put into chronic poverty were Black Africans and Black Caribbeans. During the intensified austerity programme that followed, these same groups fared worse. The report cited a recent analysis of the cycle of poverty which demonstrated that 'recessions exacerbate pre-existing inequalities, proving detrimental to those already living on the breadline. Poverty in the UK is an ever-increasing issue.'

Add to these concerns other hardships. In 2014, a *Time* magazine article written by Maya Rhodan entitled 'Hard Times Can Make People More Racist' confirmed what many people of colour know from our own lived experience. A study conducted by New York University researchers Amy Krosch and David Amodio looked at how scarcity changed the perception by lighter-skinned people of anyone with Afrocentric physical traits as being darker. In other words, when there isn't enough to go round, Black people appear blacker to white people, and therefore less like them. Those racial perceptions fed beliefs proven to promote discrimination. The study also asked participants to agree or disagree with opinions fostered during hard times, such as: 'When [B]lacks make economic gains, whites lose out economically.'

The number of people who agreed or disagreed wasn't reported, but the researchers asserted that economic hardship has been proven in many studies to adversely 'influence how people treat those outside of their own social groups'. It's not so much every man or woman for themselves, but more like every tribe. The conclusion underscored the reality that when hard times hit, racial bias escalates as the result of both individual attitudes and institutionalized white supremacy.

Three years after the Great Recession, the data told a different story. Leveraging ingenuity and a desire for change, under-represented entrepreneurs and consumers helped kickstart a sluggish economy. In 2011, the Black population of the UK was more than 1.9 million (3 per cent of the population), according to that year's census. The Centre for Research in Ethnic Minority Entrepreneurship (CREME) estimated that Black and Caribbean businesses at that time generated over £10 billion annually for the British economy. Statistics from the same period reported that the spending power of Black consumers was then more than £300 billion annually. In the US, according to the Minority Business Development Agency, 10 per cent of businesses in 2012 were Black-owned, generating $150.2 billion of annual gross revenues for the national economy, with an estimated $1.1 trillion in buying power.

This is to say that businesspeople and consumers of colour do not sit idly by waiting for rescue or permission (which may never come) out of poverty, out of crisis. This response to crisis was remarkable.

More and more, after leaving Nuance, I saw the potential that Black business, Black founders and Black communities presented, not just for creating equity and improving the lives of stakeholders but for uplifting whole economies. One of the ways in which this was made possible was by leveraging community.

When you have a shared experience within a community, you're even better able to develop a coordinated community response towards issues as pervasive as poverty and institutional racism. After being tapped by President Obama's administration to be part of the advisory council to the Small Business Association on challenges faced by under-represented businesses, I saw the way that Obama's early work as a community organizer had informed how he spearheaded policy to create change. His superpower of being able to leverage knowledge to disrupt was evident when he became the first Black editor of the *Harvard Law Review* and all the way to his election as the first Black president of the US. You could hypothesize that the instability and challenges of his early life were his training ground for managing a crisis of the magnitude of the global economic meltdown that he faced before he could even enact his policy priorities.

President Obama's brand of audacious hope, coupled with his unwavering calm focus, was exactly what the US needed at that moment. In poll after poll taken in recent years, Barack

Obama ranks by a wide margin as the best president of the last half-century. For many of us, the election – twice – of an African American to the most powerful office in the US, if not the world, was, at least fleetingly, a glimpse of the Promised Land.

If the election of an African American as president had felt like a triumph at last in the US in 2008, the same could be said for Black Britons in 1987 when four Black Labour MPs – Diane Abbott, Paul Boateng, Bernie Grant and Keith Vaz – were elected to Parliament for the first time. The first Black member of Parliament was John Stewart, elected to the House of Commons in 1832. Lord Learie Constantine became a life peer in 1969. The election of Abbott, Boateng, Grant and Vaz was a seminal moment for generations of Black British citizens, giving them a voice, representation and even legitimacy that they had been denied up until then. From that year forward, progress has come slowly, but it has come nonetheless. The general election of 2019 brought the number to a total of sixty-five non-white MPs – forty-one Labour, twenty-two Conservative and two Liberal Democrats.

The postscript, of course, is that even as Black businesses bounced back in the post-recession years, we were still a long way from the Promised Land. We weren't there because at the same time as under-represented and marginalized communities were finally achieving a degree of equality in the UK, the US and across Europe, there was a violent surge of hate crimes in response. It was in 2013, after all, that Black Lives Matter was founded in the US to protest the acquittal of George Zimmerman in the murder of Trayvon Martin, an unarmed Black teenager.

Sometimes we feel overwhelmed and wonder how we can make a difference. Trust me, you can. You can play a huge role in responding to hate and violence by leveraging your lived

164   WE DON'T NEED PERMISSION

experience to empower yourself and your community. Your knowledge may be more valuable than you know.

During the post-recession years, I started looking back at my earlier goal of becoming a VC and finally began to craft a deliberate strategy to achieve it. I had some good ideas and was eager to put them to the test. Yet nothing in my planning involved packing up and moving across the ocean to the UK, a country that was most likely responsible for shipping my forebears to the US in the first place.

7

PURPOSE + PROFIT = POWER

Step #7: Become a convener by making your mission bigger than yourself

Y'all sitting up here all comfortable. Must feel good.
Meanwhile, there's about two billion people all over
the world that look like us, but their lives are a lot harder.

ERIK KILLMONGER, PLAYED BY MICHAEL B. JORDAN IN *BLACK PANTHER*

Living up to my work mantra, 'Make it happen', the same principle was swiftly applied to my personal life when Michael and I decided to move from being partners of sixteen years to a married couple, so that I could explore working in the UK as an American. Perhaps it was a little more romantic than that but, after a quick meeting to discuss pros and cons, two weeks later a visit to the courthouse made it official. Some of our friends and family probably still have no idea.

By mid-2014 I had fulfilled all my commitments as COO of Mobile Posse, the startup founded by a former alum from AOL who had brought me on board after Nuance let me go. After nearly a decade working on mobile technology, this had seemed like a no-brainer. On top of that, it was my first official hire as COO and if I could pull it off with the rest of the team, this would be my second shot at a multi-million-dollar exit.

The opportunity to leverage what I knew was obvious from the start. What I didn't realize at first was that taking the position with Mobile Posse would allow me to become proficient at what I did not know – yet. Plus, I was about to have the challenge of playing this key role at a critical juncture in the life of the company. The other unexpected benefit from taking the job was going to be a big lesson in empowerment. That lesson yielded Step #7 – *Become a convener by making your mission bigger than yourself.*

The best way to start thinking about what it means to make your mission more than just about you is to check in with yourself about your current *why*. Look at what it is that motivates you to get up and go to work every day. Is it the money itself or is it to earn money you can use as a tool? Take it further. When you look at all the uses for your earnings, why do those things matter? Eventually, the more you continue to ask why what you hope to achieve is important, the closer you get to your purpose. If it's to own a nice home and raise your kids with security you never had, that's powerful. If it's to be able to raise your earnings in order to create more opportunities for others like yourself, that too can be empowering. If you are launching a business to deliver revenues and create a platform for your brand that can show what's possible to other entrepreneurs, you are blazing a trail. In all those examples, you've chosen a *why* that makes you a convener because you are bringing other stakeholders into your mission.

Step #7, becoming a convener by making your mission bigger than yourself, is one that works particularly well both on an individual basis and for building and running a business. For entrepreneurs, the need to figure out your startup's *why* is a given. Mobile Posse operated in a sector known as advertising technology, or adtech for short. Of all the sectors hurt by the Great Recession, the development and distribution of technology that delivers ads to your phones was not one. Mobile Posse had a driving mission – to own the home screen of every mobile phone. We wanted to be the industry leader, of course. That would yield two things. First, we would be the channel of choice for advertisers and mobile carriers to communicate with consumers. Second, it would let us protect the user experience, so that the notifications pushed to the phone's home screen would not be overwhelming (too many) or underwhelming (irrelevant) but would be able to quickly engage interest and provide returns for both consumers and companies seeking to interact with them. If we succeeded at our mission of owning the home screen, the benefits would flow to Mobile Posse plus a range of stakeholders – mobile phone carriers, brands and advertisers and, most importantly, consumers.

To be successful we had to become the best at convening those partners. Basically, this took me back to *Getting to Yes* and understanding interest-based selling. This was leveraging what I knew – as in baking a bigger pie. When you meet the interests of everyone you've convened by making the mission all-inclusive, don't forget the importance of profit. That's where we can distil the equation Purpose + Profit = Power. When you or your company learn to convene with a clearly communicated purpose *and* gain financial traction, you have the power to do big things.

An invitation to convene

Convening can be seen as attracting and assembling the right team members and resources as well as partners, investors and customers. You don't have to do this overnight. Sometimes, as we saw with speedsolve, it may take a while to find the right people and resources to be convened. You may have to play the long game at the same time as you are living up to your mission every day. At times you may feel that you are performing a trapeze act without a safety net.

When I say 'play the long game' I mean that you may have to pace yourself. The long game involves staying confident and cool, even on days where you aren't getting the exact results you want. The long game allows you to expand your view to see the lay of the land better, and to do so from vantage points you might not have been aware of before. In other words, you can view the whole forest and not just the tree in front of you. When you pace yourself, you can also pay attention to honing details so as not to undermine your moonshot launch – even if it comes later. But remain vigilant and recognize when an opportunity arises that you can't miss.

At Mobile Posse I played the long game by honing certain diagnostic, disruptive skills that would serve me later in my work on *The Money Maker* and in investment decisions with Impact X. As COO, however, I was responsible for all operations of Mobile Posse as a fast-growth market-maker – from product launch and distribution to audience acquisition and retention, market expansion, revenue attainment, margin management and ongoing customer success. That is a lot of trees. Fast action was mandatory, especially because young companies don't have much to fall back on. As with the movie *Legal Deceit*, every minute costs money, and similarly Mobile Posse did not have infinite resources. What safety net existed came from the revenues earned from a few pioneering partners willing both to take a risk on Mobile Posse's products and to write cheques at the same time, and from money raised from investors who expected a big return. As the clock was ticking, I had to learn a whole new set of business models, customs and language that were specific to adtech. I had to learn fast and would not have managed had it not been for the members of my team who helped me translate.

Pro tip – if you enter a foreign land, find a native and get some coaching.

If the mission at Mobile Posse was to own the home screen, my first job running operations was to achieve three things: 1) explosive revenue growth, 2) minimal audience churn and 3) partnership expansion. Not a minute could be wasted because, following facts not myths, I quickly learned that digital platforms that had long served up ads for revenue were being radically disrupted.

Remember, if you can, the crazy uptick in competition for consumer attention in the 2000s and 2010s? Facebook launched at Harvard in 2004 and by 2006 spread to other colleges and took off from there, commandeering countless consumer mobile and computer hours daily. Then came the explosion of apps, a plethora of social media sites drawing you in. The battle for a slice of attention on your handset was constant. With the rise of the apps and social media like Facebook, Instagram and Twitter, what we call 'walled gardens', people were spending time walled off from ad messages that weren't embedded in the actual apps. That social trend was removing another part of Mobile Posse's safety net.

Because the phone was still the key portal for home screen ads, at Mobile Posse convening partners to our cause was going to be our lifeblood. Some ideal partners were those who felt most threatened by social media's growing dominance and needed a solution to remain effective. Mobile Posse rightly decided that was the group to convene.

There are many forms of convening. There are also many ways to think about making your organizational mission bigger than either yourself or the bottom-line revenues. One of those ways is to consider the economic ecosystem that makes your business work. When you pursue growth, one aspect of making it bigger than yourself is to think how specifically the success of your enterprise contributes to other stakeholders in that ecosystem. Making it bigger than yourself can also apply to you as a founder. If you want to convene interested parties to invest with you, come to work for you, collaborate with one another, or join you in working towards a cause of mutual interest, making it bigger than yourself is the key ingredient. When everyone you have convened feels they have a stake in the company's fortunes and have a part to play in reaping those rewards, you have become a convener.

With trends that had been happening for the previous two decades, advertisers had to constantly evolve to continue connecting with consumers. My tenure at Mobile Posse was an interesting time to be learning about digital advertising. In the not-too-distant past, the impact of big-budget advertisements made for major TV broadcast events was the gold standard. In the UK, in addition to significant sporting matches, the most popular shows – think *Downton Abbey*, which debuted in 2010, and *Top Boy*, in 2011 – would predictably draw large and/or identifiable audiences. Advertisers knew roughly how many eyeballs they were reaching and their demographics. For-profit TV broadcasters gained market power by selling airtime by the second. So broadcasters converged content producers and various brands' catchy commercials with desired audience groups in desired numbers – a nice convening.

The shift happened when premium cable channels and streaming platforms came along, replacing ad revenues with subscription fees – think Netflix, HBO Max, Disney+ and BritBox. In fact, part of the appeal to viewers was that pesky irrelevant ads no longer existed on these platforms. This new frontier was clearly connected to digital media where data-tracking and unprecedented targeting were the USPs. Yet the terrain was now much harder for advertisers to navigate because the most heavily trafficked outlets like Facebook and Google weren't very transparent. They didn't give out their viewer or 'eyeballs' numbers – why would they? It was their secret ingredient.

If the object is catching consumers where they spend most of their viewing time, still nothing comes close to the mobile phone.

The statistics are staggering. The average consumer unlocks their smartphone 150 times daily. They also spend more time every day on their device (ten hours and thirty-nine minutes) than at work. Consumers tap, swipe or click on their smartphones 2,617 times per day. When I started at Mobile Posse in 2007 just as the world was increasingly convening on mobile phones, connecting with consumers on their home screen was a route which marketers were eager to try. Would consumers react positively to being targeted in such an immediate and personal way? And if so, for how long? We had to move fast. Incidentally, June 2007 saw the launch of a consumer-centric smartphone blockbuster – the iPhone – heralding another market condition that impacted Mobile Posse.

A quick aside – in time, social media facilitated all kinds of ways for under-represented founders to become conveners without being given permission. They just needed to identify the right platform. Social media influencers and content creators who come from nowhere to gain multi-million followings are able to monetize their content, from ad revenues, sponsorship and merchandise sales, to an astonishing degree. They become their own programmes and networks. This dynamic came to its full realization much later in Mobile Posse's lifecycle.

Mobile Posse had the technology to own the home screen,

which remains the first port of call for every owner of a smartphone every time they unlock their device. We quickly established relationships with manufacturers like Samsung and US carriers like T-Mobile, Verizon, AT&T and others. We established media buying relationships with ad agencies and brands such as Walmart, Unilever, Starbucks, Ford and Coca-Cola, to name a few, while developing further strategic partnerships with other digital and mobile companies. Ultimately, we grew the audience with which brands could connect. All in all, this was an effective convening. Most tellingly, we multiplied revenue over twenty times where it had been when we began.

Here was a proof of concept of the equation Purpose + Profit = Power, which kept us humming along with an easy-to-communicate recipe. Profit is how to objectively measure the impact of operations. Startups, like corporations, are in the business of making money. As they say – the bottom line is the bottom line. Yet purpose animates profit. Purpose, above all, is the key ingredient for extraordinary growth. Profit makes growth possible and leads to power.

Purpose is that part of the equation that helps in convening stakeholders and making the mission of the startup bigger than the founders. When you think about the purpose of your business – which can be the same as the mission – the words you choose can refer to what the company does, its purpose for existing, and its ongoing purpose or mission into the future. It becomes bigger than you when you see your purpose as a reason to join forces with someone else's success. And vice versa. As others connect to your success and you to theirs, you'll deliver that much more than what was possible with just one success driver, and probably faster.

When your mission is clear, that lets you explain your narrative to investors and to the marketplace.

As a VC, I also look at two other 'p' words – *Potential* and

Process – when choosing whether to invest in a startup. Most of all, I ask how the product, service, technology or commodity is going to matter to consumers and/or companies – and by extension to the world. That says a lot about potential for fast growth too.

The big lesson that I had to learn from this first official stint in the C-suite at Mobile Posse was that growth is absolutely consequential. When numbers are spiking as you intended, that can give you a lot of power and influence. However, if growth starts to level off, there's where the vulnerabilities begin. In a fast-growth market there are so many hard-to-control variables. So if growth of top-line revenue starts to level off and expenses continue to stay where they are, it falls to the COO to address that levelling off. I'm not even talking about a drop in revenue. I'm talking about how you reverse a trend and keep the growth line going up on a continuous basis.

During tough times, my advice is that you constantly convene. Leverage what you and your team know, convene whom you know, listen to diverse voices to come up with different solutions. The Mobile Posse ride was not all roses, but convening stakeholders to come up with breakthrough ideas was almost always the right strategy. Eventually, all the elements aligned and Mobile Posse was sold via trade sale exit to a publicly listed company, Digital Turbine.

This experience taught me that knowledge and learning are two different things. If you are operating from a knowledge base, that's important. I'll repeat: *leverage what you know*. But if you can continually learn, based on changing inputs, that's what keeps you relevant.

After departing Mobile Posse, the timing was right for a long-overdue break. I don't remember who suggested spending Christmas in England's beautiful countryside, only that it sounded wonderful. Something about the short, rainy and quiet days appealed to me. We would visit friends in London, fly to Ireland, explore areas we'd never seen. And I could take some time to contemplate what was next.

More than just getting on with it

In general temperament, something about Brits felt familiar to me. What used to be described as a 'stiff upper lip' has been modernized with the familiar expression 'Just get on with it.' This means that if you are hurt or sick, best not to complain but simply get your tasks done. The benefit of the 'Just get on with it' attitude is that in the British workplace, at least, there seems to be limited operatic drama upon which some business cultures thrive. No histrionics or 'palaver', as the British version of the Portuguese word for fuss goes.

But I worry that the downside to 'just get on with it' can be too much acceptance of the status quo or a lack of real desire to fundamentally disrupt.

I heard inklings of acceptance sometimes when I spoke with Black and other minority entrepreneurs. Almost all would bemoan the lack of equity in access to capital, especially when it meant taking hundreds of meetings and suffering countless rejections, often having to meet with at least twice as many folks as their white counterparts and then raising a fraction of the capital that the non-minority founders received. Others would admit their frustration, but 'just get on with it' and look for alternative means.

An American like me doesn't have to be in the UK long to learn that under-represented communities of colour, categorized together by the government under the very unhelpful umbrella of BAME, are not a unified assembly at all. Even among Black Britons there is a curious distinction that I hadn't experienced before between those identifying as Black African (just under a million, 1.8 per cent), those who identify as Black Caribbean (0.6 million, 1.1 per cent), and others like African Americans who made up the remainder. Diversity UK reported further that in 2018 14 per cent of the UK population was from a minority ethnic background.

It's worth digesting the numbers in full:

- Total UK population – 56.1 million:
    7.5 per cent of the population is made up of Asian ethnic groups
    3.3 per cent of the population is made up of Black ethnic groups
    2.2 per cent of the population is made up of mixed/ multiple ethnic groups
    1.0 per cent of the population is made up of other ethnic groups
    86.0 per cent of the population is white

- The Asian ethnic group population of 4,213,531 (7.5 per cent) is broken down as follows:
    ○ Indian: 1,412,958 (2.5 per cent)
    ○ Pakistani: 1,124,511 (2.0 per cent)
    ○ Asian other: 835,720 (1.5 per cent)
    ○ Bangladeshi: 447,201 (0.8 per cent)
    ○ Chinese: 393,141 (0.7 per cent)

- The Black ethnic group population of 1,864,890 (3.3 per cent) is broken down as follows:
    ○ Black African: 989,628 (1.8 per cent)
    ○ Black Caribbean: 594,825 (1.1 per cent)
    ○ Black other: 280,437 (0.5 per cent)

- The Mixed/Multiple ethnic groups population of 1,224,400 (2.2 per cent) is broken down as follows:
  - Mixed white/Asian: 341,727 (0.6 per cent)
  - Mixed white/Black Caribbean: 426,715 (0.8 per cent)
  - Mixed white/Black African: 165,974 (0.3 per cent)
  - Mixed other: 289,984 (0.5 per cent)

The power and presence of people of colour in the UK is all the more astounding when you look at the numbers broken down like that and think of the enduring contribution by Black, Asian and other minority ethnic Brits to education, the arts, letters, science, technology and government. And now this is where it gets interesting:

Diversity in the UK – individuals in politics and local government:
- 8 per cent of MPs are Black, Asian and minority ethnic (as of 1 May 2019)
- 5.8 per cent of Members of the House of Lords are Black, Asian and minority ethnic (as of 1 May 2019)
- 17 per cent of local councillors are Black, Asian and minority ethnic – that's 1,235 out of 7,306 councillors in 123 local authorities in England (according to the OBV Black, Asian and minority ethnic Local Political Representation Audit 2019)

In previous years – when business had brought me to the UK for brief stays – many of my British colleagues of colour had expressed surprise that I had followed Black British history as closely as I had. Most African Americans they had met apparently seemed to be unaware of the violent white supremacist assaults on the UK's Black and minority citizens. In this, their attitude was not one of 'Just get on with it'. In fact, many were all the more traumatized that so little was known about Black British civil rights leaders and the activism they had inspired. Most troubling for them was the acceptance of the status quo by most white Brits, who claimed not to be racist yet took no stand as anti-racists.

There were so many parallels to my US experiences. Issues of police violence towards Black citizens were ones I had followed closely in the UK. In 1970, for instance, there had been the trial of the Mangrove Nine. Police harassment was the trigger leading to the arrest of the nine young Black protestors out of more than 150 who non-violently had taken to the streets of Notting Hill, in west London. The *Guardian*'s coverage stated that the trouble began when police raided the Mangrove restaurant, which was owned by the Trinidadian-born entrepreneur and well-known civil rights campaigner Frank Crichlow. A central figure in the Notting Hill Carnival, Crichlow had established the restaurant in 1968 and it had become a frequent haunt for Black activists, as well as an important meeting place for recent immigrants from the Caribbean. It was also popular at the time with Black celebrities, including Jimi Hendrix and Nina Simone. The police raided the Mangrove no fewer than twelve times in just eighteen months, always on the pretext of searching for drugs, despite a lack of evidence. They never found any. The protestors were sick and tired of being sick and tired. Enough was enough.

All nine protestors, including Crichlow himself, the broadcaster Darcus Howe, former British Black Panthers member Barbara Beese and British Black Panthers leader Altheia Jones-LeCointe were acquitted. And the trial at the Old Bailey – which lasted fifty-five days – became a rallying cry for Black power. Judge Edward Clarke used his stature to declare that the case revealed racial hatred within the Metropolitan Police Force.

Several traumatic events in the collective memory of Black Britons were ones I'd read or heard about, one of which was the New Cross Fire, which took place in January 1981 in southeast London during a terrible period in Britain's history that was marked by escalating far-right nationalism. A January 2021 feature in the *Guardian* recalled the neighbourhood of 439 New Cross Road where the fire broke out as having long been called the 'capital of race hate in Britain'. Tragically, thirteen young Black people, aged fourteen to twenty-two, were killed. More than fifty more were injured. Yet the media, the police and two inquests have, while finally accepting that the fire was started deliberately, refused to name the crime as arson or conclude that the crime was racially motivated. To this day, no one has been charged. Each of the deaths remains an open verdict.

The New Cross Fire marked a turning point between Black Britons, the press, law enforcement and government. There had already been a lack of trust between Black communities and the police, and you can point back to the Mangrove Nine to see why. But, as the *Guardian* article asserted, the fire fuelled a greater distrust of authorities and the convening of an 'intergenerational alliance to expose racism, injustices and the plight of Black Britons'.

Two years later, on 12 January 1983, twenty-one-year-old Colin Roach died in the foyer of a police station in circumstances that could be called mysterious at the very least but, more aptly, suspicious and even sinister. Colin's death was deemed to be the result of a single shotgun blast through his mouth. The police from the Stoke Newington station claimed that Colin had committed suicide even though he'd apparently been shot in the back of the head. This was only one of the discrepancies in the police officers' accounts. A police forensic surgeon reported that Colin's condition was not consistent with suicide. Other evidence showed that he would not have been able to bring a shotgun into the station inside the sports bag he was carrying.

In a time before news could spread virally and virtually via social media, the streets got the word out immediately and protestors began demonstrating soon after Colin's death. In an article published decades later in 2018 in the *Hackney Gazette*, the poet Benjamin Zephaniah recalled the spontaneous eruption and demand for answers:

> The mood in the community at the time wasn't just about Colin Roach. It was about all the other cases of racial injustice taking place at the time, and he represented the extreme. There was a tangible feeling of: 'Who is next? It could happen to me.'

This sentiment had come on the heels of an uptick in the number of citizens in Black communities being stopped and searched by police for no reason other than 'they appeared to be acting suspiciously'. The *Gazette* piece noted the outrage being stoked by the police using unnecessary and unlawful force, arresting people who had committed no crime, racially abusing people, using the stop and search (sus) law, which was particularly prevalent in the 1980s, and raiding people's homes. All of this came to light as serious police abuses in an inquiry later commissioned by supporters of Colin's family.

Benjamin Zephaniah described those experiences:

> We didn't have much money and we were walking the streets. You would be stopped so many times in one night, and sometimes they would lock you in the station all night. It was so outrageous. I got a bit of money and I bought a white

BMW off a friend, and I drove it from Ladbroke Grove to East Ham, and I got stopped four times . . . The Black community would have no business with the police – it was really sad. The National Front was rampant at the time, so you had these racist skinheads walking around the streets at night, and you would get beat up or chased by them but you couldn't go to the police. We were really on our own.

Looking back from the vantage point of 2020 and 2021, there is clearly a similarity between the impact of the Black Lives Matter marches galvanized by George Floyd's murder and photographs of the rallies and protests that had their epicentre in Hackney in the aftermath of Colin's death. A movement had begun, spurred on by the Roach family, who simply wanted to know, 'Who killed our son?' An inquiry ensued, with many findings pointing to police culpability, but without individual names or convictions. Forty years later their question remains unanswered.

It was left to the Lawrence family, ten years on in the early 1990s, to pick up the torch, when their son, an eighteen-year-old schoolboy named Stephen, was murdered – stabbed to death – while waiting at a bus stop in south-east London. Evidence showed that Stephen had been on the ground and that, despite deep stab wounds to his lungs, he managed to get up and tried to run, throwing the contents of his pockets out as though to appease thieves, before he collapsed and died. Despite tip-offs and a witness, Stephen's murderers evaded conviction for almost twenty years. The two main suspects had been known for acts and threats of racial violence against Blacks and Asians. One of them had been recorded as wanting to skin Black people alive and mow Asians down with a machine gun. Yet the police and prosecutors couldn't provide the evidence for a conviction.

Refusing to 'just get on with it', Stephen's family worked with private detectives and a hired legal representative, unprecedented at the time, who helped see to it that an investigation of the Metropolitan Police was conducted. The conclusion was that the force had been incompetent and racially biased in their efforts to gain justice for Stephen. The investigation also recommended and succeeded in repealing the rule of double jeopardy in murder cases – the law which means you cannot be tried twice for the same criminal charge. Considered by many to be 'one of the most important moments in the modern history of criminal justice in Britain', as the BBC's coverage described it, a new trial went forward, soon leading to the conviction for murder of Gary Dobson and David Norris.

Imran Khan, the Lawrence family lawyer, summed up for a *Guardian* reporter in 2012 what had happened and how it would change the UK:

> . . . what we have now is an acceptance within mainstream society that racism is a problem, that people can complain about it and that there is legislation that allows you to do something about it.

Of course, it remained to be seen whether there was, in fact, broad acceptance within mainstream society that institutionalized racism – aka systemic white supremacy – was a problem in urgent need of confrontation. For my part, I had seen the short attention spans of too many people from all backgrounds who care about racism and are concerned when presented with lived-experience evidence, but who move on when other headlines draw them away.

Another challenge in the UK is the tendency to rush to overlook white supremacy by conflating race with class. To be clear: race and class overlap a great deal. It's worth repeating that the racial face of UK poverty is that one in two Black families suffer from it versus one in five white families. Race receives a unique treatment that doesn't happen across class in housing, education, policing, hiring, pay, etc. etc. ad nauseam. In the UK, education is an area of particular concern. All you need to know about rampant elitism is that no fewer than twenty British prime ministers have attended Eton!

In 2013, after the 2012 re-election of President Barack Obama, a lot of folks pointed to his popularity as a sign of a new America. One that began to be described as post-racial. I and many others were encouraged that America had turned an important page. A closer look revealed concurrent spikes in hate crimes, threats on the president's life and full-frontal attacks by none other than Donald Trump in his continual attempts to delegitimize a Black president with a variety of false claims including a charge about a foreign birthplace. Hope and optimism are important, without question, as are remembering history and looking at the facts.

Many UK folks, then and now, want to parse differences in the Black experience on both sides of the Atlantic. I always say that, no matter the nuance of their treatment, enslaved people are oppressed and slight distinctions in the style of oppression are irrelevant – though, of course, the specific local manifestations of oppression should be used very effectively to inform the dismantling strategies.

It occurred to me then, as it does every day, that without clear purpose and deliberate action to topple those forms and styles of oppression, sustainable changes do not occur. That was a message to myself that I needed to hear. And perhaps it's a message we all need to hear to empower ourselves for the times when there's no choice but to move from inertia to action.

Wherever you are in your entrepreneurial journey, don't let anyone take away that which gives you purpose. Power up.

Don't get disheartened or distracted. Don't let temptation, discouragement, failure, delays, persecution or racism hold you back. True, there are things which are not equitable. You can change those things. How you choose to be of purpose and to create your own opportunities, as you convene others for the cause of your enterprise or join them in theirs – that will give you power.

Where you were when you first started out many steps ago doesn't determine where you end up. Your current address doesn't determine how far you can go. Your place on the map right now doesn't exclude you or make you less than, or not as smart as or as capable of having success as, the folks who are hitting it big already. You are just warming up. Your GPS coordinates right now are not your final destination. My colleague Ursula Burns, the first Black woman to head a Fortune 500 company, Xerox, and a founding member of Impact X, is a constant reminder that where you are does not have to define you. So when you ask yourself the question *Am I serving a purpose greater than myself in my current position?* be aware that you may already be on your way and don't even know it.

We as people of colour have faced dragons of fire and hatred and racism that seem baked into everything we encounter. We don't have to listen or wait for permission. We can be successful and let our success become contagious.

Remember, everything you do is bigger than yourself.

Across the pond

Becoming a convener can also be a lofty way of saying *Don't be afraid to leverage your connections.* Though I hadn't come to the UK that Christmas to find purpose in my career or to job-hunt, others in my network decided that would be an interesting thing to do. A former colleague suggested that I should spend some time with the two founders of a startup called SwiftKey. They were not founders of colour, but they had a young team and came with the reputation of being the nicest, smartest, most collaborative, purpose-driven tech entrepreneurs I would ever meet – Jon Reynolds and Ben Medlock.

As a regular churchgoer, I was intrigued that Jon and Ben were religious. Cambridge-educated and family-focused, they were passionate about their mission 'to enhance interaction between people and technology'. As a leading UK startup founded in 2008, SwiftKey used machine learning and AI to deliver 'optimal predictive input'. This meant that SwiftKey's products helped mobile users to text and search more efficiently and effectively. Not unlike Tegic, SwiftKey and its core tech capacities had come about in order to accommodate the limitations of people with disabilities, language barriers, or who lacked technical fluency. We got along well and they were eager to have me come on board. My challenge was that they were in talks with someone else to become COO, which was the job I wanted. What to do?

Here was a dilemma that you may have faced before, or will at some time later on your journey. The purpose in this offer was right up my alley. But the position wasn't what I wanted. When I did some future-casting, however, and asked myself if this experience would enrich me or not, I realized that I would be missing out if I passed up a chance to have fun and work with the right people. Don't forget, whenever you future-cast and see how an opportunity might serve you, having fun is no small consideration. You can have cake and eat it too.

Even without the right role, SwiftKey seemed like a good fit on both sides and a great adventure for me; however, nothing was settled by the time Michael and I finished our holiday and returned to the US. The one concern I had was that there wasn't as much diversity at SwiftKey as I like to see. The tech world is notoriously dominated by white males from prestigious schools and with family connections. At SwiftKey there were many white guys, even though they were a great group of white guys. Otherwise I was interested, but waited a while to hear about their interest in me.

For all of you who are waiting for actual offers, and the process feels slow going, leaving you uncertain as to whether or not you're really wanted, remember that it ain't over till it's over. Finally, Jon, Ben and I agreed that I would join the leadership team as a Chief Revenue and Distribution Officer. There was one hitch. I'd have to move to Silicon Valley or the UK, and the sooner the better.

For a lot of people that's a big move. But it wasn't a hitch to me. I'd travelled to so many different countries for so many years in different capacities and had never lowered anchor for any length of time. I was excited to take a position and put down some semi-permanent roots. This was going to be an adventure that I was sure would be beneficial. If the long game for me was to become a VC with capital to invest in under-represented founders and my eye was firmly on that prize, I believed that SwiftKey would be a profitable investment of my time. I could do well by SwiftKey and vice versa.

Michael was a bit of an Anglophile, had close relatives in the UK and is always up for an adventure. Being with the right partner is an investment which keeps reaping benefits – though I'm not sure I can give you any advice as to how to make that happen. He also started to receive a number of opportunities soon after the decision was made to move to the UK. A plan was hatched to come for two to three years and return stateside for other promising endeavours on the horizon.

As he had done from Nuance to Mobile Posse, Scott Kim made the move with me to SwiftKey and, with the team already there, we convened a global network of colleagues (former and new) who helped us hoover up partners eager to benefit from doing business with SwiftKey, whose keyboards would soon be ubiquitous in the Android market.

So much felt familiar, and yet I also experienced many moments of culture shock when I first arrived in the UK. For example, I was hired on my US contract with a UK visa which gave me, as US standard, two weeks' vacation per year, while almost everyone working with me was on their UK contract and had at least four weeks' holiday. Something unexpected. This was very telling of a value I had not cultivated. Work/life balance had never been my priority, yet I came to appreciate that downtime is necessary for regrouping, regeneration and restoration.

In startup world, where I'd spent many years, it's all about Team Execution. Getting things done. At its extreme it is relentless and around the clock: no sleep, or people taking power naps in the office in high-tech sleeping pods; always at the office eating your meals, exercising and showering at work, having your clothes sent out and washed from the office; constant travelling, sometimes called being a road warrior – achieving legendary status for your work ethic. Basically, spending little time at home. Somehow, having that all-in mentality had come to be a sign of success. Why? Because the thinking in the US and elsewhere was that 'We are all in this together', building the next disruption that will transform the world. In the back of everyone's mind is that there is some competitor out there working equally hard to beat us. When I joined SwiftKey, in the UK and Europe that was thought to be unnecessary, if not unproductive. The change of culture was welcome. Weekends became a chance to decompress, go to the movies and museums, see shows, play tennis or socialize with friends. When Monday morning rolled around, I could be as intense and as productive as ever.

However, the mood in the UK is shifting. Covid-19 has told

WE DON'T NEED PERMISSION

us that we can work twenty-four hours a day but that we don't have to go to the office all the time. Lines blur. Still, the reality is that for anyone starting a business, sacrifices have to be made. That's something to remember as you get going and feel overwhelmed. I encourage you to remember that having a business you intend to make profitable and purposeful is not for the faint-hearted. But remember that it's a marathon, not a sprint. Self-care when you can.

The true test of how at home I had become in the UK arrived in 2016 with SwiftKey's highly successful exit by enterprise acquisition to Microsoft (for $250 million) and my response to the job offer that was given to me. I had been flown to Redmond, Washington, driven around the Microsoft campus in a Tesla, and experienced several days full of riveting meetings with tech and marketing geniuses. Having had the red carpet rolled out and received an offer to join an important group at Microsoft working on the internet of things that would shape SwiftKey's future as well, I couldn't do it.

When you go to work for a behemoth that can say 'Money is no object', you will be well compensated. In 2021, the average salary for a US starting engineer, someone right out of university or the equivalent, was around $100,000. But there is a hierarchy to which you must answer, and it was clear that at Microsoft I would not be high in the hierarchy. This was a sticking point.

In these instances, when you have to assess whether an offer is all that you're looking for, your sense of purpose is your best advisor. You have to weigh up what you want, what you need and what you're being offered. The more success you have, you'll most likely be making more of these types of difficult decisions. Or at least decisions which appear difficult on the surface or to the outsider, but you probably already know deep down which way you're going to jump.

At that stage in my career, I wanted the challenges of significantly helping make a difference to the company's bottom line. There was no particular turnaround needed at Microsoft. No void in competency that I could fill meaningfully. Not every temptation is an opportunity.

The time had come to take up the cause of under-represented founders, either in the C-suite or, at last, as a VC. Besides all that, the UK was where I'd lowered anchor for the time being and I wasn't ready to pick up and leave so soon.

Microsoft was not the Promised Land. It's exactly that for plenty of others. But for me, promise was where I already was in the UK – with a small company in Clerkenwell called Touch Surgery, which later became Digital Surgery, founded by two extraordinary men of colour, Dr Andre Chow and Dr Jean Nehme. For much of my life I'd been drawn to discovering under-represented entrepreneurs, but I hadn't expected to find them so readily in the UK.

Imperial College-educated, their incredibly disruptive, purpose-driven startup was already democratizing surgical care both in developed countries and in the developing world. The two of them had met during their medical training. As in many immigrant and minority families, their parents sent them off to be educated and to become doctors or lawyers. In the process, the two had noted a huge inefficiency in surgical training around the world: the apprenticeship model depressed the number of new doctors who could be trained. As they began to calculate the numbers of lives that could be saved with more efficient and effective training, they looked into ways to leverage technology to train thousands of doctors globally online using digital training tools, especially gamified simulations. Jean and Andre didn't know the tech business intimately, but they taught themselves to code and launched their enterprise.

This was a definitive opportunity to support the work of a purpose-built company that was bigger than just us. Not only did the founders disrupt the training of surgeons from the apprentice model that had persisted for so long, it was also a way to convene stakeholders from multiple fields to save lives, empower surgeons, create uniform standards in operating rooms, ease public and private costs for supplying healthcare in poor areas, help usher in the era of widely used medical robots, and more.

Digital Surgery took off as a technology-augmented training platform that allows more surgeons to train better and faster. As COO I was able to play a role in establishing and growing Digital Surgery to become the leading platform for mobile surgical simulation. In 2020, the company exited with a sale to the robotics division of a big medical device firm for $400 million.

Two years before the exit, I wrapped up my role as COO and was getting ready to fly to the US for one of my last meetings when the fateful phone call came in from Tom Ilube. The power of tying purpose to profit isn't something you have to wait to get an important phone call to try. Had I been waiting for permission? Maybe. But no longer.

Give yourself permission to make your goals bigger. You don't have to alert the press or get on Twitter unless that's what you choose to do. Your successful execution of a plan against the odds can also be a great cause. That's what it means to extract as much opportunity as possible where you are, and it's a smart move. You don't have to sail your ship elsewhere to find good water. Sometimes you simply 'cast down your buckets' or your fishing nets where you are. Other times you don't have to leave the Pharoah's land, the place of your oppression, to prosper. If you want to overturn Pharoah, tie that great purpose to an enterprise that enriches and empowers you as well as others. Then you will have the means, and the team, to make the Promised Land where you already are.

When you shift from your own goals and outcomes to shared goals and outcomes, then, well – you're in business.

8

BLACK WOMEN ARE AN EXCELLENT INVESTMENT

Step #8: Invest in women to create Alpha

If they don't give you a seat at the table, bring a folding chair.

SHIRLEY CHISHOLM, FIRST BLACK US CONGRESSWOMAN

Let us propose the possibility that you've already put the steps in place which we've covered so far and are ready to launch your own business. Or perhaps you've already started your company and are looking for meaningful third-party investment to expand. Or maybe you're gainfully employed by a company, hoping that you will soon be moving on up. It could be that you're coming through a difficult time in your career and are attempting to find a new and better situation for yourself and your family. Or you've decided to collaborate with others to disrupt the status quo and fight for an urgent cause together.

In all these situations, permission is *not* needed but investment *is*.

Of course, I'm talking about *investment* writ large. For example, to build and grow your business, it's usually necessary to seek investment *from others* – not only in capital but in terms of time, advice, support, connections, partnership and knowledge. You are also invariably investing *in others*, whether it's hiring them to be part of your team, or bringing them on board as a partner, paid advisor, consultant or support professional, or as fellow leaders in a movement for change you are shaping together. More than anything, your most important investment is in yourself. In my experience, there is magnetic power in the investments you make in yourself and your business, project, or in any bold, forward move. This is a lesson I learned over and over – invest in yourself then investments from others can follow.

Investing in your venture, especially when you are on your own in the early days, is known as bootstrapping. Your venture won't get far without an investment of your own time, energy, passion, lessons learned and priorities. There are very few investors who will share their resources with you if they don't see you committing your resources. As we've seen all along, there is nothing quite as contagiously investable as self-belief demonstrated well by bootstrapping.

There is another, often overlooked yet verifiably profitable and powerful investment strategy that is so important I have made it a step unto itself. Whether you're hiring and building teams, forming boards, investing in startups or becoming investable yourself, one of the timeliest principles you can apply is Step #8 – *Invest in women to create Alpha*. A tried-and-true phenomenon in finance, Alpha refers to a measure of performance, indicating when an investment strategy, trader or portfolio manager has managed to beat the average market return over a certain period.

The likelihood of creating Alpha increases when investors take advantage of market inefficiencies, for example by investing in startups founded by under-represented entrepreneurs. In every investment sector and in every under-represented population group, women – especially Black women – are vastly more under-represented than their male counterparts, creating an even more acute market inefficiency that can likewise lead to even greater financial returns for wise investors. Just to put it plainly, that's why women of colour are excellent investments – and investors.

This was a point raised on the business and tech site www. urbangeekz.com in December 2019 by Sian Morson, an entrepreneur and VC. Morson used the recent troubles for Silicon Valley's behemoth-sized bets that had received massive VC investments – like WeWork, the startup that had plummeted over the course of just six weeks from a $47 billion valuation in January to near-bankruptcy – to ask where the economy might be if only people of colour, especially women, were to receive a modest percentage of those investments. Now that diverse teams have been proven to have a 30 per cent higher return rate than all-white male teams, Morson made the case for paying greater attention to Black and other female founders of colour who not only make up a group of entrepreneurs growing faster than any other but who are 'starting businesses that ultimately contribute jobs and dollars to the overall economy'. She went on to bemoan the fact that, despite these facts, Black, Latinx and other under-represented female founders were being overlooked by investors. Her solution? Increase the number of female VCs of colour.

As it so happened, that thinking had been in play back in the spring of 2018, when Impact X was in its infancy, as our growing core of founders and investment team members convened a series of meetings. From the start, we agreed on the basics of what would become our calling card as a double-bottom-line venture capital company, founded to support under-represented entrepreneurs in the UK and across Europe.

A few of those terms merit explanation. All companies have goals. Most times the primary goal in for-profit companies is financial returns to shareholders. And that is our primary bottom-line goal at Impact X. A secondary goal that we prioritized from the start is making the world a better place, in part by creating meaningful, highly valued jobs for women and people of colour. Not just any jobs, but the kind that remain critical in all economic cycles – software jobs, for example. In growth sectors – healthtech, among others – these are jobs that get recruited and the folks in those positions are developed and promoted, generally, whereas workers in food and hospitality services have much greater turnover. So, having a primary and a strong secondary goal is a double-bottom-line approach to business.

The term 'under-represented' for us refers to the superset of entrepreneurs not found in the portfolios of other VCs in percentages that correspond to the presence of those groups in the general population. These founders are under-represented in the capital allocation of generalist VCs. Impact X chose to invest in under-represented founders because whenever there is an acute market inefficiency it increases the probability of a greater Return on Investment. The ongoing McKinsey studies on gender and racial diversity have shown persistent market-beating returns over time – take a look at *Diversity Matters* in 2015, *Delivering Through Diversity* in 2018, and *Diversity Still Matters* and *Diversity Wins* in 2020. Statistics in 2019 showed that companies with gender diversity in decision-making positions were 25 per cent more likely to have above-average profitability; that was up from the 2014 data, which put the figure at 15 per cent. Teams with greater ethnic diversity overall, as we've noted, were shown to be 35 per cent more likely to have above-average profitability in 2014 and were up at 36 per cent in 2019.

At Impact X we also prioritize investing in women and under-represented founders because of added benefits to the economic growth of larger under-represented communities and wider business-propelling ecosystems. The Borgen Project, a non-profit tackling global poverty, has for many years been tracking the results of women's financial empowerment through micro-credit in the form of small loans. Investors care about returns on their investments, but they also see putting money into the hands of women in developing countries as a way to solve poverty and elevate the overall economy for those nations. A 2018 paper from the International Monetary Fund reported that countries with higher gender equality – 70 per cent and above – see a 13 per cent growth in their GDP. Women comprise 80 per cent of recipients of microfinance loans worldwide and rate more favourably than men in every risk area. The long-term benefits of investing in women – who tend to use their business earnings for their family's food, housing, healthcare and education – are proof positive that when women from poor and marginalized groups have access to even small amounts of capital, money gets reinvested in local communities and whole economies grow.

A virtuous circle

You may have picked up on the starring roles that Black women have played in my life personally and professionally – from my mother Adeline Collins to my mentor Irma Tyler-Wood, from my colleague and fellow Impact X founder Ursula Burns to Impact X's chief investment officer, Paula Groves (whom you'll meet shortly). We've also looked at examples of unstop-pable Black female entrepreneurs and disruptors like Pat McGrath of Pat McGrath Labs and Cathy Hughes of Urban

One. Each woman I've highlighted has returned capital dramatically and each embodies the theme that Black women are always an excellent investment.

When we look at the unprecedented numbers of women, here and in the US, flooding into entrepreneurship, in both traditional and non-traditional sectors, it's clear that VCs have been put on notice. Ignoring the opportunity and untapped potential comes at the peril of investors and, frankly, does harm to the overall economy. For years, however, we've witnessed inequities in access to funding even with a growing awareness of the problem. In fact, as underinvested as the businesses of male founders of colour have been, Black women with startups have had it even worse. One statistic from a 2020 Extend Ventures study shocked me – that over the last ten years, only 0.24 per cent of all funding from VCs went to Black startups (a total of thirty-eight founders), and that only 0.02 per cent went to Black female founders. We can deduce the fact that a huge percentage of Black-owned businesses received no VC investment at all.

This investment reality exists for most under-represented founders, especially women, at all the usual stages that we can define, whether pre-seed (idea conception), seed (product built and market established), growth companies (developed and/or grown) and exit (company sold). Whenever I'm asked about the attributes I most value in founders, the top two qualities I seek are nearly always present with Black entrepreneurs. The first is tenacity. Most of us know about why tenacity can become the coin of the realm. It's that refusal to give up and persevere no matter what. Tenacity is the thing that makes you knock on enough doors until the right one opens.

The second attribute is the ability to stay lean. By that, I'm talking about the focus and urgency that come from being prudent stewards of capital. Lean founders know they have to hustle and use their resources with absolute care, not wasting one iota of them and leaving no margin for error. Certain founders are prepared to rough it. Staying lean means you will survive and thrive, by necessity. Lean founders also don't spend on splashy offices or private chefs or ping-pong tables to distract them when they take breaks. Recognizing their investable strength, their lived experience, is key; often it's a result of the systemic racism and sexism they've had to face that has excluded them from some of the easy-glide paths, so they've learned to find other ways. Also, they tend to create companies premised on early and sustained revenue generation which mirrors what most funders expect, outside a few pockets. Or that's how it used to be when Silicon Valley VCs left room in their portfolios for losses they could write off – as though a billion here or a billion there couldn't hurt. These days, the name of the game is making sure that your investment in a startup really flies when the company gets more infusions of capital at the next investment rounds. That's why staying lean gets you through the gauntlet.

Maybe some of this sounds familiar to you. If you are a woman founder of colour, you probably know that in the UK under-represented entrepreneurs raise the least funding from all categories – personal funds and third-party funds (banks, private equity, friends and family). And yet, as we've seen, female founders of colour are the fastest-growing group of entrepreneurs launching new businesses. Many are self-funded and use company revenues instead of getting third-party capital infusions. The dangers are that you never have enough free cash to invest, for instance, to expand your staff, product line or to target a new geography. If you have no cash reserves, you lose flexibility and potentially are not sustainable. In venture capital, the narrative says that each time you raise more capital, the higher the value of your company and the more investable you are seen to be. In the UK, according to the 2020 Extend Ventures report, there have only been three Black women between 2009 and 2019 who have raised £1 million from institutional investors. Only one woman raised significantly more than £1 million and that was Sharmadean Reid, the founder of Beautystack, in 2017.

Reid is a former salon owner and brand consultant, and her startup, as described by TechCrunch, is a booking app for beauty professionals which first raised pre-seed funding and then 'picked up £4 million in seed funding led by Index Ventures'. The combination of social media marketing and appointment-booking technology lets users discover a beauty look they love and then immediately make an appointment with a professional to achieve it. Participating salons, many of them owned or staffed by women of colour, also get to see a boom in their businesses.

You can see how three different constituencies can profit in one booking – Beautystack, the beauty professional and the consumer. Although Beautystack has pivoted to another business model and become The Stack, I encourage you to look at your own business model to check how many constituencies are getting paid with every transaction. Then look at how that money spills over into another set of transactions that use the currency for something else.

This is what Impact X recognizes as a world-changing 'virtuous circle' that is created when global venture capital is strategically directed to under-represented founders – which is especially efficient when investing in women of colour. The concept of a 'virtuous circle' was formulated in our early conversations in 2018, when my colleagues and I envisioned our own double-bottom-line VC startup as a supercharged turbo engine for change. In creating this model, aimed at disrupting economic infrastructures built on institutionalized white supremacy, we wanted to turn our concept into proof that could be applied by individuals as well as by fellow investors. The idea of a virtuous circle comes with a reminder that when you choose to start a business of your own or break through barriers erected to keep you from advancing, you're firing up that engine.

Think about it. The creation of a company in turn creates opportunities for others in the form of jobs or as suppliers of materials, sub-contractors, advisors. As women and people of colour have proven to over-index in hiring women and people of colour, those positions are created and lead to better wages, higher skills, leadership advancement and robust pedigree. Often the progression includes work experience in non-traditional professions, seats at decision making tables, P&L responsible roles, and prominence in professional/community circles. The virtuous circle reshapes an economic landscape even faster by creating future-resistant jobs in fast-growth companies. As the original creator of such a company, you've now empowered and enriched your employees to advance, work elsewhere and even start a company of her or his own. At some point exits occur and capital is released that can be used to pay off student loans, buy a home, support entities charitably, politically or culturally *and* invest in the next generation of entrepreneurs, not to mention your own children. A flywheel is created.

Under-represented women founders understand the potential of a virtuous circle. So do Black women, Latinx women, Asian women, immigrant women, Native American women in the US, indigenous women the world over, refugee women, LGBTQ+ women, as well as women with disabilities, women from religious/cultural minorities, and women who experience bias because of their age. We know that women in the workplace are the most overworked and undervalued. Yet they are also most often the ones mainly raising children, doing the household work, frequently managing finances, also making time to volunteer as church mothers, school helpers, community activists and unpaid social connectors for friends and family. They are the mother lionesses protecting their pride, seeking out any and all opportunities to create generational wealth so their daughters and sons can have it a little easier. They are awe-inspiring and possess formidable superpowers.

When called on to confront increasingly violent and tacitly permitted racism, women of colour have every right to be sick and tired of being sick and tired. They are not. In fact, there is an African proverb that says when sleeping women wake, mountains move.

My absolute conviction is that when we invest in under-represented women, mountains will move. Which mountains? Let's examine the data.

More women VCs = more women founders

In October 2019, a study published by Bloomberg from Kauff-man Fellows (a family foundation funding research to produce a next generation of superinvestors) analysed over 90,000 US startups over a period that went as far back as 2001. The report, which confirmed other data that my colleagues and I at Impact X had used in our funding guidelines, noted that, at all levels across the 400,000 employees working in these startups, only 60,000 were women. However, the research found that teams with one or more female founders often accumulate more investment capital than teams with all-male founders. The report underscored the fact that studies have long shown how founders tend to hire employees who are culturally similar to themselves. The conclusion was that if women aren't in charge of hiring, women will continue to be 30 per cent less likely to be hired than men.

The Kauffman Fellows research further concluded that as the main activity for startups had been increasingly expanding outside of tech hubs in Silicon Valley, the time was ripe for creating strategies to attract more diverse teams.

The title of the second report of the same study said it all: 'Startups With At Least 1 Female Founder Hire 2.5x More Women'. When a company has a female founder and a female executive in charge of hiring, the statistics go up even more, to *six times* more women being hired. In other words, gender diversity often flows from the top down. More female VCs of colour will lead to more funding for women founders of colour.

Those are great solutions. It's also good to know that when teams with a female founder, one at least, attract VC investment, more capital is typically raised. In the UK, firms with more women senior executives have typically higher EBIT (Earnings Before Interest and Taxes).

But lest we forget the roadblocks, the study also found that, overall, teams with all-male founders were still much more likely than all-female teams to raise VC investment.

Here is the data that stands out to me:

- A CEO is more likely to be named John or David than be a female CEO; women account for only 4 per cent of Fortune 500 CEOs.
- A woman has a better chance of being hired when gender-blind applications are filed. Founders often hire people who look like versions of themselves. Men most often hire other men; women most often hire other women. These biases are wired deep in our DNA.

In another study on ethnic diversity from 2020, Kauffman Fellows research pointed to the 'selection bias problem' in the investment world, with the data showing that 80 per cent of VCs are white, compared to just 3 per cent being of colour, and for this reason 77–80 per cent of investment is directed towards companies with white founding teams.

The data that points us in a new direction comes from a pre-pandemic three-year study reported in 2019 by McKinsey, the main message of which was that the greater the representation of women overall, the higher the likelihood of outperformance, or the Alpha phenomenon. McKinsey's analysis recommended that companies should focus on getting diverse talent into top roles, including management and on the board, and to ensure that practices of Inclusion & Diversity are taken seriously. The report presented some recommendations that resonate for me in the world of VC investing:

- *Enable equality of opportunity through fairness and transparency.* To move towards a true meritocracy, it is critical that companies ensure a level playing field in advancement and opportunity. Also, companies should look at the data regularly to assess where opportunity is not fairly distributed and employ strategies to correct the inequities immediately.
- *Promote openness and tackle microaggressions.* Companies should uphold a zero-tolerance policy for discriminatory behaviour, such as bullying and harassment, and actively help managers and staff to identify and address microaggressions (the subtler techniques directed at under-represented people to let them know they are not wanted and do not belong). They should also establish norms for open, welcoming behaviour and ask leaders and employees to assess each other on how they are living up to that standard.

- *Foster belonging through unequivocal support for multivariate diversity.* Companies should build a culture where all employees feel they can bring their whole selves to work. Managers should communicate and visibly embrace their commitment to multivariate forms of diversity, building a connection to a wide range of people and supporting employee resource groups to foster a sense of community and belonging.

In a pre-pandemic UK, the picture of gender equality can be said at best to have been muddled for many complicated reasons. Although Britain ranked at number five on the EU Gender Equality Index in 2019, as the *Guardian* reported, rankings of various measures – health, education, pay equity and so on – had barely budged from year to year. By 2021, the *Guardian* noted, despite progressive laws allowing for paid leave for new mothers, childcare assistance and regulations enforcing equal pay (something yet to pass in the US), women's rights seemed to be stalled under the misapprehension that chauvinism and outright misogyny were things of the past. Not so. In addition to which, none of this takes into account the toll taken by Covid-19, Brexit and an economic contraction in the UK the likes of which hasn't happened since the early eighteenth century.

These trends have been all the more crushing for women of colour in the UK at a time when Black people and immigrants are being marginalized more than ever by the rightward-shifting, Brexit-driven pro-white rhetoric.

These are the mountains that have to be moved urgently.

If it's daunting for you to contemplate starting your own enterprise *and* creating opportunities for others to join you, while also needing to topple systemic white supremacy, your reaction is normal. We question our own power all the time.

But don't let that self-doubt be yet another barrier. Name your mountain – the one that stands in your way – and start your own business, cause, movement, endeavour or project. When you think of who you want along with you in the process, you needn't wait to become the CEO of your enterprise – which is quite possibly still nothing more than an idea. Start interviewing and recruiting well in advance, so that when you do open up for business you'll have an array of the best of the best to choose from. Remember to invest in Black women to create Alpha.

That's a page taken right out of the playbook for how we turbocharged our efforts to get Impact X off the ground in record time.

If you build it, they will come

Let me back up briefly to provide and emphasize the context for how the convening and proceeding of Impact X came together.

In 2018, nothing 'new' was happening. The unequal impacts of austerity were deepening daily, Brexit was becoming more real, and white supremacist activity was intensifying from the PM down. The economy was chugging along, but not for everyone. It was effectively the same old same old.

The UK's Black Hand Gang already had aspirations to change the narrative. This group had become increasingly outspoken on equality issues for people of colour, although nothing had sparked a larger movement. The Black Hand Gang included Lenny Henry, who needed no permission from an early age (exemplified by sneaking out of his mother's house at sixteen to audition for and win the *New Faces* talent show), and who saw the time was ripe to invest in self. When Lenny read the names on the *Powerlist* it led him to Tom Ilube, who called me, and others.

Finally, here was a group who were saying 'No more conversation.' These Black creatives and athletes wanted to address continuous and soul-crushing inequities. Forever, folks had been compelled to go hat in hand to persuade people with limited accountability that it made sense to invest in Black projects. They saw the role gatekeepers and commissioning executives play in closing doors to opportunity and were ready to do something about it.

I don't wish to be overly simplistic or overly dramatic (perhaps the producer in me is still there), but there was a sense from the very beginning of that old saying, 'If you build it, they will come.' Our founding members, including our executive founders and our investment team, are 100 per cent under-represented. We are diverse in our interests, lived experiences and nations of origin. Several of us are US-born while also seeing ourselves as transplants to the UK, where we now live. Among our founders and executives, women and men play key roles. In our day-to-day operational team of five, women outnumber men three to two. They have given us wings, helping to achieve goals and milestones more quickly. They are the reason why all the companies in our funding portfolio are excellent and under-represented.

We began with the thesis, which we see as our purpose, to invest in under-represented entrepreneurs in Europe to achieve large financial and job creation returns in three key sectors. The first is Digital and Technology startups, which have become the most valuable companies in the world. This sector is known for huge profits and wealth being created and released. The second category is Health, Education, Lifestyle. These are areas where people of colour and women over-index. There is always space for more disruption and innovation in this broad category. (This may help to explain the raucous disruption of Farfetch, a British/Portuguese online luxury fashion retail platform promoting under-represented designers that sells products from over 700 boutiques and brands from around the world and employs over 4,500 staff.) The third category, Media and Entertainment, is a bottomless well of revenues and a staple for centuries for people of colour and women, provided the right funding and curating is available.

Once our thesis was in focus – that is, our sense of purpose was clear – I began to build the team. One of the issues I faced as a first-time fund manager was an expected amount of scepticism about my lack of a track record. My solution came from learnings over the years about how to partner with folks who can bring complementary skills to the table. To that end I called Paula Groves – whom I had known since my speedsolve days. Paula had distinguished herself in the course of serving as general partner in two VC firms with almost $1 billion of cumulative assets under management. Paula not only said 'Yes' but embraced how our efforts would galvanize a virtuous circle for disrupting the status quo, and she did a lot to help articulate that.

In a recent podcast in which Paula Groves was interviewed, she raised the distinction between social-impact investing and charitable giving. Paula emphasized that investing capital to confront poverty and inequality was a more expedient approach to creating change. This would be a move away from a form of charity ('give a person a fish') towards social-impact investment ('teach a community how to fish'). She described the virtuous circle, saying: 'Entrepreneurship creates jobs, builds wealth and then, through reciprocity, these successful entrepreneurs can then fund the next generation of entrepreneurs who create jobs and build wealth.'

It was also Paula – indefatigable and infinitely curious – who proposed a firm set of guidelines that have been indispensable to us in helping to attract and screen candidates for funding. The Impact X brand has been defined by our investing in companies with the following characteristics:

- Large market opportunity with demonstrable customer traction.
- Differentiated and defensible competitive position.
- Strong management which has invested time and money.
- An established board and/or credible team of advisors.
- Exceptional job creation potential.
- The ability to positively impact lives on a global scale.
- Compelling exit opportunities.

Two more female team members came on board. Yvonne Bajela – who would be named on the *Forbes* '30 Under 30' list for her record of accomplishment in finance and investing in European, Middle Eastern and African under-represented startups – is a deal-sourcing machine. She has uncovered some of our best returning investments. Yvonne has spoken many times about how her recipe for success was shaped by the racial barriers put in front of her. Entertainment veteran Erica Motley, who wrote the book on funding for direct-to-streaming TV projects, brought strengths to our investment team that gave us a leg-up as a venture capital firm. Erica's unmatched contact list makes her a connector who brings along a seat at the table for other powerful Black women. She can package projects like nobody's business, getting the right people to attach themselves to projects at the earliest stages – a VC's dream.

Our fifth team member, Ezechi Britton, arrived in our midst

as a seasoned Chief Technical Officer and business founder who had scaled lots of technologies and raised lots of money at financial technology (fintech) innovator Neyber. He is the perfect complement to the four of us and one of the best operating executives in the fast-growth ecosystem.

Among our executive founding members, I persuaded Ric Lewis to serve as Chair. That was a huge win. Ric epitomizes the lack of need for permission from anyone. He has lived in the UK for twenty years. He also had a long track record in private equity, had billions of assets under management on behalf of clients, and enormous investment credibility in many industrial sectors. Ric also has the largest Black business in the UK and is known for not wasting his time. Lenny Henry, one of the main instigators for Impact X, would continue to remain active as a founding member and Vice-Chair for Media and Entertainment. Lenny has been an asset at every turn. Beyond the fact that he is beloved, with a broad-based multi-generational following, he continues to provide access to local founders and funders alike.

When Ursula Burns came aboard, accepting a position as Vice-Chair of Digital and Technology, I knew we were in business to last. It's not only Ursula's unparalleled access to allies in our cause; she is also an all-round smart strategist. Early in her tenure at Xerox, Ursula drew from her engineering background to ascend the ranks in Alpha style. She went from starting as an assistant to a division head to being named CEO of Xerox in 2009. It's worth repeating that she was the first Black woman to hold that title at a Fortune 500 company.

In her first year as Xerox's CEO, Ursula oversaw the turn-around of a behemoth-sized corporation that was in trouble. Her tenure kicked off by helping the company close its largest acquisition up to that time, in turn enabling Xerox to evolve into a services firm rather than just a hardware and consumables firm. Ursula has credited her success to always being available and to digging into everything in the way only an engineer can.

After we got to know each other better through Impact X, I had the opportunity to sit down and talk at length with Ursula after she agreed to be the very first guest of my podcast, 'The Recipe'. On it I unfurl the narratives of well-known and emerging business leaders who share the ingredients they use to get results. As someone who is so oversubscribed, overscheduled and over-committed, Ursula Burns is nonetheless always the one person who finds time to help in the biggest and most personal of ways.

Ursula is refreshing. The two main ingredients of her recipe, she said, were, 'grit and appreciation'. Grit is a familiar ingredient claimed by Black women. We call them fierce, we call them queens, we call them fearless. Grit sums up a power source I see in many women of colour. Appreciation is also powerful and something I hear more and more Black women and men weaving into conversations. The turn of the phrase 'I appreciate you' seems so much more personal than just 'Thank you'. Give it a try the next time you see someone going out of their way to deliver results.

Ursula and I also talked about the fact that attainment of wealth should not be seen as a measure of her having anything especially exceptional that others don't have. For Ursula, money turned out to be a tool that she understood could be leveraged to disrupt the status quo – much as we covered in Chapter 2. These points are reminders to all of us that we each bring added value to our business dealings that has little to do with the bottom line. We each can do great things no matter where we began.

Something else I've also heard Ursula mention is the importance of giving voice to opinions and insights that aren't motivated by a desire to appease anyone who might be threatened by a confident woman of colour. Her feeling was, 'I realized I was more convincing to myself and to the people who were listening when I actually said what I thought, versus what I thought people wanted to hear me say.'

Incredibly, the planning phase at Impact X lasted only six months. We began in May 2018 when our conversation started, conducted research from June to August, and plunged into fundraising from August to November, with our First Close on 27 November 2018. All that was for fund formation and fundraising. Our Second Close for investing took place in May 2019 and in June 2019 we made our first investment – in underrepresented male founders in the fintech arena.

When the opportunity arose to invest in R.grid, a UK startup developed by a Black female founder, we were excited. R.grid's founder, Dr Amber Michelle Hill, had an academic background in translational neuroscience along with a social-impact background focused on creative and digital strategies in healthcare to improve outcomes. As if those combined areas of expertise weren't enough, Dr Hill's desire to delve more deeply into the practical application of research, development and data science led her to further her education in engineering and entrepreneurship. After developing research programming used in the UK, Germany, the US, China and Africa, Amber conceived of R.grid as a means of creating efficiencies in clinical testing. The outcome was to reduce administrative workloads for healthcare providers from months to minutes. In the world of Covid-19 and the need for validated vaccine solutions produced at record pace, R.grid could be the answer.

Proving our principle that Black women are an excellent

investment, R.grid is already changing the world of research studies. Impact X has found success with investments in many companies that have women founders as well as executives across multiple sectors. In media and entertainment the companies include Little Black Book, Chudor House, Lion Forge and Scope. We have even added Impact X Studios as an investment home for our media and entertainment projects. We are not a production studio per se but a company that invests in projects from production companies and content creators.

We built it and they came.

We have a female-founded Welsh company in the healthtech arena called Health & Her, and in the beauty/lifestyle sector we've invested in companies such as Afrocenchix and Beautonomy. All these companies over-index for women in key decision-making roles. The expectation is that Alpha will be produced. Where before there have been few female board members and C-suite executives of colour, that narrative is now being turned on its head.

If there is only one piece of inspiration you take away from a discussion about the good business sense of investing, hiring and enlisting the talents of under-represented women, I hope it is this: that you will look more closely for ways that women in your circle can contribute as part of your team.

Indra Nooyi, a woman of colour born in India and the former CEO of PepsiCo, is a champion of empowering women in the workplace. She points out that while women are largely understood by companies to be the 'end users', very few of those companies are fully across the idea of their female employees being uniquely placed to innovate for female consumers. She says: 'When women are empowered in the design and innovation process, the likelihood of success in the marketplace improves by 144 per cent!'

In other words, women – especially women of colour – are

a secret power source who, when invested in and empowered, can lead an economic revolution. However you choose to say it, there is nothing like a once-in-a-millennium catastrophic pandemic to make change not only meaningful but absolutely necessary – as we'll consider next.

WE DON'T NEED PERMISSION

9

UNDERDOGS BECOME UNICORNS

Step #9: Sell your vision, make time-appropriate asks and don't forget to recruit allies

... more people can achieve success when they think that others view them as underdogs – if they view others as less credible and channel their motivation to prove them wrong toward performing better.

SAMIR NURMOHAMED, 'THE UPSIDE OF BEING AN UNDERDOG',
HARVARD BUSINESS REVIEW

In venture capital, a unicorn is a privately held startup company that is valued at more than $1 billion. It's a term that's become common, but where did it come from and why are these companies called unicorns?

PITCHBOOK

Many years ago, I toyed with the idea of becoming an actor. I'd done shows in high school and university and had been encouraged to investigate the possibilities. Then, one evening, while attending a Broadway production, caught up in the spectacle, I realized that the only way for me to work would be to get cast. That is, someone else – or several others – would be in charge of determining how far I could or couldn't go. It occurred to me that while being an actor might be creatively fulfilling, my bigger interest was in determining my own path and having autonomy, responsibility and power over my own future. Why willingly choose to be beholden to someone else's mercurial choices for my well-being?

The answer which came eventually was that, as the underdog, I didn't always have the resources to be the top dog – as in the actual impresario who foots the bill for those shows. Then it occurred to me that even impresarios are beholden to investors or partners. The reality is that in all forms of business, wherever you are in the food chain, there will always be obligations – as in the old-fashioned quid pro quo. If you work for someone, you are beholden to them for employing and paying you, but they are beholden to you for supplying your services.

Shonda Rhimes – known for creating and producing *Grey's Anatomy*, for creating the cheeky political thriller *Scandal* and for producing the massively successful Netflix series *Bridgerton* – has spoken often about learning to respect actors as partners in an aligned vision. So even though she has the power to cast an actor or not, the actors who bring her storytelling to life have the power to influence how successful she is.

This points to a strategic way of thinking about your role in a larger firm that employs you. You might be seen in this context as an *intrapreneur*. If you are given a green light to develop a project or concept for the company, along with resources and the potential for sharing to some degree in the success, you are using the same talents you might put to use for your own company – although you won't have the same risks or rewards as the actual owner. Some of the most successful startups have come from intrapreneurs-turned-entrepreneurs.

All that said, if we as Black businesspeople want to transform our lives, our communities and our world, the fastest and most direct route to greater autonomy, freedom and power is by owning our own businesses. You know by now, of course, that you don't need permission to do so. But let me add that you are free to give yourself permission to ask for help if you need it. There is an abundance of how-to seminars, incubators and accelerators that can get you going or help you grow your business if you've already started. Give yourself permission, if you're further along, to help someone else start her or his business. This is your flywheel in action.

If you find yourself wavering – not sure whether to go for it full-on or take it slow – an effective exercise is to map the steps you'll need to take to get where you want to be. As you've seen, it took me a little while to get to do the job I'd declared at eighteen years old would one day be my purpose. Yet there I was, still in the early days of launching Impact X, suddenly with the dream job of VC, investing money, time and counsel in the futures of others.

The kinds of companies we seek for Impact X are different in ambition (Impact X businesses always think globally) from some of the smaller and mid-sized startups that I have advised on television and podcasts, as well as in business seminars. If you happened to watch *The Money Maker*, you may remember that all the entrepreneurs could be seen as underdogs. By that, I mean few of them had easy paths to success, for example having limited access to investment and advisors. In the case of each business with which we worked, there were two messages I emphasized that can offer practical help and can be applied regardless of the scope and scale of your enterprise.

The first bit of wisdom, learned the hard way by me, is

simply the exciting reality that underdogs can become unicorns. The term was first coined in 2013 by VC Aileen Lee, who had reviewed outcomes for 60,000 internet and software companies around the world that had received funding over the previous decade. Just thirty-nine of these startups were valued at $1 billion or more. Lee chose the mythical animal to represent just how rare such successful ventures really are. However, since that time, a pitchbook.com post noted, unicorns have become less rare. In April 2021, the total number of startups achieving unicorn status was up at 602.

The underdog power play you can choose to use isn't to accept underdog status forever. Rather, I see underdogs as those who toil in obscurity – imagining and then actualizing solutions that make life better for untold numbers of others, often from having experienced those same problems themselves.

The second bit of wisdom is that with all your autonomy, allow yourself to receive incoming opportunities and practise getting past hurdles. There are going to be many variables that will determine the trajectory from underdog to unicorn and many pitfalls that will undermine that trajectory. Anyone who claims that there is only one route is wrong. Just as wrong as those who think that unicorns are recognizable from inception. They aren't. The path to unicorn status claims countless victims along the way who never reach the $1 billion threshold – with Lee's 2013 analysis showing us that just 0.065 per cent make it.

Without a good sense of timing – with respect to getting help – it is almost impossible to grow a company valued at $1 billion in a short amount of time. Contrary to the heroine and hero stories that we hear about successful entrepreneurs, no founder is an island. As much as you may think that Steve Jobs built Apple on his own or that Meg Whitman built eBay by herself, it doesn't work that way. So no matter how much you want to DIY your startup, there will come the time when you have to reach out and become comfortable with Step #9 – *Sell your vision, make time-appropriate asks and don't forget to recruit allies.*

If so much about successful growth is timing, then when is the right time? I'd like to answer that question with insights from team members of the four businesses I had the pleasure of introducing to audiences in the UK, Europe and even beyond.

First, I'll set the stage as to just how unpredictable timing can be.

Now is the time

In February 2021, towards the end of filming the four-part series I had agreed to do a seeming lifetime earlier, we were paused in production. In my home office, between Zoom meetings, I saw an Associated Press headline pop on to my laptop screen. It read: 'UK economy suffers biggest drop since 1709'.

For a moment I thought – *That's impossible! I must have misread it.* Then I looked again. Sure enough, that's what the headline said. The piece, written by Danica Kirka, which was picked up and run by other outlets as the day went on, assessed the damage to the British economy as the biggest decline it had suffered in 312 years. With the toll taken by Covid-19 and the shutdown of many industries, the Office for National Statistics reported that the drop was 9.9 per cent – more than two times the economic decline experienced in the Great Recession of 2009. The last time anything of this magnitude happened had been in the early eighteenth century, when the agriculturally based economy was literally frozen – caused by the Great Frost, a sudden cold snap that destroyed farms and food stores.

Obviously, I knew that the economy was in bad shape, but not as bad as this data suggested. The news had arrived during what was actually a third lockdown in England, with severe restrictions also imposed in Wales, Scotland and Northern Ireland. The UK was doing nearly twice as poorly as Germany (whose GDP shrank 5 per cent in the same time period). Worse, the drop in GDP in the UK was around three times the US decline of only 3.5 per cent.

The AP story quoted government representatives urging patience and optimism, predicting that the vaccination rollout, already under way, would allow businesses to come roaring back. As reported by Kirka, Shadow Chancellor Anneliese Dodds blasted that overly sunny outlook by saying, 'These figures confirm that not only has the UK had the worst death toll in Europe, we're experiencing the worst economic crisis of any major economy. Businesses can't wait any longer. The Chancellor needs to come forward now with a plan to secure the economy in the months ahead, with support going hand-in-hand with health restrictions.'

Two contrasting reactions hit me in fast succession. The first was one of concern. I knew both from the data and from direct observation that the UK's communities of colour had already been traumatized by bearing the brunt of Covid-19, suffering more than twice as many deaths as white Britons. In June 2020, Reuters research showed that the percentage of employed Black, Asian and other minority ethnic people had fallen from 72 per cent in February 2020 to 67.4 per cent in April 2020. For non-Black, Asian and other minority ethnic people the decline was less severe: from 81.1 per cent to 79.4 per cent.

My second reaction, to my surprise, was the same empowered, resolved feeling I had experienced in the summer of 2020 when Black Lives Matter and Stand Up to Racism marches took place over a period of months in 260 cities and towns across the UK.

George Floyd had pleaded for permission to breathe and

died waiting. Nor was permission needed by any of the thousands of people who took to the streets, most of them young, to make sure their voices were being heard. An article about the impact of the marchers appeared in the *Guardian* on 13 November 2020, which explained that although the British marchers looked to the US movement and what was happening there, their anger was very much based on their experience of being Black in Britain. Rather than the names of George Floyd, Trayvon Martin, Ahmaud Arbery and Breonna Taylor, their placards carried the names of Mark Duggan, Sean Rigg and Sheku Bayoh – casualties of police brutality in the UK. In June 2020, the *Guardian* had reported that, while constituting only 3 per cent of the population, Black people accounted for 8 per cent of deaths in police custody. One aspect of the abuse of power by the police was their ability to stop and search anyone for any reason – a practice, remember, stretching back to the 1980s. Impassioned protestors carried signs broadcasting the truth that, according to gov.uk, between April 2019 and March 2020 there were six stop and searches per 1,000 whites and fifty-four per 1,000 Blacks. Black people were angry about the mistreatment of the Windrush generation. And they were angry about the stats around disproportionate Black deaths from Covid-19.

As if there wasn't enough insult being piled upon injury by a combustible mix of Covid-19, an economic collapse, scapegoating of immigrants and people of colour by authorities and right-wing activists, let's also not forget that many Britons of colour had been barely surviving for over a decade since the 2008–9 global financial collapse. According to data produced for Bloomberg by the Office for National Statistics and reported in May 2021 by Olivia Konotey-Ahulu, over the past decade in the UK the median accumulation of wealth through home ownership by a Black family was zero. In comparison, the median accumulation of property and land wealth over the past decade by a white British family was about £115,000 ($163,000). One of the main reasons for this disparity is that only about 30 per cent of Black families are home owners.

The righteous anger was like a jolt of adrenaline for me, and maybe for you. Despite a traumatizing pandemic and an economic near-wipeout, Brits of colour and our allies had come out in force, armed with facts and history, to disrupt the status quo. For every flash of concern, I kept looking at another set of data points that told a different story – one of resilience.

At the end of 2020, the *Financial Times* had reported that the pandemic was leading to a boom in new businesses. The main cause for hope came from the fact that entrepreneurs saw opportunities to address a new set of business and individual needs that resulted from rapid changes in how everyone was working and living. New approaches to social distancing created business opportunities, as did innovative delivery methods for services and goods. Another positive trend was that many workers who had been furloughed were starting businesses.

None of this news about a surge in new businesses necessarily promised economic equity to under-represented founders. But throughout 2020 there had been significant statements of commitment of capital and support for Black entrepreneurs and workers, all made from an array of institutional and private equity sources. The time had come to make sure those commitments were kept.

There was not a moment to waste.

In other words, conditions have never been better to sell your vision of a more equitable future, particularly as an underdog. Now is the time. You don't have to be a unicorn to do what unicorns do, but have the goal that your business will attain unicorn status. Map your plan and practise selling your idea to doubters while in the shower or when you talk to yourself in the mirror, or to your most trusted confidantes. Predict the questions of naysayers and be able to address them in advance. Make your vision the greatest breakthrough since the discovery of fire. It's momentous. Sell your vision to yourself. Make sure that you understand its need and what it will take to scale it. Know your audience. Do your homework and collect data to make your case. Prepare for pushback. Practise listening to advice and putting it to use.

Making time-sensitive asks means that, when you have an opportunity to ask for a favour or a key introduction or a major investment, it's best to first assess the appropriateness. Can your potential investor or helper provide the assistance you seek? Does this person have a demonstrated record of support in their past? It is not a complete waste of everyone's time if your target supporter does not invest in businesses in the ways you need. At the very least you can get feedback on your pitch. Even with rejection, you stand to learn more from an investor historically predisposed to supporting businesses like yours.

Take a little extra time if needed to get to know that person's interests and how your ask fulfills those interests. When in doubt about timing, I suggest you first build a working relationship. Make engaging with you a two-way street. Providing your connection with some value is one way to do this. If an investment is your target outcome, introduce them to something which helps them invest better. Help educate them about your sector by providing third-party-validated research and articles. You might also introduce them to other investors or investable companies. All of these steps add value without you making an ask. And in this way, you are building a working relationship so they become more receptive to your pitch. The operative idea is to establish a working relationship rather than a casual relationship.

Recruiting allies is something to consider at every stage of the development of your startup and its growth. Allies, in my view, are folks who might not share the same instigating impetus but will join you to achieve your goals. Recruiting the right allies is like adding booster rockets to your spaceship. They provide a huge lift. Allies exist along a continuum: there are those who are easy to recruit and those who are more challenging. Some allies should come with a warning label because, although allies are generally a benefit, managing the overheads of relationships can suck up resources. I've found that letting allies lead in defining what my goals are leads to compromise in goals, process, speed and/or team. So pitching allies is rarely an early step. My key allies share some critical values, but with their own motivations. I've found that having these key allies to help me achieve my goals creates magic. Ideally, allies have complementary strengths, talents and assets that they can contribute.

Knowing whom and when to call – or when not to call – is both a skill and an art.

The three women who founded Black Lives Matter in 2013 – Patrisse Cullors, Alicia Garza and Opal Tometi – had a goal and understood, in 2020, how to recruit allies who were not people of colour, plus how to harness the energy of support. During the summer of 2020, allies deliberately patronized Black-owned businesses and consumed Black-created and -curated content in their reading, viewing and listening choices. The best BLM allies recognized that they needed to be educated as to how to become not just not-racists, but rather anti-racists.

In business, allies can be your customers. You should be recruiting them and keeping them engaged at every step. They are your extended posse – people you know, people who are recommended to you by people you trust, your good friends, close colleagues and friends of friends. The best places to find allies are where you find your friends.

The next place to find allies and customers is by leveraging a platform. Otherwise, how are customers and allies going to find you?

Marketing for underdogs and unicorns

When I first set out to select the startups to be featured on a business reality TV show, I was primarily interested in finding underdogs who had potential but who were struggling. My goal was to choose diverse businesses, so that the solutions we found would help a range of stakeholders, including other business owners or would-be entrepreneurs.

My first trek was to Manchester, where I met Jasen Jackiw, founder of Prymo, a terrific niche service offering invisible repairs to damaged surfaces within the booming construction industry. Jasen and his team were enormously confident and capable of selling their vision. The materials and restoration processes they used to invisibly repair marble, granite, plastic counter tops, flooring, wood, plaster – you name it – were remarkable. Seeing was believing. But there was a problem with the financials – not much profit, therefore very little cash to invest in growth. The real problem was that Jasen didn't realize that, although he was busy, his business was stagnating. Or he did realize it but was hard-pressed to admit that the allyship he wanted from me (passive investment and some scale-up guidance when requested) came with lots of my opinions, at my pace and at least some of my outcomes. Ouch.

The big challenge for the business was to try new ways to solve a persistent problem – which in this case was the recruitment of new technicians from non-traditional backgrounds. They needed to scale up, but at a reasonable cost, and couldn't find enough staff to do the skilled work. This was where the disruption came in. We set up a recruiting process designed to give opportunities for trainees to learn a new trade. Jasen was amazed that the underdogs among the prospective trainees, with little to no background in construction or repair, worked twice as hard to master the techniques. With more employees hired and fantastic word of mouth, Prymo's business shot up. New alliances in the apartment construction and housing industry were soon struck. Even before the Prymo episode aired the business's financial picture had improved, only to improve even more after becoming known to new customers and allies post-broadcast.

Next, I met Alex Jacobs of The Sussex Kitchen. Right from the start I saw the promise of this multi-award-winning independent craft bakery specializing in some of the most delicious bread, savouries and fresh pastries I had ever tasted. Alex and his team had figured out how to navigate the challenges of Covid-19 by pivoting from supplying hotels and restaurants, which were now shuttered in line with government restrictions, to delivering freshly baked goods straight to customers' doors early in the morning. However, selling their vision to grow the business and recruit new customers and allies wasn't happening. To give Alex a feel for how much more he could accomplish, I brought in a team of social media experts from Jellyfish, the marketing performance specialists, who galvanized engagement many times over. When Alex saw the possibilities, he grasped the potential of reaching new customers but was not in his comfort zone. The surest way to scale up and grow the business was to build a robust social media following. He did not have the skill set to do that, for one thing, but mainly he didn't trust the power of social media to convert into product sales.

After he rejected several attempts to steer him towards modernizing and scaling up his efforts, it became clear that the reason for his reluctance was that he saw The Sussex Kitchen as his business and, having worked so hard, giving up equity, even a small amount, in return for investment and guidance was too big a step for him.

If you are content staying an underdog, doing things your way as you always have, that's fine. My advice, though, is to be creative about taking on help when it's offered. Otherwise it may not come again and, if it does, it could be too late. Alex and I parted ways on a positive note, however, with Alex determined to take some of what he had learned to grow his business his way.

The third business to receive my attention was Winny's Meals in Birmingham, which had tremendous potential. Founded by Shaun Sookoo, a medical student-turned-personal trainer-turned-entrepreneur, this prepared Caribbean meal business, which delivered to homes around the country – worth potentially millions as part of a £9-billion-a-year industry in the UK – had been inspired by Winny, Shaun's mum, and the Caribbean cooking he'd grown up with. Shaun had a devoted, talented team, knew where he wanted to lead them and could passionately lay out his vision. Missing was a mastery of his core business, which we overhauled in every detail – from reworking the recipes to rebranding Winny's Meals as Winny's Kitchen to new packaging, going from black and white geometric shapes to bright, colourful labels summoning the feel of an imagined Caribbean home. We revamped the menu and launched a new hero product – bottled jerk sauce, a proof-of-concept that got the brand into the supermarket.

Once the reinvention was accomplished and data (that people loved it) was provided, we secured a time-sensitive opportunity to make a presentation to the buyers at Morrisons supermarket chain. The key was knowing that, even though we were outside their usual new products testing cycle, they often have extra time to experiment with something not on the market anywhere else. Shaun and his team delivered big-time and left with a commitment to continue the relationship so that

Morrisons could get to know Winny's Kitchen meals for possible stocking in their freezer aisles and shop shelves. The meals the buyers loved the most were the ones that were truly the most authentic, spicy, delicious and unique. The meals that were created to appeal to more moderate, mainstream palates were questioned. The takeaway is a reminder to capitalize on what's authentic to you and your culture. It's another form of leveraging what you know.

The fourth business in which I intervened was called Trim-It, an app allowing you to order a mobile barbershop direct to your doorstep. It was a vision that needed little selling. In the UK, men's barbering represents billions of pounds in annual revenues. But the pandemic had shut down all of that trading, so the idea of booking an appointment on your phone and having a skilled barber park at your office or home at the appointed hour was timely.

Darren Tenkorang, the twenty-six-year-old founder, had started Trim-It while at university after wasting time waiting for his haircut at the barbershop one day. There are echoes of Branson's delayed flight that led to the founding of Virgin Atlantic here, and I loved that he had observed a problem and discovered a gap in the marketplace. He had a young, smart tech team around him – all friends from university. Frankly, I didn't need the sell. That was an easy investment decision. Whatever I asked, Darren and his team overdelivered in half the time. It was a reminder that a great team is the best risk mitigation strategy there is.

Darren and his team were excited about my suggestions for scaling the business but had an unclear roadmap for making it happen. They would need a business model that could scale, yet at the same time maintain quality in a highly evolving personal-services business where hair-styling preferences change frequently and one poor haircut would mean the permanent loss of at least one customer (and potentially more from word of mouth). It's a difficult balance that very few services businesses master. Getting more vans throughout London and beyond required more barbers. Trim-It needed a franchise business that could work.

For inspiration, I asked Darren if he would like to meet with some of my connections, including the head of Uber in the UK. He and his team leaped at the opportunity. Then came the hard work of preparing for that key meeting. We ran a few mock presentations with some of my colleagues from Impact X. Initially the team was unprepared and things didn't go well. But, as always, the Trim-It guys went back and made changes and seemed to be in a good place. However, when we went to the Uber meeting, Darren was clearly nervous. While trying to come up with numbers in response to a question, he floundered. I called for a quick break and pulled him and the team aside to get him refocused and delivered a brief pep talk focused on being himself. He was then able to go back to the meeting to talk about data and why explosive growth potential existed for Trim-It. This included discussing the 17,000 satisfied end users they already had, showcasing their sophisticated scheduling technology and making clear that Trim-It's true customers were the folks giving the trim, not the recipients of the service – such a smart move.

In that shift of energy, from seeing Darren caught in the headlights to witnessing him being able to speak with deep authority about the potential of his business, the two Uber executives fully engaged. They offered their support and guidance, inviting Darren and the Trim-It team to learn from them. After all, they said, the founders of Uber had once been underdogs too.

The gift of expertise that an ally brings can sometimes be more valuable than a financial investment.

In the case of Trim-it, particularly, and the two other companies I invested in on *The Money Maker*, I have not ruled out fast growth that can lead to unicorn status for them. However, I know that becoming a unicorn is not for everyone. They are called unicorns because they are that rare.

Despite all those bad economic tidings flooding our shores in 2020, 2021's astonishingly good news was revealed in certain investment sectors in the UK. Here are some Tech Nation stats from June 2021 from which to take encouragement and even inspiration:

- By mid-2021 the UK's tech industry had raised £13.5 billion – about three times what was invested in the same period the year before.
- By late 2021, the UK's venture capital investment in tech ranked third in the world (behind only the US and China), and more than double the next biggest market – Germany (with £6.2 billion).
- By Fall 2021 venture capital investment in the UK went to 1,700 tech startups.
- Outside London, Oxford and its biotech businesses make it the top city for venture capital investment, followed by Bristol, Birmingham and Cambridge.
- UK tech companies are collectively valued at £428 billion and climbing.
- The countries that produce the most tech unicorns are the US and China, with the UK coming in in third place with more unicorns than any other country in Europe.
- The UK's 105 tech unicorns include twelve decacorns (a privately held company valued at $10 billion) – seven of which were so declared in 2021.
- The UK's tech companies employ 9 per cent of the workforce, or nearly 3 million people.

- Fintech dominated 2021's investment rounds and the UK, second in the world for attracting fintech venture capital investment, received £4.2 billion by mid-2021.

Don't tell me as you look at those statistics – even if only 0.2 per cent of venture capital investing has gone to Black founders and only 0.02 per cent to Black women founders – that the likelihood of an underdog becoming the next major unicorn is a crap shoot. It's not magic, either. But there is a playbook, as you can see by all those compelling statistics and opportunities.

Likewise, there is a playbook for how Black business can be increased to have world-changing impact.

Now.

10

IMPACT NOW!

Step #10: Always bet on Black

. . . What if we launched an initiative on the scale of the Marshall Plan or the space race to eradicate white supremacy? . . . What if?

BARBARA SMITH, 'THE PROBLEM IS WHITE SUPREMACY'

Shortly before I arrived at law school, one of my professors, Derrick Bell, wrote and published a seminal work, *And We Are Not Saved: The Elusive Quest for Racial Justice.* In it he uses a series of parable-like stories and fictional conversations to present his main argument – that despite the gains of civil rights in terms of laws and policy precedents, the work is far from done. His proof that we are still in the struggle for racial justice and equality can be highlighted by differences in income, wealth and life expectancy.

The book's title is a biblical allusion to Jeremiah 8:20, which, in full, reads: 'The harvest has passed, the summer has ended, but we have not been saved.' Theological interpretations vary, but the message Bell implies is that it's not enough to expect deliverance just because the hard work has been completed. What I took from the reading was a reminder that justice will be reached – like the Promised Land – when all who seek it are involved in the daily toil for it.

The question to ask ourselves, then, is what *work* have I accomplished today to create that all-important virtuous circle? What part have I played investing in the summer's harvest or making possible the economic intervention that for too long has been the critical missing piece in the quest to dismantle white supremacy?

Other questions to ask were posed by Black feminist pioneer, activist, author and professor Barbara Smith in a June 2020 op. ed. in the *Boston Globe* entitled 'The Problem Is White Supremacy'. The piece posed a series of 'What if?' scenarios, starting with the proposal to mount an effort against white supremacy on the scale of the commitment made by the US to Western Europe to build back at the end of the Second World War. Smith argued that a starting point would be to address the refusal by the powers that be to recognize the existence of white supremacy as an institution; the term itself, she pointed out, seems not to be understood by many people. Her clarification was that white supremacy is 'not merely the individual delusion of being superior to Black people', but rather a deeply entrenched, centuries-old institutionalized operating system designed to give privilege to white people and disadvantage people of colour. As for a plan on the scale of a moon landing or a Manhattan Project, Smith asked: *What if the effort was led by experts with lived experience of how white supremacy functions?* For this plan to succeed in ending white supremacy for good, *What if the poor and working-class folks of colour were able to work in tandem with other experts in the fields of research and advocacy?*

Barbara Smith followed up those 'What ifs?' in a longer

piece for the *Nation* magazine in August 2020, into which she added the necessity for economic intervention to eradicate white supremacy once and for all. This would include ending poverty, tackling the racial wealth gap, guaranteeing employment and investing in communities of colour.

Well, what if we each played a part in such a plan? What would that look like for you? On any given day?

My late father, who, much to our sorrow, passed away in the Fall of 2020, was fond of reminding us after church, 'If you want your prayers answered, get up off your knees and hustle.'

In this last chapter I want to echo that sentiment and urge you on in your entrepreneurial enterprise, which will power your own virtuous circle. As a daily mantra, the last principle is one that has been woven throughout the book: Step #10 – *Always bet on Black*. Your success as an under-represented founder or an ally or a champion of an economic empowerment movement will in turn fuel the success of every stakeholder in the world, because my concept is that instead of merely creating a Black Silicon Valley, for example – a business company *town* – we are disrupting old paradigms and creating a Black business company *world*.

We can start by creating the conditions that lead to recyclable wealth in our own families and in our own backyards. My approach comes from the school of 'You can't take it with you.' So my focus has never been on passing along money at death. The bequeathing of family wealth, if we are lucky enough to have the capital, usually happens late in life for the inheritor. This is one option. But I'd argue that this type of wealth transfer often comes too late and misses the chance to incubate new talent and new opportunities. For me, this is a concept that began with my parents and one that we have learned through some of the stories told in the preceding pages. Small amounts today can deliver outsized returns.

After all, what is the purpose of leaving money to your kids? Is it to make their life more comfortable and give them some security? If you have your first kid when you are 28.9 years old (the UK average) and you die at the average age of eighty, your child will be fifty at the time of wealth transfer, which is currently sixteen years shy of UK retirement age. By this point in life, many opportunities will have passed. That is the bane of an investor, missing a great opportunity for Return on Investment.

Intergenerational wealth transfers are fine at any point, but many Black folk can still only dream of being able to leave their children anything. This is why I say: invest small amounts all along the journey.

However you choose to be empowered and create wealth, it probably goes without saying by now that we don't need permission. We don't have to wait to be saved. There are all kinds of ways to always bet on Black. Let's look at some of them to hopefully stir your imagination.

Solve for impact

At some point in our younger lives, many of us most likely had occasion to come across one of those classic toys known as Russian dolls. Every time you open up one doll, there's another inside, right? This is how I see the insidiousness of white supremacy: we are unable to fully comprehend it because it goes so deep and touches on so many aspects of daily living.

With the first doll, Stage One, we ask ourselves – *What is the impact of so many families of colour living in poverty? Of one in two Black British families living in poverty, barely above or even below the breadline?*

We know that poverty has arisen as the result of multiple factors. We can spend time addressing and trying to solve those problems. But the solutions to poverty itself may not be as readily effective in creating sustained change as coming up with solutions to address the toll taken by poverty. That is, alleviate the symptoms and then cure the disease.

We then open the doll, see Stage Two and ask – *What is the impact of people of colour having lower rates of home ownership and other sources of recyclable wealth to pay for education and transportation and provide a sense of security and potential for the next generation?*

With the next doll, we arrive at Stage Three – *What is the impact of institutionalized white supremacy that denies credit and other means of getting loans to self-support based on the supposedly objective criteria of income level and asset ownership?*

You can see where this is going. The fact that during Covid-19 Black families have had to borrow money for funeral costs for loved ones ought to be unacceptable to everyone. The fact that people of colour have as little as a tenth of the assets held by white families with the same median income should be intolerable. Assets, according to www.Investopedia.com, means anything of value or a resource that can be converted to cash.

How do we change all that? I propose we do so in the same way we address the fact that access to VC investment has been so elusive for founders of colour. It's the same way Impact X bets on Black to remedy the plague of there being no Black-owned/founded companies in the Fortune 500 or the FTSE 100, or so few women of colour in the C-suite and on governing boards of major corporations.

We have to address the enemy of change: inertia. When Black Lives Matter summoned millions upon millions to march in the streets in the middle of Covid-19, when they'd been directed by governments to shelter at home, they showed the world that protesting peacefully is still potent. Getting people to a march is not a small effort, and the ability to mobilize for voter rights, anti-lynching, protesting police brutality and more is not only powerful but remains necessary.

The onslaught of Covid-19 demonstrated to me the lengths to which the world is willing to go if its existence is at risk. In some ways it helped me to see, as we showed in Chapter 3, that I was thinking too small. When a microscopic enemy first started to kill us in late 2019, governments, businesses and individuals mobilized to defend humanity. Then, in March 2020, something happened which most of us never imagined possible: the UK shut down, closed its borders, decreed that businesses could not trade, that churches could not congregate, households could not convene, families could not meet, individuals could not travel or even leave home except for medical help, food and limited exercise. The stakes were so high and the potential negative outcomes so dire that an unprecedented strategy was imposed.

It is this level of intervention we need to put in place to dismantle white supremacy.

We have all witnessed that when the will is there, people, business and governments find a way. White supremacy may never be felt to be sufficiently dire to unite all humanity in its eradication because, as Barbara Smith puts it in the *Boston Globe* piece, 'the power structure has always refused to acknowledge the institution'. And we can't simply wait and pray for that intervention. The costs are too high. George Floyd's murder unified many allies, highlighted critical issues and silenced many haters – for a time. But the fight continues and, as with Covid-19, we are battling for our empowered existence. Let's use this period of disruption to the fullest and take a lesson from the Covid-19 pandemic: throw everything and everyone we have at the problem.

By the same token, it is important to mobilize allies and backers of initiatives to halt the paralysis by analysis and to bet on Black as never before. In the digital age, we know that it's possible to grow a global village that is bigger than any one person or leader. So the challenge to consider is how we can get every stakeholder in the world to come to the table. To begin with, we have to get the word out that white supremacy is pervasive; we have to convince those who do not believe it exists that it is in their interest to see it and combat it, and be completely confident that it can be fought. Climate change activism is a parallel movement from which strategies can be incorporated.

The proposition that empowering Black businesses can be a boon to entire economies is not new. In 2020, a McKinsey study reported the estimate that every year the US economy incurs losses from the Black–white wealth gap of $1 trillion. Projects that promote healthy Black businesses, community-based entrepreneurship and develop concentrated community wealth will shift national economies. We have a track record and are that much more investable.

In fact, in some cases Black business successes have been so powerful that they seem to have posed an existential threat to white supremacy: instead of welcoming the enrichment to all, some people have attempted to halt or destroy Black progress. In the US, of course, it wasn't enough to pass Jim Crow laws to reverse any socio-economic strides made by African Americans during Reconstruction after the Civil War. Instead, a regime of intimidation, isolation and murder was instituted, particularly in the South.

Lynching wasn't restricted to the South, as we know, but the majority of the violence took place in the same states that had fought on the side of the Confederacy. There were a recorded 4,000 murders of Black men, women and children in those states between 1877 and 1950. These included not only the killing, maiming and torture of individual Black citizens but full-on race massacres, many of which targeted wealthier African Americans and their businesses in the bustling cities of the South.

In 2021, many in the UK and the rest of the world learned about the anniversary of the destruction of Black Wall Street in 1921, which was part of the race massacre in Tulsa, Oklahoma. Long considered the worst act of domestic terrorism committed in the US, it was carried out by an armed and organized white mob that was activated by the resentment of African American prosperity. That was the fuse, the official record now says. At the time, the spark that lit the massacre was a report of a white woman who claimed to have been assaulted by a Black man on his way out of a segregated bathroom. A group of Black men sought to protect the accused man from being lynched and were all gunned down. Hundreds of residents were murdered, more than a thousand homes burned to the ground, and almost all the Black businesses were destroyed.

As described in May 2021 by the *New York Times*, the main target was the Greenwood neighbourhood, a flywheel of opportunity aimed at counteracting the racial hatred of the era. As many as 10,000 Black residents enjoyed the thriving city built in the early 1900s. Comfortable, gracious homes nestled in well-tended residential areas that surrounded the business section – complete with churches, banks, theatres, hotels, grocery stores and doctors' offices. All of it was gone by the end of the massacre.

During this same period, a different set of circumstances had led to what began as the 1919 race riots in the UK. In its account, blackpast.org describes the violence in the seaport areas of cities like Liverpool, Cardiff, Hull and South Shields. The riots were stoked by economic 'anxieties and anger by white union workers and demobilized white servicemen' and it was directed at Black, Arab and Chinese people, at marginalized communities and, importantly, the businesses they had established.

As recounted in the national archive of gov.uk, in this period of economic downturn the white working-class former servicemen had no means of challenging ship owners for better wages. With their power removed, it was all too easy to turn that frustration towards those in an even less stable position than their own. Ginned up to blame immigrants and other men of colour for their own disempowerment, they rationalized that it was not just their jobs being threatened but that these Black and brown men were out to steal their white women. A young Afro-Caribbean, Charles Wootton, was lynched by white rioters while businesses and homes belonging to Black, Arab and Chinese citizens were destroyed by fires. After the riots, five people had been killed, hundreds of arrests and injuries had occurred, and more was to come – the government's reaction of deporting colonial citizens for fear of a 'Black backlash'. To sweeten the deal, the government offered a repatriation settlement, and between 1919 and 1921 around 3,000 Black and Arab seamen, along with their families, were effectively sent home. In addition, Caribbeans who were employed by various shipping companies were fired, and then returned to the West Indies. The aftermath of the First World War was already a time of economic hardship, but this period of sustained racism and changes to the legal status of Black and Arab people meant that life was made incredibly difficult for people of colour.

One full century later, here we still are. Britain's Black population is a testament to the stubborn tenacity of the generations of people of colour who chose not to leave the UK when they could have. They stayed, retrenched, and didn't wait to be saved. Similarly, in the US after the Tulsa massacre, with the Great Migration under way – between 1916 and 1970 – many (not all) who survived the destruction stayed in Oklahoma, determined to rebuild. The flight to Northern and Midwestern states in the US – to industrial, urban centres that promised better lives and employment opportunities – is considered the greatest mass movement of people in US history, aside from the forced migrations of Native Americans and including the importation of enslaved people. Yet many who fled the Jim Crow laws that made institutionalized white supremacy legal found that it existed equally in the North, but just had a different accent.

In the histories of both the US and the UK, the scapegoating of immigrants and people of colour is a recurring illness. The fact that policies are enacted to try to build walls to keep the 'others' out tells us that the economic value of immigrants, mostly of colour, is still not recognized. Despite it all, Black citizens and other marginalized people continue to strive to make meaningful contributions.

And yet, in the UK, at the Tory 2021 party conference the Prime Minister used the code of rampant migration as a means to animate the Conservatives' base of supporters. Despite ample criticism, Boris Johnson continues to foment the view of 'us versus them' and points to migrants as bogeymen and worse. It is a wrong, dangerous and yet often recycled and galvanizing white strategy.

At a time when London is considered one of the most multicultural cities in the world – with one third of its residents not born in the UK and 200 different languages spoken – it should not be surprising that modern multiculturalism is a marker of improved living standards. Studies reported in Bloomberg as far back as 2011 connected multiculturalism to thriving economies for the main reason that diverse cultures lead to more innovative and adaptive ways of thinking, which are proverbial gateways to opportunity.

Herein lies one of the reasons, perhaps, why the rise of Black and multicultural communities seems to pose a threat to the sterility of the white race. In the UK, many are familiar with Enoch Powell and his 1968 'Rivers of Blood' speech. Although

I already knew of it, hearing the speech recently, at a time when white nationalism is being justified and normalized, was a chilling experience. By no mere coincidence, Powell, a Conservative MP, stood in opposition to a Labour Party-promoted Race Relations Bill in 1968 that provided greater protections for Black Britons.

The most famous lines from the speech spoke of his fears of Black and immigrant people taking over the country. He referred to a coming war that would pit whites against Blacks and saw it as inevitable. With a nod to Virgil's *Aeneid*, he said that this certainty filled him with foreboding. 'Like the Roman, I seem to see "the River Tiber foaming with much blood",' he said. Powell insisted that closing the UK's borders was not enough to stem the tide. Rather, immigrants would need to be forcibly returned to their countries of origin. Allegedly quoting one of his constituents, Powell said that if actions weren't taken, within two decades the Black man 'will have the whip hand over the white man'. He also told a story of an elderly woman who complained about her neighbourhood being overrun by Blacks and immigrants. She was advised to avoid voicing racial prejudice – which Powell described as her right. He attacked journalists who were in favour of anti-discrimination laws, much as other demagogues have done in recent years. A 2018 piece in *The Atlantic* magazine looked at Powell's lingering influence and pointed to how his anti-immigrant rhetoric was easily recycled during the debate over Brexit.

At the same time, against the odds, big, promising changes are already in motion.

When I first arrived in the UK I was taken aback by the fact that there were no Black universities, as there have been for well over a century in the US. Nor were there any Black banks that had been founded in the UK. The good news is that in 2019, the first Black – and a woman – Baroness Valerie Amos was promoted to head one of the colleges at Oxford; Sonita Alleyne assumed a similar position at Cambridge, and was recently joined by Simon Woolley, also at Cambridge. (Let's for now gloss over that the job title is generally Master of the specific college.) In March 2021, news broke that Atmen would become the first British-led Black banking startup in the UK. In these ways, betting on Black continues to yield success.

What if our economic disruptive revolution is right on time? There are challenges. As we wrestle with the massive problem of white supremacy, we have to be careful to coordinate and make sure we are all pulling in roughly the same direction to solve it – and we know from Covid-19 that to solve a problem of such magnitude requires a universal response. When you grapple with problems that other people are trying to solve too, differences in approach or style are inevitable. But as long as the strategies are complementary, we can all be right. There can be more than one valid solution, and they might all be investable, profitable, scalable and ready for impact now.

I'd like to show you some examples.

In it to win it, together

Whenever I hear that there are other VC firms opening up for business, I cheer. There will always be friendly competition, but when it comes to betting on Black the more we are in it to win it together, the better. This experience of collaborating with allies has given me a new awareness that might be helpful as we seek to build alliances for a common cause. I think of this as a flow of different degrees of separation.

The First Degree of Separation. Within the infrastructure of Impact X, we found our first set of allies within our own network. These are folks who share very similar, if not overlapping views of the world. Because time is of the essence and staying close to home makes sense, I call this top tier 'friends and family'. They arrive first and have few concerns that will stop them from investing.

The Second Degree of Separation are those folks who have a demonstrated commitment to shared values. Their track record, like ours, evidences an ability and dedication to put their money where their mouth is. They have allocations, processes, people in place to institutionalize the full integration of others. This generally has some longevity. Let's call these angel investors.

The Third Degree of Separation are those folks with an articulated interest but no demonstrated commitment. They may hop in if all the metrics are fully demonstrated and most risk is removed, for example if the government guarantees to take it on. Let's call these downstream allies fast followers.

The Fourth Degree of Separation are those folks with no interest or demonstrated commitment. They will come aboard after generations of proof and after many others have piled on. These downstream allies are called slow followers.

Not all VC investor allies are meant for every adventure. So much of an entrepreneur's time, which is not disposable, is spent trying to create alliances with the wrong folks. My caution to founders is to seek out funders as carefully as those funders seek you out. Make sure there is a consensus that all are on board for the same adventure. All money is not created equal, and having the wrong investor involved (reticent, not aligned, with different risk tolerances, a different return timeline), no matter how well funded, will impede you in achieving your goals.

Some of Impact X's UK VC allies whom we've invested alongside are 10x10 (Afrocenchix), Cornerstone (Beautonomy), Ada Ventures (R.grid), LocalGlobe (Business Score) and Passion Capital (Marshmallow). It is worth noting that two of these firms are headed by women, one of whom is Asian, and 10x10 and Cornerstone are both headed by Black Brits. Among our earliest investments, R.grid is already changing the world of research studies and is growing customers. Our second-ever investment, Pace, is rapidly redefining how business is done in the hospitality field, supporting small and mid-sized hotels by helping them optimize their room pricing. Raylo, our very first investment, uses a leasing model to ensure folks can afford smartphones and remain connected, thus helping alleviate the digital divide that lockdown poignantly highlighted. At the time of writing, all eyes are on Raylo's last fundraising round, which puts it into strong growth contention.

Just as many of the companies we bet on have adapted to the challenges of the pandemic, our inability to travel and a realization, thanks to Zoom, Google Meets and so on, that we didn't have to do so meant that Impact X could increase the number of companies we talked to and met with – even exponentially. An upside of less travel, beyond reduced jet lag. Much more could be done in a compressed period, meaning more meetings per week – virtual rather than physical.

Not everyone feels the same way about communicating via our computer screens. For me, it has added to productivity immensely. That said, meeting face to face in real time is always nice when possible. Nice, but not essential, especially when those meetings are used mainly to assess intangible comfort and fit – how much like me these people are.

We also happened upon some surprises. For example, our

portfolio of media and entertainment projects led by teams of under-represented founders increased during lockdown. We took on projects that could withstand lockdown and periods of self-isolation, which we identified as 'Covid-resistant' or even 'Covid-enhanced' projects – productions you'll be hearing about soon, from companies including Chudor House, FxF, Little Black Book Co., YouNeek Studios, GoodGate Media and Three Tables.

At a time when people are particularly conscious of their health but have constrained access to healthcare, a problem that isn't going away any time soon, the startup Health & Her delivers practical expert advice and select products for women experiencing perimenopause and menopause. Yet they are so much more than a retailer of soothing solutions and sage counsel. They are a digital destination where information is disseminated and dissected by experts as well as communities of women with lived experience. The data this community generates is an accessible depository of wisdom.

Similarly, Score the Business could not be more timely. Developed for early-stage entrepreneurs, the founder used his own frustrating experiences as a first-time business owner to create a solution for other harried business owners looking for anything from working capital to legal services to accounting support. Where does a first-time entrepreneur find what they need? Sometimes network, sometimes their VCs and advisors. Now they also have Score the Business.

When I'm asked how we choose which startups to fund, as if Impact X has a crystal ball or special intuitive gifts to foresee how valuable a company will ultimately become, I refer people to the data. I don't rely on guesswork, gut or on my people-assessment skills. For me, it's all in the data. That said, when I first heard about identical twins Oliver and Alexander Kent-Braham, I knew their startup – the digital-first insurance provider Marshmallow – was a standout. In the UK, they recognized challenges and barriers to obtaining car insurance, especially if you are an immigrant or young. Insurance premiums for these groups can be up to five times what is paid by an older Brit. Their business started as a broker helping to match drivers with hard-to-find affordable rates. They have now expanded to become their own insurance company.

Tenacious and lean – winning traits in founders – Oliver and Alexander, along with their Chief Technical Officer, managed to fly under the radar by choosing not to brand Marshmallow to the public, but offering services through other brands. In doing so, they kept their technology and model for success all to themselves. In September 2021 the news broke everywhere, including on *Sifted*, a *Financial Times* newsletter, that Marshmallow had received an $83 million Series B investment after being valued at $1.25 billion. Marshmallow had just become the UK's second Black unicorn and the first for Impact X. This was thrilling to us, of course, and for everyone in the venture capital ecosystem who had decided to bet on Black.

It was important to us, too, that in the *Sifted* coverage Marshmallow acknowledged the issues Black founders had long been facing, even successful ones. The article pointed to recent reports which had highlighted that Black people constituted just 3 per cent of the European venture capital and private equity industry – something we at Impact X are all too aware of, but many aren't. And the key takeaway was this: Marshmallow had taken on an entrenched insurance industry and was winning.

More gratifying yet for Impact X was that Marshmallow had achieved its current levels of success with a workforce that was 50 per cent female and 20 per cent people of colour. The scale of its success, and the full team behind that success, tells an important story.

As if to remind us that we are not yet saved, during the week when the unicorn news came out, our celebration coincided with the fortieth anniversary of the New Cross Fire, as of yet 'unsolved'. It had also been almost forty years since the suspicious killing of Colin Roach, and was almost the thirtieth anniversary of the murder of Stephen Lawrence. The contrast between where we had come from and where we were going made me feel that we were on a new trajectory. While we can no longer expect to be saved by law enforcement and a government that still refuses to acknowledge that white supremacy is rampant, we have started a new virtuous circle of empowerment for change. And we are doing this ourselves, and by working with our allies.

Impact X has focused on creating an infrastructure which can support any movement that Black people want – the financial means for independent thought and action. We do not talk about being part of a movement. Yet Impact X is funding wars on many fronts – the war against intolerance, white supremacy, racism, misogyny, ageism and more. We are recruiting others to do the same.

My own journey has been a case study of the flywheel effect made possible by an ever-increasing group of people who work with me across opportunity, sector, challenge and ocean to get to the Promised Land. Yours can be too. Follow the playbook for betting on Black and creating your own flywheel for change. These strategies are sustainable because together they generate more and more momentum as time goes on.

Here are the key action points as I see them, and I leave them with you to change the world. I can't wait to see what you accomplish.

- Start and invest in Black companies.
- Create opportunity for others in these companies (employment).

- Let those folks thrive internally, colonize other firms or start their own new businesses.
- Help some of these companies exit and release massive resources.
- Let that flood of resources fund anything it wishes, from politics to arts to education to housing to health to seeding new companies (a virtual flywheel).
- Continue the process indefinitely.

A short time after the good news arrived about Marshmallow, I attended London Tech Week 2021. This was the first opportunity I'd had to meet Oliver Kent-Braham in person and hear him speak on a panel sponsored by a research firm. Unable to suppress my pride, I heard him talk about disrupting the insurance sector and all the work Marshmallow is doing to achieve outsized returns. Oliver was fantastic. Afterwards, as we spoke in person for the first time, a picture was taken of us.

Not a bad photo. The two of us are both tall and had the same 'What's next?' expression that might once have been captured on the face of Reginald Lewis. When I looked at the two of us smiling into the camera, I thought back to my parents. This young man is changing the world and I can only take credit for injecting a bit of capital. Yet in a small way Marshmallow, Oliver and Alexander are my legacy – as I am my parents'. I am so glad that Impact X invested in them early. Well, them and all those other women and men who are changing the world. For good.

Join us.

EPILOGUE: YOUR TRUMP CARD

During the last chorus of 'Lovely Day' by Bill Withers, sung at the *Powerlist* dinner held at the Savoy Hotel on 15 October 2021, I felt many emotions, but especially an overwhelming sense of validation. Three years earlier, those of us who had met to form Impact X had done so with the belief that capital was the missing link needed to upend white supremacy for good. By using our own resources, putting our money where our mouths were, we set a strategic plan in action to enrich and empower Black and other under-represented founders, businesses and communities in the UK and in Europe. Despite an increasing level of political and racial violence, amid the ongoing upheaval caused by Covid and its variants, complicated by a turbulent global economy, we were helping shift a balance of power. On faith and through action, we demonstrated that creating greater access to capital for entrepreneurs of colour could be our proverbial trump card.

That was not the only reason I felt validated. While rising to my feet along with the rest of those in attendance, I could hardly believe that the same questions I'd asked in my youth about Black entrepreneurship had blessedly directed me to these shores and were creating purpose for me and others.

Amazing, I thought, *how is it possible that I'm in the ballroom of a 5-star hotel in London singing a Bill Withers song at the top of my lungs along with hundreds of other Black Britons?* As an American son of the embattled deep South, I had been born into an insidious system of segregation and racial division, one which for centuries had implied that only by being granted permission from outside forces could I hope to rise. In fact, I had been the first Collins since our forced arrival in the US who had been guaranteed the right to vote from birth. It finally occurred to me as I left the Savoy that night what the distance travelled to this moment of confronting white supremacy really meant.

Nothing is as liberating as throwing off the mental shackles that form alongside the need to ask for permission. In a sense, the freedom you give yourself to be powerful is your true trump card. I don't use the 't' word casually, by the way, mostly because of the demoralizing impact conjured by the mere mention of the name Trump. I use it as a galvanizing call to action. For this reason, I heartily encourage you to activate your own trump card over Trump and his ilk and the backward-looking forces being ginned up if we ever lack the courage to harness powers already at our disposal.

Throughout this book, I have shared my playbook for empowerment and entrepreneurial success and have encouraged you to join in the movement. In whatever way you choose to participate, and at whatever scale you start, the point is that you *do* start – and you could not choose a better moment to do so than now. Don't know how, where or when to get started? Begin by taking the smallest step wherever you are. Buy Black. Support women-led organizations. Stop putting your resources into places and people that are backward forces. Practise a daily mantra of giving yourself permission to become the next unicorn.

Because we all have shorter attention spans and ever-growing lists of things to do, I'm happy to recap and remind you of the *10 Steps of Empowerment* – for easy access – along with a few takeaways I'm glad to underscore:

- Step #1: *Embrace the unexpected.* If you were to make a list of every challenging experience you've had to endure in your life, I'd wager good money that on the other side of that ledger was a hidden opportunity. When you jostle yourself out of complacency, habit or sheer exhaustion to get out of a place of feeling stuck, you open your senses to new opportunities you might never have encountered otherwise. Let every day reveal new possibilities to you. Embrace them.

- Step #2: *Engage in consistent and continuous acts of disruption.* If you have played it safe or followed the rules for most of your life, choose to follow the example of the disruptors and entrepreneurs who practised the art of disruptive change first by defying tradition or other required ways of moving forward. Feel free to borrow from the Collins family values – a commitment to achieving social justice and a recognition that hustle and action should be your watchwords. Call yourself a disruptive visionary who sees a distinct path toward achievement. Recognize that money is a tool for disruption. You don't need unlimited amounts of investment as long as you use your money with purpose.

- Step #3: *Let go of small – think bigger, think global and prepare for pitfalls.* Think big. Continually expand your vision. Do not limit your imagination. Give yourself permission to imagine new solutions to old problems. Be prepared for bumps in the road and plan for them with creativity, commitment and innovation. Leverage lessons from loss and hardship. Practise getting past hurdles. Listen and learn. When mentors give you their guidance, honour them by using it well and passing along lessons learned. A global vision includes a respect for all parties who come to the table.

- Step #4: *Take risks and use data to mitigate the downside.* Allow yourself to receive incoming opportunities. Recruit allies. Leverage your connections. Leverage the experiences that fuelled you. Listen, watch and learn. Facts get you further than myths. Three measures of risk include defining the actual risk, assessing the amount of exposure and determining the potential reward. Don't forget that there are lessons that come from shortfalls and even from failures. In that sense, there is no such thing as failure.

- Step #5: *Put your money where your mouth is and make your resources matter.* No matter how dire or challenging your current circumstances, remember Ursula Burns's motto (and memoir title) that where you are is not who you are. When you choose to believe that you deserve a turnaround – whether it's your life, your business, your community or the economy as a whole – you shift your focus to your value. Look for the silver linings of timing, even in economic crises. Become a student of the causes of the cycles of boom and bust. Be prepared. Be tenacious. Stay lean to survive and thrive. Be a prudent steward of capital. Practise making your values and your resources matter.

- Step #6: *Leverage what you know.* When you lean into your lived experience and into the knowledge gained from expertise and education, you activate an underused superpower. The ability to leverage what you know – including knowledge gained from loss and struggle – is a key leadership trait. It's also important when assembling diverse teams to recognize the various strengths being brought to the team by all. Allow them to leverage what they know. To disrupt oppressive systems, leverage every ounce of knowledge from all quarters.

- Step #7: *Become a convener by making your mission bigger than yourself.* Whenever you have been denied a seat at the table, you may choose to become a convener by building a table of your own. That gives you power, especially when you combine your purpose with profit. One purpose of your business should be that all stakeholders win. As a convener, your job is to make sure that all parties' interests are aligned and addressed, so that everyone wins. Purpose is your guide. Make it matter.

- Step #8: *Invest in women to create Alpha.* Everyone wants to beat the market by taking advantage of inefficiencies that lead to outsized financial returns on wise investments. Yet, judging by the same cast of mostly white males dominating in tech sectors, the power of women, especially Black women, to create Alpha is continually overlooked. Investing in under-represented women – through funding, hiring, promoting and mentoring – is a policy that yields immediate and lasting dividends.

- Step #9: *Sell your vision, make time-appropriate asks and don't forget to recruit allies.* Even when we operate in a no-permission-needed ecosphere, we must still bring others on board if we truly want Black business to elevate entire communities and economies. Of utmost importance is the ability to excite partners, investors and allies whose interests align with ours. We have to maintain our unifying vision and harness the help in a timely fashion.

- Step #10: *Always bet on Black.* As we have learned from all the steps, betting on Black and all under-represented entrepreneurs creates a flywheel for sustainable progress while also proving to be good business in general. We no longer need to wait for the boom days to thrive. The potential we have to successfully disrupt old, oppressive systems will be realized when we choose to rewrite the history we are charting together. What we do today has consequences and will create opportunities for others who will continue moving the ball forward. Always betting on Black is a choice, a movement and a revolution.

I'm also betting on you. When your life and the lives of your loved ones and community members depend on changing the status quo, it's astonishing what you can accomplish. All that matters now is the courage to act. None of this is easy, I know, but I have never been so hopeful about the change for the better that is in front of us.

So what and whom are you waiting for? C'mon, let's do this! Name your river, the biggest one you know, and remove the constraints to your imagination. Take out your trump card, charge it up, and let's go change the world for good. You don't need permission.

REFERENCES

Prologue: The Promised Land

3   **'Black and minority ethnic (BAME) households . . . in poverty as their white counterparts'**: Patrick Butler, 'Nearly half of BAME UK households are living in poverty', *Guardian*, 30 June 2020. https://www.theguardian.com/society/2020/jul/01/nearly-half-of-bame-uk-households-are-living-in-poverty

3   **nearly one in two Black households . . . can be classified as poor**: ibid.

3   **the face of Covid-19's worst destruction is female and non-white**: see Francesca Donner, 'How women are getting squeezed by the pandemic,' *New York Times*, 20 May 2020. https://www.nytimes.com/2020/05/20/us/women-economy-jobs-coronavirus-gender.html.
    Also see John Eligon, Audra D. S. Burch, Dionne Searcey and Richard A. Oppel Jr, 'Black Americans face alarming rates of coronavirus infection in some states', *New York Times*, 14 April 2020. https://www.nytimes.com/2020/04/07/us/coronavirus-race.html

4   **Britain's far right was growing more openly racist . . . a shift in the direction of much more 'openly racial politics'**: Lizzie Dearden, 'British far right "becoming more racist" after Black Lives Matter protests, report finds', *Independent*, 15 August 2020. https://www.independent.co.uk/news/uk/home-news/far-right-black-lives-matter-protests-racism-patriotic-alternative-hope-not-hate-a9672401.html

5   **In 2018, only 3 per cent of VCs in the US were Black**: see
     Megan Rose Dickey, 'Venture capital's diversity disaster',
     TechCrunch, 30 July 2018. https://techcrunch.com/2018/07/30/
     venture-capitals-diversity-disaster/

5   **Less than 1 per cent of venture capital goes to Black
     founders worldwide**: see James Norman, 'A VC's guide to
     investing in Black founders', *Harvard Business Publishing Education*,
     19 June 2020. https://hbr.org/2020/06/a-vcs-guide-to-investing-
     in-black-founders

5   **Extend Ventures, a not-for-profit whose remit . . . only 0.2 per
     cent of capital was going to Black entrepreneurs**: see Natasha
     Lomas, 'UK report spotlights the huge investment gap facing
     diverse founders', TechCrunch, 2 November 2020. https://
     techcrunch.com/2020/11/02/uk-report-spotlights-the-huge-
     investment-gap-facing-diverse-founders/

5   **Only 0.02 per cent went to Black female teams**: ibid.

5   **In February 2021 . . . over a third are still in America's Silicon
     Valley**: see Kenny Herzog, 'Why are venture capitalists still
     funding mostly white, male entrepreneurs?', Entrepreneur.com, 11
     February 2021. https://www.entrepreneur.com/article/365079

5   **Five months later . . . increasing numbers of VCs of colour
     and also women**: see Marlize van Romburgh and Gené Teare,
     'Funding to Black startup founders quadrupled in past year, but
     remains elusive', CrunchBase, 13 July 2021. https://news.
     crunchbase.com/news/something-ventured-funding-to-black-
     startup-founders-quadrupled-in-past-year-but-remains-elusive/

5   **More good news . . . in the process of founding their own
     business**: see Shelley Zalis, 'Black female entrepreneurs are
     launching more businesses than ever: Here's what they need to
     help them mature', *Forbes*, 25 May 2021. https://www.forbes.com/
     sites/shelleyzalis/2021/05/25/black-female-entrepreneurs-are-
     launching-more-businesses-than-ever-heres-what-they-need-to-
     help-them-mature/?sh=3b5b3a336bc0. Also see Donna Kelley,
     Mahdi Majbouri and Angela Randolph, 'Black women are more

likely to start a business than white men', *Harvard Business Review*, 11 May 2021. https://hbr.org/2021/05/black-women-are-more-likely-to-start-a-business-than-white-men

8   **That's the big takeaway . . . tireless fight for the rights of the Windrush generation**: see Aamna Mohdin, 'Jacky Wright and Marcus Rashford in Top 10 most powerful Black Britons', *Guardian*, 14 October 2021. https://www.theguardian.com/world/2021/oct/15/jacky-wright-and-marcus-rashford-in-top-10-most-powerful-black-britons

1 Capital Is the X Factor

11   **'People are more comfortable with a familiar discomfort than they are with an unfamiliar new possibility'**: Lisa Nichols @2motivate, www.twitter.com, 19 July 2021. Bestselling author, founder, motivational speaker. https://www.motivatingthemasses.com

14   **We'd seen them unmasked in Charlottesville . . . and shouted racist and anti-Semitic slurs**: see Michael E. Ruane, 'Freedom and slavery, the "central paradox of American history"', *Washington Post*, 30 April 2019. https://www.washingtonpost.com/local/freedom-and-slavery-the-central-paradox-of-american-history/2019/04/30/16063754-2e3a-11e9-813a-0ab2f17e305b_story.html

14   **Inflaming the rhetoric . . . 'watermelon smiles'**: see Boris Johnson, 'If Blair's so good at running the Congo, let him stay there', *Telegraph*, 10 January 2002. https://www.telegraph.co.uk/politics/0/blairs-good-running-congo-let-stay/

15   **Among ongoing racist and xenophobic slurs over the years . . . they could be mistaken for bank robbers**: see Boris Johnson, 'Denmark has got it wrong. Yes, the burka is oppressive and ridiculous – but that's still no reason to ban it', *Telegraph*, 5 August 2018. https://www.telegraph.co.uk/news/2018/08/05/denmark-has-got-wrong-yes-burka-oppressive-ridiculous-still/

19   **In a September 2021 . . . getting home loans**: https://www.
independent.co.uk/news/uk/home-news/ethnic-minority-
housing-inequalities-report-b1919371.html; https://www.
bloomberg.com/news/features/2021-05-18/uk-propety-wealth-
data-2021-show-big-gap-between-black-and-white-homeowners

23   **For example, there's a great story about how . . . have disrupted the record industry and changed culture**: see Steven Tweedie,
'How Jimmy Iovine ran into Dr. Dre on the beach and convinced
him to start Beats instead of a sneaker line', *Business Insider India*, 16
October 2014. https://www.businessinsider.in/how-jimmy-iovine-
ran-into-dr-dre-on-the-beach-and-convinced-him-to-start-beats-
instead-of-a-sneaker-line/articleshow/44830797.cms. See also Steve
Stoute, *The Tanning of America: How Hip-Hop Created a Culture That
Rewrote the Rules of the New Economy* (Gotham Books, 2011).

2 Money Is a Tool

29   **'If you always do what you always did, you will always get what
you always got'**: attribution unknown. Quote is variously credited to
Albert Einstein, Henry Ford and Tony Robbins, among others.

29   **'Personal disruption is the vehicle through which success
and economic growth travel'**: Nicky Verd, international keynote
speaker, Tech MC, podcast host and author of *Disrupt Yourself or Be
Disrupted*. https://nickyverd.africa

29   **Berry Gordy persuaded his family to give him a loan**: unless
otherwise noted, insights drawn from Berry Gordy, *To Be Loved:
The Music, the Magic, the Memories of Motown* (Grand Central
Publishing, 1994).

30   **I'm using the term 'disruption' . . . to changing entire
systems of doing business**: see Andy Rachleff, 'What disrupt
really means', TechCrunch, 16 February 2013. https://techcrunch.
com/2013/02/16/the-truth-about-disruption/

31   **It's common knowledge that The Beatles . . . especially by
Motown artists and songwriters**: see Paul McGuinness, 'Best

Motown Beatles covers: When Motown met the Beatles', UdisoverMusic.com, 5 May 2021. https://www.udiscovermusic.com/stories/best-motown-beatles-covers/

32 *Black Enterprise* – founded by Earl Graves in 1970 . . . document Motown's meteoric rise: Jeffrey McKinney, '45 great moments in Black business – no. 28: Berry Gordy sells Motown Records', *Black Enterprise*, 29 October 2017. https://www.blackenterprise.com/45-great-moments-in-black-business-no-28-berry-gordy-sells-iconic-motown-records/

32 Formula One's most successful racing-car . . . using his fame, platform and money to campaign against white supremacy: Gary Younge, 'Lewis Hamilton: Everything I'd suppressed came up – I had to speak out', *Guardian*, 10 July 2021. https://www.theguardian.com/sport/2021/jul/10/lewis-hamilton-everything-id-suppressed-came-up-i-had-to-speak-out

33 'The shackles have been broken . . . The greatest problem is we are afraid to offend our oppressors': John Carlos 1968, cited by Gary Younge, ibid.

34 Enter Litey Collins, my entrepreneurial ancestor: for this and all references to Collins genealogy and history in this chapter see Noah 'No-nie' Collins, historian, and Joseph Satchell, artist, ed. Elsie B. Francis, *The Collins Family: A History and Roots from the 18th Century (1724–1990)* (1990).

36 Given all of that, I was alarmed . . . top grades: Dana Beltaji and Bethan Lewis, 'University offers less likely for more diverse students', BBC News, 22 September 2021. https://www.bbc.com/news/uk-wales-58640992

37 For centuries British bonding, indenturing and serfdom . . . did not exist under English law: see Krista J. Kesselring, 'Slavery and Cartwright's case before Somerset', Legalhistorymiscellany.com, 10 October 2018. https://legalhistorymiscellany.com/2018/10/10/slavery-and-cartwrights-case-before-somerset/

38   **The moment when it happened . . . to be a landowner in America**: see George Tucker, 'Ambitious slave-turned-slaveowner enjoys farm success', *The Virginian-Pilot*, 21 August 1994. https://scholar.lib.vt.edu/VA-news/VA-Pilot/issues/1994/vp940821/08190821.htm. Also see https://www.facinghistory.org/reconstruction-era/anthony-johnson-man-control-his-own (refuting claims by white supremacists that Johnson was the first slaveowner in the New World).

40   **This story was recently dramatized . . . Juliet Gilkes Romero**: see David Jays, 'The scandal of the £20bn bailout to slave-owning Brits', *Guardian*, 26 January 2020. https://www.theguardian.com/stage/2020/jan/26/juliet-gilkes-romero-the-whip

40   **It is also told by Professor David Olusoga . . . while ex-enslaved people were allotted no reparations**: see Omar Alleyne-Lawler, 'Recap: Britain's forgotten slave owners', 24 August 2015 original airdate. https://www.blackhistorymonth.org.uk/article/section/history-of-slavery/recap-britains-forgotten-slave-owners/. '[The] first episode focused around the latest discoveries made by Professor Catherine Hall and her team at UCL. By using this database and following the claims, Olusoga begins to explain how the money was distributed, who received it and why such a large amount was needed.'

40   **Whenever Black history . . . 'Black people have been living in Britain since at least Roman times'**: Paul Edwards, 'The history of Black people in Britain', *History Today*, 9 September 1981. https://www.historytoday.com/archive/history-black-people-britain

40   **'famous among buffoons'**: ibid.

40   **In 2012 *New African Magazine* . . . the Beatles song 'Being For The Benefit Of Mr Kite'**: see Prof. Gima, 'History of success for African entrepreneurs in UK', *New African Magazine*, 19 February 2012. https://newafricanmagazine.com/619/

41   **Perhaps the most famous example . . . New Granada, a Spanish colony**: see Abdul Rob, *Ignatius Sancho: The composer*, www.blackhistory.org.uk, 4 February 2016, reprinted October 2021.

https://www.blackhistorymonth.org.uk/article/section/bhm-heroes/4181/

42 **A government report (ons.gov.uk) . . . eight times that much in white ones**: Carla Kidd, 'Household wealth by ethnicity, Great Britain: April 2016 to March 2018', Office for National Statistics, 23 November 2020. https://www.ons.gov.uk/peoplepopulation andcommunity/personalandhouseholdfinances/incomeand wealth/articles/householdwealthbyethnicitygreatbritain/april 2016tomarch2018

45 **One important leader . . . outlawing acts of discrimination within employment, housing and advertising**: see Angela Lynch, 'Black History Month: Let's talk about the UK civil rights movement', London Youth, 1 October 2020. https://londonyouth. org/black-history-month-lets-talk-about-the-uk-civil-rights-movement/

45 **the lasting damage from what became known as the Windrush Scandal . . . Few of the oppressive policies were subsequently changed**: see BBC News, 'Windrush generation: Who are they and why are they facing problems?', 24 November 2021. https://www.bbc.com/news/uk-43782241

49 **The three entrepreneurs I studied . . . Reginald Lewis of Beatrice International Foods**: Eric D. Collins, 'African American Entrepreneurship: A Historical Analysis' (1988). Unless otherwise cited, the thesis covers three profiles. Additionally, sources for this paper include: Jerry Schwartz., 'After three years of high hopes, Air Atlanta is out of cash,' *New York Times*, 12 April 1987; Linda Williams, 'Air Atlanta seeks Chapter 11 protection', *Wall Street Journal*, 6 April 1987; Daniel F. Cuff, 'McCall's Pattern's head is pleased by takeover,' *New York Times*, 10 July 1987; Jonathan P. Hicks, 'Beatrice unit brings $985 million: International Food is sold to TLC Group', *New York Times*, 10 August 1987.

49 **John H. Johnson (1918–2005) represents . . . in sumptuous, aspirational images**: see Bruce Glasrud, 'John H. Johnson (1918–2005)', Blackpast.org, 3 December 2007. https://www.blackpast. org/african-american-history/johnson-john-harold-1918-2005/

55   **A short time later . . . ten times bigger than the McCall sale**:
Alfred Edmond, Jr, 'I'm proud to be part of the legacy of
Reginald F. Lewis', *Black Enterprise*, 30 November 2012. https://
www.blackenterprise.com/im-proud-to-be-part-of-the-legacy-of-
reginald-f-lewis/

57   **'to be a force for economic and social justice . . . where
opportunity comes more equally'**: https://reginaldflewis.com/
foundation/

3 What's in a Name? Why Amazon and Not Thames

59   **'Judgement hinders imagination'**: Roger Fisher (1922–2012),
Harvard Law professor, co-founder of the Harvard Negotiation
Project, pioneer of modern negotiation and conflict resolution,
best-selling author of *Getting to Yes: Negotiating Agreement Without
Giving In* (Penguin Books, 1981).

59   **'An open mind is not an empty one'**: ibid.

62   **'The fastest way to expand . . . but really aren't'**: Michael
Mamas, 'The importance of adapting your worldview to reality',
Entrepreneur.com, 26 October 2016. https://www.entrepreneur.
com/article/283711

63   **In business . . . 'make or break' your entire enterprise**: see
Adam Fridman, 'Why your company name is as important as your
company function', www.Inc.com, 6 August 2015. https://www.
inc.com/adam-fridman/why-your-company-name-is-as-
important-as-your-company-function-adam.html

63   **Actually, as the story goes . . . first settled on the name
Cadabra**: see Shana Lebowitz, 'How Amazon got its name',
Business Insider, 8 May 2018. https://www.businessinsider.com/
amazon-jeff-bezos-chose-company-name-2018-5

63   **More details about how the name was finally chosen**: Tavis
Andrews and Roxanne Roberts, 'The love affair between Jeff Bezos
and "Star Trek"', *Washington Post*, 13 October 2021.

https://www.washingtonpost.com/arts-entertainment/2021/
10/13/jeff-bezos-star-trek-william-shatner/

64   **Nothing especially disruptive stands out . . . significant investment from his parents**: unless otherwise noted, see Brad Stone, *The Everything Store: Jeff Bezos and the Age of Amazon* (Little, Brown & Company, 2013).

64   **'I'd never seen or heard . . . was very exciting to me'**: Jeff Bezos on seeing data for opportunity in e-commerce in a speech, 'We Are What We Choose', at Princeton, 30 May 2010. https://www.princeton.edu/news/2010/05/30/2010-baccalaureate-remarks

65   **'Bezos pored through the A section . . . "It blows all other rivers away"'** Stone, *The Everything Store.*

65   **Similarly, in 1998, after two Stanford grad students . . . turned out to be genius**: see Nathan McAlone, 'The true story behind Google's first name: BackRub', *Business Insider*, 6 October 2015. https://www.businessinsider.com.au/the-true-story-behind-googles-first-name-backrub-2015-10

66   **Take the name of 'Acorn' . . . sold 1.5 million, many of them for use in schools**: see Tony Quested, 'Arm the mighty oak that grew from Acorn', *Business Weekly UK*, 4 June 2020. https://www.businessweekly.co.uk/tech-trail/tech-profiles/arm-mighty-oak-grew-acorn

66   **Acorn co-founder Andy Hopper . . . increasingly influential tech hub**: Nick Heath, 'Acorn co-founder on the BBC Micro and the early days of personal computing', *Zdnet.com*, 7 October 2009. https://www.zdnet.com/article/acorn-co-founder-on-the-bbc-micro-and-the-early-days-of-personal-computing/

68   **In April 2021, *Forbes* reported . . . all billionaires around the world:** Kerry A. Dolan, 'The 2021 Forbes 400 list of richest Americans: Facts and figures', *Forbes*, 6 April 2021. https://www.forbes.com/sites/kerryadolan/2021/04/06/forbes-35th-annual-worlds-billionaires-list-facts-and-figures-2021/

68   As for the top Black firms in the US . . . warehousing as well
as business integration: '5 Black-owned companies you've never
heard of that make $500 million or more a year', *Black Enterprise*,
18 July 2020. https://www.blackenterprise.com/5-black-owned-
companies-youve-never-heard-of-that-make-500-million-or-more-
a-year/

69   Bezos knew there would be pitfalls . . . lose money on their
investment: Stone, *The Everything Store*.

69   A June 2021 *Business Insider* piece . . . could barely be given
away for free: Dennis Green and Mary Meisenzahl, 'Jeff Bezos
famously embraces failure. Here are the biggest flops Amazon has
overcome under his watch', *Business Insider*, 29 June 2021.
https://www.businessinsider.com/amazon-products-services-
failed-discontinued-2019-3

70   the deal that saved Amazon . . . especially merciless to
e-commerce companies: see Timothy B. Lee, 'The little-known
deal that saved Amazon from the dot-com crash', *Vox*, 5 April
2017. https://www.vox.com/new-money/2017/4/5/15190650/
amazon-jeff-bezos-richest

73   only one in eight of the most successful . . . graduate-level
degrees: see Rachel Premack, 'Billionaires like Bill Gates and
Mark Zuckerberg reached success after dropping out of college,
but experts say the average person should take the opposite
approach', *Business Insider*, 26 October 2018. https://www.
businessinsider.com/billionaire-college-dropout-zuckerberg-bill-
gates-2018-10; article cites data from www.adview.com.

77   When Roger Fisher passed away . . . end of apartheid in
South Africa: see Caroline M. McKay, 'Harvard Law School
Professor Roger Fisher dies at 90', *The Harvard Crimson*, 1
September 2012. https://www.thecrimson.com/
article/2012/9/1/roger-fisher-law-obituary/

80   would become ground zero . . . the online publication for
Black innovation: see Vic Motune, 'Black-led tech firm Calendly
valued at $3 billion after $350m Series B Raise', Urban Geekz,

27 January 2021. https://urbangeekz.com/2021/01/black-led-tech-firm-calendly-valued-at-3-billion-after-350m-series-b-raise/

4 Facts Work Better Than Myths

89   **'The pawn can only move . . . coming into the industry':** Funk Butcher, aka Kwame Safo, DJ/producer/activist

89   **In fact, a *Forbes* analysis by . . . by whether you are able to 'manage risk properly':** see Chris Carosa, 'Why successful entrepreneurs need to be calculated risk takers', *Forbes*, 7 August 2020. https://www.forbes.com/sites/chriscarosa/2020/08/07/why-successful-entrepreneurs-need-to-be-calculated-risk-takers/?sh=263ede062f5b

92   **A piece in Deadline Hollywood . . . 13 per cent of the UK workforce:** see Jake Kanter, 'Damning new report reveals that BAME representation went backwards in British TV last year', Deadline Hollywood, 28 January 2021. https://deadline.com/2021/01/cdn-bame-representation-backwards-tv-1234682277/

92   **The facts spoke for themselves . . . 'painful reminder of why casting is so important':** see Sir Lenny Henry Centre for Media Diversity, *Race Between the Lines: Actors' Experience of Race and Racism in Britain's Audition and Casting Process and On Set*, Personal Managers' Association Racial Diversity Group. Survey conducted between March and April 2021. https://bcuassets.blob.core.windows.net/docs/diverse-actors-surveyv1-132742714535244780.pdf

92   **He told Jonathan Dean of the *Sunday Times* . . . the colour of his skin:** see Jonathan Dean, 'The British star of *Get Out* and *Black Panther*, Daniel Kaluuya, on his new film about racial prejudice', *Sunday Times*, 12 January 2020. https://www.thetimes.co.uk/article/the-british-star-of-get-out-and-black-panther-daniel-kaluuya-on-his-new-film-about-racial-prejudice-5orvntwqw

93   **Another award-winning Black British actor . . . James McAvoy or Benedict Cumberbatch:** Mark Brown, 'Roles in UK

for black and minority ethnic actors worse than ever, claims David Oyelowo', *Guardian*, 28 September 2015. https://www.theguardian. com/film/2015/sep/28/roles-uk-black-minority-ethnic-actors-worse-than-ever-claims-david-oyelowo

93   **In an interview with Ellie Phillips . . . asking him if he has ever breathed**: see Ellie Phillips, '"I experience racism as often as I breathe!" Idris Elba reveals his parents taught him that in order to make it "you have to be twice as good as the white man"', *Daily Mail Online*, 26 June 2020. https://www.dailymail.co.uk/ tvshowbiz/article-8463373/Idris-Elba-says-success-not-negated-experience-racism.html

94   **As reported in Indiewire . . . storytelling lacked authenticity**: see Zack Sharf, 'Idris Elba's Luther isn't "authentic" because "he doesn't have Black friends," says BBC exec', IndieWire, 14 April 2021. https://www.indiewire.com/2021/04/idris-elba-luther-black-authentic-bbc-exec-1234630309/

94   **Elba didn't respond to the comments . . . focus was only on moving forward**: Isobel Lewis, 'Idris Elba says "we must not pull ourselves backwards" as BBC diversity chief claims Luther isn't an "authentic" Black lead', *Independent*, 15 April 2021. https://www. independent.co.uk/arts-entertainment/tv/news/idris-elba-luther-miranda-wayland-b1831794.html

95   **Reed Hastings, co-founder of Netflix . . . 'adapts to the individual's taste'**: see Jena McGregor, 'High-tech Achiever: Netflix', *Fast Company*, 1 October 2005. https://www.fastcompany. com/54186/high-tech-achiever-netflix

95   **In a 4 December 2018 Ideas.TED.com piece . . . bubble burst in 2000**: see Brian McCullough, 'A revealing look at the dot-com bubble of 2000 – and how it shapes our lives today', Ideas.TED.com, 4 December 2018. https://ideas.ted.com/an-eye-opening-look-at-the-dot-com-bubble-of-2000-and-how-it-shapes-our-lives-today/

95   **Twenty-odd years later we have an estimated 4.9 billion users**: see Joseph Johnson, 'Number of internet users worldwide from 2005 to 2021', Statista, 22 December 2021. https://www.

statista.com/statistics/273018/number-of-internet-users-worldwide/

96 **Reported by Jeff Green in *Bloomberg Business* . . . Black and Latinx combined:** see Jeff Green, 'Diverse startups raise more cash, return more to investors', Bloomberg, 5 February 2020. https://www.bloomberg.com/news/articles/2020-02-05/diverse-startups-raise-more-cash-and-return-more-to-investors. Also see Collin West, Gopinath Sundaramurthy and Marlon Nichols, 'Deconstructing the pipeline myth and the case for more diverse fund managers', *Kauffman Fellows Journal*, 4 February 2020. https://www.kauffmanfellows.org/journal_posts/the-pipeline-myth-ethnicity-fund-managers

97 **That's another myth . . . more discomfort *and* better performance:** see David Rock, Heidi Grant and Jacqui Grey, 'Diverse teams feel less comfortable – and that's why they perform better', *Harvard Business Review*, 22 September 2016. https://hbr.org/2016/09/diverse-teams-feel-less-comfortable-and-thats-why-they-perform-better

97 **In a 2016 LinkedIn piece . . . deliver the fastest 'legitimate' money you can make:** see Carla Morales, 'How risky is investing in entertainment?', LinkedIn, 29 January 2016. https://www.linkedin.com/pulse/how-risky-investing-entertainment-carla-morales

98 **The conversation about the need for greater representation . . . Academy Award for Best Actress:** see 'Experience over nine decades of the Oscars from 1927 to 2021', Academy of Motion Picture Arts and Sciences. https://www.oscars.org/oscars/ceremonies

98 **A 2018 analysis of the BAFTAs dating back . . . Frances McDormand in *Nomadland* who won the award:** see Professor Binna Kandola, OBE, and Dr Jo Kandola, 'Analysis of BAFTA film awards by ethnicity & gender', Pearn Kandola, February 2018. https://pearnkandola.com/app/uploads/2018/07/BAFTA-Analysis-New-House-Style.pdf. Also see 'Awards database', British Academy of Film and Television Arts. http://awards.bafta.org/

100 **For instance, in 1991 the film . . . had been released to much acclaim**: see Michon Boston, 'The filmmaker who sweetened Beyoncé's "Lemonade" guides a new generation', *Washington Post*, 12 January 2017. https://www.washingtonpost.com/lifestyle/magazine/the-filmmaker-who-sweetened-beyonces-lemonade-guides-a-new-generation/2017/01/11/63b19bd0-c3dc-11e6-9578-0054287507db_story.html

101 **With a string of 1980s smash hits . . . (Sidney Poitier was the original when he was the #1 box office draw of 1968)**: see Laura Jacobs, 'Sidney Poitier, 1967, and one of the most remarkable runs in Hollywood history', *Vanity Fair*, 1 February 2017. https://www.vanityfair.com/hollywood/2017/02/sidney-poitier-remarkable-run-in-hollywood-history

101 **Samuel L. Jackson had made his movie debut . . . total gross for all Jackson's movies is more than $27 billion**: see Seth Abramovitch, '120 movies, $13 billion in box office: How Samuel L. Jackson became Hollywood's most bankable star', *The Hollywood Reporter*, 9 January 2019. https://www.hollywoodreporter.com/movies/movie-features/how-samuel-l-jackson-became-hollywoods-bankable-star-1174613/

102 **Most newspapers had publicized her appointment . . . joined the BBC**: see Ellen E. Jones, 'Barbara Blake-Hannah: How Britain's first black female TV reporter was forced off our screens', *Guardian*, 7 January 2021. https://www.theguardian.com/society/2021/jan/07/barbara-blake-hannah-how-britains-first-black-female-tv-reporter-was-forced-off-our-screens. Also see Barbara Blake Hannah, 'It wasn't Trevor or Moira – I was the first black British TV presenter', *Guardian*, 22 October 2008. https://www.theguardian.com/commentisfree/2008/oct/23/television-raceandreligion

102 **In an October 2020 profile of her in the *Guardian* . . . exclusively white and possibly conclude that you don't belong**: see Aida Edemariam, 'Margaret Busby: How Britain's first black female publisher revolutionized literature – and never gave up', *Guardian*, 22 October 2020. https://www.theguardian.com/

society/2020/oct/22/margaret-busby-the-uks-first-black-female-
publisher-everyone-assumed-i-was-there-to-make-the-tea

104   **In 1980, BET was founded by Robert Johnson . . . a BET
co-founder, the first Black female billionaire**: see 'Robert
L. Johnson', *Encyclopedia Britannica*, 4 April 2021. https://www.
britannica.com/biography/Robert-L-Johnson. Also see Peter Perl,
'His way', *Washington Post*, 14 December 1997. https://www.
washingtonpost.com/wp-srv/business/longterm/post200/
stories98/bet.htm; Erik Gruenwedel, 'ViacomCBS launches BET
Studios', *Media Play News*, 15 September 2021. https://www.
mediaplaynews.com/viacomcbs-launches-bet-studios/; Geraldine
Fabrikant, 'BET Holdings to be bought by Viacom for $2.34
billion', *New York Times*, 4 November 2000. https://www.
nytimes.com/2000/11/04/business/bet-holdings-to-be-bought-
by-viacom-for-2.34-billion.html

105   **The story of Cathy Hughes and Radio One/Urban One . . .
publicly held corporation**: see 'Cathy Hughes', The History
Makers, 21 September 2004 and 2 March 2005. https://www.
thehistorymakers.org/biography/cathy-hughes-39

107   **In the UK a similar pattern existed . . . *Empire Road, Mixed
Blessings, The Lenny Henry Show* and *Desmond's***: see Professor
David Hendy, 'The Black and White Minstrel Show', https://www.
bbc.com/historyofthebbc/100-voices/people-nation-empire/
make-yourself-at-home/the-black-and-white-minstrel-show

113   **In 2018, more than twenty years later . . . the global box
office**: see Box Office Mojo, '2018 worldwide box office',
IMDbPro. https://www.boxofficemojo.com/year/world/2018/.
Also see Pamela McClintock, 'Box office: "Black Panther"
becomes top-grossing superhero film of all time in U.S.', *The
Hollywood Reporter*, 24 March 2018. https://www.
hollywoodreporter.com/movies/movie-news/box-office-black-
panther-becomes-top-grossing-superhero-film-all-time-us-
1097101/; Elahe Izadi, '"Black Panther" keeps smashing records,
exceeding box-office expectations and making history',
Washington Post, 25 February 2018. https://www.washingtonpost.

com/news/comic-riffs/wp/2018/02/25/black-panther-keeps-
smashing-records-exceeding-box-office-expectations-and-making-
history/

119   **CRM is ubiquitous . . . over \$80 billion by 2025**: see
Christopher Sirk, 'Current state of CRM 2020', CRM.org, https://
crm.org/crmland/current-state-of-crm-2020

5 Everything Deserves a Good Turnaround

121   **In 1987, in a lengthy *Harvard Business Review* . . . sharpened
the main skills required**: see John O. Whitney, 'Turnaround
management every day', *Harvard Business Review*, September 1987.
https://hbr.org/1987/09/turnaround-management-every-day

122   **For example, by the summer of 2021 . . . driven the startup
boom for most of 2020**: see Yusuf Berkan Altun, 'Pandemic fuels
global growth of entrepreneurship and startup frenzy', *Forbes*, 9
April 2021. https://www.forbes.com/sites/forbestechcouncil/
2021/04/09/pandemic-fuels-global-growth-of-entrepreneurship-
and-startup-frenzy/?sh=44cb730f7308

123   **All of which is not to downplay . . . communities of colour
brutally hit by Covid-19**: see Robert Booth and Caelainn Barr,
'Black people four more times likely to die from Covid-19, ONS
finds', *Guardian*, 7 May 2020. https://www.theguardian.com/
world/2020/may/07/black-people-four-times-more-likely-to-die-
from-covid-19-ons-finds. Centers for Disease Control and
Prevention, 'Health equity considerations and racial and ethnic
minority groups', United States Department of Health and Human
Services, 30 November 2021. https://www.cdc.gov/coronavirus/
2019-ncov/community/health-equity/race-ethnicity.html

123   **In the US, between February and April 2020 . . .
'accumulating such wealth'**: see Kemberley Washington,
'Covid-19 has had a disproportionate financial impact on Black
small businesses', *Forbes*, 3 June 2021. https://www.forbes.com/
advisor/personal-finance/covid19-financial-impact-on-black-
businesses/

124   **When I checked how things stood . . . amassed wealth of £1.087 billion**: see 'The *Sunday Times* Rich List 2021', *The Sunday Times*, 21 May 2021. https://www.thetimes.co.uk/sunday-times-rich-list

124   **Strive Masiyiwa was putting his money . . . more than 1.3 billion Africans at risk**: see Silence Charumbira, 'Rich countries "ran off and secured supplies" of Covid vaccines, says Africa envoy', *Guardian*, 24 June 2021. https://www.theguardian.com/global-development/2021/jun/24/rich-countries-deliberately-keeping-covid-vaccines-from-africa-says-envoy

124   **In the US, the numbers for African Americans . . . access to credit and capital**: see Charisse Jones, 'Latest Forbes richest list shows Black billionaires remains a rare club', *USA Today*, 6 April 2021. https://www.usatoday.com/story/money/2021/04/06/jay-z-kanye-west-and-tyler-perry-seven-richest-african-americans/4579811001/. Also see Brett Mons and Amanda Ballantyne, J.D., 'Breaking barriers to credit and capital access for Black, Latinx, and women-owned businesses', The Rockefeller Foundation Blog, 26 August 2020. https://www.rockefellerfoundation.org/blog/breaking-barriers-to-credit-and-capital-access-for-black-latinx-and-women-owned-businesses/

124   **Those same barriers were evident . . . slow progress in the first place**: see 'The colour of power', Operation Black Vote, 26 July 2021. https://thecolourofpower.com/

124   **In the US Crunchbase stated that the amount was $300 billion**: see Gené Teare, 'Global VC report 2020: Funding and exits blow past 2019 despite pandemic headwinds', Crunchbase, 13 January 2021. https://news.crunchbase.com/news/global-2020-funding-and-exit/

125   **In the UK, KPMG reported . . . Tech Nation put the number at £13.5 billion**: see Bina Mehta, 'Q2 2021 global and UK analysis of venture funding', KPMG, 21 July 2021. https://home.kpmg/uk/en/home/insights/2021/07/q2-2021-global-and-uk-analysis-of-venture-funding.html. Also see Simon Neville, 'UK tech sector raised record-breaking £13.5bn in first half of 2021', *Independent*, 20 September 2021. https://www.independent.co.

uk/business/uk-tech-sector-raised-recordbreaking-ps13-5bn-in-first-half-of-2021-b1923077.html; 'The future UK tech built: Tech Nation Report 2021', Tech Nation. https://technation.io/report2021/#key-statistics

125   **Adding to that potential was an unprecedented . . . police brutality – as 'one of us'**: see Tracy Jan, Jena McGregor and Meghan Hoyer, 'Corporate America's $50 billion promise', *Washington Post*, 24 August 2021. https://www.washingtonpost.com/business/interactive/2021/george-floyd-corporate-america-racial-justice/

126   **Startups that were launched . . . Uber and WhatsApp**: Callum Burroughs, 'The 2008 financial crisis heralded giants like Uber and Airbnb. We asked top investors what they are looking for during a downturn', *Business Insider India*, 13 April 2020. https://www.businessinsider.in/tech/news/the-2008-financial-crisis-heralded-giants-like-uber-and-airbnb-we-asked-top-investors-what-they-are-looking-for-during-a-downturn-/articleshow/75119654.cms

127   **Shockingly, in the US . . . homophobic remarks and policies**: see Ruth Igielnik, Scott Keeter and Hannah Hartig, 'Behind Biden's 2020 victory', Pew Research Center, 30 June 2021. https://www.pewresearch.org/politics/2021/06/30/behind-bidens-2020-victory/. Also see Cassie Barton, 'GE2019: How did demographics affect the result?', House of Commons Library, 21 February 2020, https://commonslibrary.parliament.uk/ge2019-how-did-demographics-affect-the-result/

130   **A matter-of-fact distillation of what happened later . . . 'taught us to live online'**: see Brian McCullough, *How the Internet Happened: From Netscape to the iPhone* (Liveright Publishing, 2018). Also see Brian McCullough, 'A revealing look at the dot-com bubble of 2000 – and how it shapes our lives today', Ideas.TED.com, 4 December 2018. https://ideas.ted.com/an-eye-opening-look-at-the-dot-com-bubble-of-2000-and-how-it-shapes-our-lives-today/

131   **By January 2021 there were 4.66 billion . . . number of website addresses was 1.86 billion**: see Joseph Johnson,

'Number of internet users worldwide from 2005 to 2021', Statista, 22 December 2021. https://www.statista.com/statistics/273018/number-of-internet-users-worldwide/. Also see 'Total number of Websites', Internet Live Stats. https://www.internetlivestats.com/total-number-of-websites/

133 **The co-COO at that moment was Dick Parsons . . . music landscape in the form of Warner Music**: see David Carr, 'No use crying over spilled billions', *New York Times*, 20 June 2004. https://www.nytimes.com/2004/06/20/business/no-use-crying-over-spilled-billions.html

138 **A 2020 report from the UK's Tech Nation . . . 71 per cent men and 29 per cent women**: see 'Diversity and inclusion in UK tech companies', Tech Nation, 17 March 2020. https://technation.io/insights/diversity-and-inclusion-in-uk-tech-companies/

138 **www.diversityintech.co.uk estimates . . . in the general workforce**: see 'Representation of BAME in tech', Diversity in Tech. https://www.diversityintech.co.uk/representation-of-bame-in-tech

139 **In the UK, Jackie Wright . . . women to join her ranks**: see Walé Azeez, 'Microsoft's Jacky Wright had to leave the UK to become its most influential Black person', CNN Business, 14 October 2021. https://www.cnn.com/2021/10/14/tech/jacky-wright-microsoft-powerlist/index.html

140 **The foes of workplace inclusion . . . stronger cases for gender and racial diversity**: Cedric Herring, 'Does diversity pay?: Race, gender, and the business case for diversity', *American Sociological Review*, 74(2), pp. 208–24. http://www.jstor.org/stable/27736058

140 **Such findings were included in a later report . . . evident in companies with the highest women's representation**: see *The Bottom Line: Connecting Corporate Performance and Gender Diversity (Report)*, Catalyst, 15 January 2004. https://www.catalyst.org/research/the-bottom-line-connecting-corporate-performance-and-gender-diversity/

140	In a speech on the topic . . . 'be as successful as you could be': see R. Thomas Unstead, 'Parsons: Diversity not happening fast enough', Nexttv, 17 September 2003. https://www.nexttv.com/news/parsons-diversity-not-happening-fast-enough-100585

144	Recently I read a book written in 1952 . . . Oh, we don't have the problems of white supremacy the US has: see Roi Ottley, *No Green Pastures: The Negro in Europe Today* (Scribner, 1952).

144	In the UK, by the time of the pandemic . . . 'solitary, poor, nasty, brutish, and short': see Tendayi Achiume, 'Visit to the United Kingdom of Great Britain and Northern Ireland Report of the Special Rapporteur on contemporary forms of racism, racial discrimination, xenophobia and related intolerance', United Nations Human Rights Council (41st session, 24 June–12 July 2019). https://undocs.org/A/HRC/41/54/ADD.2. Amelia Gentleman, 'Austerity has fuelled racial inequality in the UK, says UN expert', *Guardian*, 14 June 2019. https://www.theguardian.com/business/2019/jun/14/austerity-has-fuelled-racial-inequality-in-the-uk-says-un-expert

145	And yet I can see the emergence of a turnaround . . . Chancellor of the University of Portsmouth, are UK exceptions): see Laura Morgan Roberts and Anthony J. Mayo, 'Towards a racially just workplace', *Harvard Business Review*, 14 November 2019. https://hbr.org/2019/11/toward-a-racially-just-workplace. Also see Don Lee, 'The pandemic saw a boom in new Black-owned businesses – the largest surge in the last quarter-century', *Los Angeles Times*, 28 June 2021. https://www.latimes.com/politics/story/2021-06-28/pandemic-silver-lining-black-owned-business-startups-surge-to-25-year-high. Also see 'Racial diversity stagnated on corporate boards, study finds', CNBC, 10 June 2021. https://www.cnbc.com/2021/06/10/racial-diversity-stagnated-on-corporate-boards-study-finds.html; Tiffany Burns, Jess Huang, Alexis Krivkovich, Ishanaa Rambachan, Tijana Trkulja and Lareina Yee, 'Women in the workplace 2021', McKinsey & Company and Lean In, 27 September 2021. https://www.mckinsey.com/featured-insights/diversity-and-inclusion/women-in-the-workplace

6. Superheroes Don't Need Permission

148 **The UK's Pat McGrath . . . beautiful Black people represented in culture:** see Jenny Bailly, 'The genius of Pat McGrath', *Allure*, 12 January 2021. https://www.allure.com/story/pat-mcgrath-cover-interview-february-2021. Also see Alyx Gorman, 'Pat McGrath becomes first makeup artist to receive damehood from the Queen', *Guardian*, 31 December 2020. https://www.theguardian.com/fashion/2021/jan/01/pat-mcgrath-becomes-first-makeup-artist-to-receive-damehood-from-the-queen

150 **Still, Pat prioritized product value . . . care most about quality:** see Lisa Niven-Phillips, 'Pat McGrath Labs becomes Selfridges biggest-selling beauty line', *Guardian*, 1 June 2019. https://www.theguardian.com/fashion/2019/jun/01/pat-mcgrath-labs-becomes-selfridges-biggest-selling-beauty-line

150 **However, one of the areas . . . making speedy purchases on Amazon:** see Chip Bayers, 'The inner Jeff Bezos', *Wired*, 1 March 1999. https://www.wired.com/1999/03/bezos-3/

151 **It follows logically that . . . store could be built to contain that many choices:** see Mathias Döpfner, 'Jeff Bezos reveals what it's like to build an empire – and why he's willing to spend $1 billion a year to fund the most important mission of his life', *Business Insider*, 28 April 2018. https://www.businessinsider.com/jeff-bezos-interview-axel-springer-ceo-amazon-trump-blue-origin-family-regulation-washington-post-2018-4

151 **In June 2021 – with Amazon . . . Walmart's $566 billion in total sales during that time:** see Matt Krantz, 'Here comes the third $2 trillion company after Microsoft and Apple', *Investor's Business Daily*, 25 June 2021. https://www.investors.com/etfs-and-funds/sectors/sp500-here-comes-the-third-2-trillion-company-after-microsoft-and-apple/. Also see Jim Zarroli, 'There's rich, and then there's Jeff Bezos rich: Meet the world's centibillionaires', NPR, 10 December 2020. https://www.npr.org/2020/12/10/944620768/theres-rich-and-theres-jeff-bezos-rich-meet-the-members-of-the-100-billion-club

151   **This victory, explained by Shira Ovide . . . merchandise from location to location**: see Shira Ovide, 'The on tech newsletter: How Amazon won shopping', *New York Times*, 17 August 2021. https://www.nytimes.com/2021/08/17/technology/how-amazon-won-shopping.html

152   **In February 2000, David Neeleman . . . even in those challenging years**: see Bill Saporito, 'How JetBlue founder David Neeleman launched a new airline during a pandemic', Inc. https://www.inc.com/magazine/2021006/bill-saporito/david-neeleman-jetblue-breeze-airline-serial-entrepreneur.html. Also see Sumit Singh, 'The impressive history and rise of JetBlue', Simple Flying, 28 October 2021. https://simpleflying.com/jetblue-history/

153   **'Using the same skill we'd developed . . . but it got us noticed'**: see 'Our story', Virgin Atlantic. https://corporate.virginatlantic.com/gb/en/our-story.html

153   **As the story goes, Branson's lived experience . . . choose to fly if you wanted an adventure**: see Karen Gilchrist, 'How Richard Branson started Virgin Atlantic with a blackboard selling $39 flights', CNBC Make It, 29 December 2019. https://www.cnbc.com/2019/12/30/richard-branson-started-virgin-atlantic-with-a-board-and-39-flights.html

155   **When Berry Gordy sold Motown Records . . . had announced his retirement**: see Jem Aswad, 'Motown founder Berry Gordy to retire', *Variety*, 24 September 2019. https://variety.com/2019/music/news/motown-founder-berry-gordy-to-retire-1203347182/. Also see Mick Brown, 'Berry Gordy: The man who built Motown', *Telegraph*, 23 January 2016. https://s.telegraph.co.uk/graphics/projects/berry-gordy-motown/index.html

156   **Reginald Lewis didn't stop for a moment . . . leveraged everything he had learned**: see Mary Corey, 'The amazing ascent of Reginald Lewis', *Baltimore Sun*, 14 April 1991. https://www.baltimoresun.com/news/bs-xpm-1991-04-14-1991104174-story.html

157   **After years of hip-hop couture . . . a nice change of pace for the boardroom**: see Guy Trebay, 'Maturing rappers try a new

uniform: Yo, a suit!', *New York Times*, 6 February 2004. https://
www.nytimes.com/2004/02/06/nyregion/maturing-rappers-try-a-
new-uniform-yo-a-suit.html

158   **So much so that in 2021 Microsoft paid $19.7 billion . . . most
prized divisions**: see Dina Bass and Liana Baker, 'Microsoft to
acquire Nuance for $19.6 billion in health-care bet', Bloomberg, 12
April 2021. https://www.bloomberg.com/news/articles/2021-04-
12/microsoft-buys-nuance-for-19-7-billion-in-bet-on-health-care

160   **In 2012, a study from the University of Warwick . . . but
didn't bring it to fruition**: see Jerker Denrell and Chengwei Liu,
'Top performers are not the most impressive when extreme
performance indicates unreliability', *Proceedings of the National
Academy of Sciences*, 109(24), pp. 9331–6, 12 June 2012. https://
www.pnas.org/content/109/24/9331.abstract. Also see Anna
Blackaby, 'To be a winner, learn from "losers" ', Futurity,
20 June 2012. https://www.futurity.org/to-be-a-winner-learn-
from-%E2%80%98losers%E2%80%99/

160   **For instance, during the global financial meltdown . . . a
historically high amount of personal debt**: see 'The great
recession', Investopedia, 23 October 2020. https://www.
investopedia.com/terms/g/great-recession.asp

161   **A 2015 report from the Immigration Advice Service . . .
'Poverty in the UK is an ever-increasing issue'**: see Paul Fisher
and Alita Nandi, 'Poverty across ethnic groups through recession
and austerity', The Joseph Rowntree Foundation, 30 March 2015.
https://www.jrf.org.uk/report/poverty-across-ethnic-groups-
through-recession-and-austerity

162   **In 2014, a *Time* magazine article . . . both individual
attitudes and institutionalized white supremacy**: see Maya
Rhodan, 'Study: Hard times can make people more racist', *Time*,
9 June 2014. https://time.com/2850595/race-economy/. Also see
Amy R. Krosch and David M. Amodio, 'Economic scarcity alters
the perception of race', *Proceedings of the National Academy of
Sciences*, 111(25), pp. 9079–84, 9 June 2014. https://www.pnas.
org/content/111/25/9079

162   **In 2011, the Black population of the UK . . . more than £300 billion annually:** 'Buying power and the power of business ownership', Black Business Champions 2021. https://black businesschampions.com/the-facts/. Cites population at census 2011. Also https://www.ons.gov.uk/peoplepopulationand community/culturalidentity/ethnicity/articles/2011censusanalysisethnicityandreligionofthenonukbornpopulationinenglandand wales/2015-06-18

162   **In the US, according to . . . $1.1 trillion in buying power:** see Minority Business Development Agency, *The State of Minority Business Enterprises: An Overview of the 2012 Survey of Business Owners*, US Department of Commerce, 2018. https://www.mbda.gov/ sites/default/files/media/files/2019/mbdastateofminority businessenterprises_2012data.pdf

163   **In poll after poll . . . best president of the last half-century:** see Mason Bissada, 'Best recent president? Obama wins overall and Republicans pick Reagan over Trump in poll', *Forbes*, 20 December 2021. https://www.forbes.com/sites/masonbissada/ 2021/12/20/best-recent-president-obama-wins-overall-and-republicans-pick-reagan-over-trump-in-poll/?sh=61695 dd36e57

164   **Black Britons in 1987 . . . legitimacy that they had been denied up until then:** see 'The first Black Parliamentarians of our times', *Black History Month* 2021, 19 August 2015. https://www. blackhistorymonth.org.uk/article/section/history-of-politics/the-first-black-parliamentarians-in-our-times/

164   **The general election of 2019 . . . two Liberal Democrats:** see Elise Uberoi and Richard Tunnicliffe, 'Ethnic diversity in politics and public life', House of Commons Library, 26 November 2021. https://commonslibrary.parliament.uk/research-briefings/ sno1156/

164   **It was in 2013, after all . . . an unarmed Black teenager:** see 'Black Lives Matter', *Encyclopedia Britannica*, 14 September 2021. https://www.britannica.com/topic/Black-Lives-Matter.

7 Purpose + Profit = Power

173   **The average consumer . . . 2,617 times per day**: see John
       Brandon, 'These updated stats about how often you use your
       phone will humble you', Inc., 19 November 2019. https://www.
       inc.com/john-brandon/these-updated-stats-about-how-often-
       we-use-our-phones-will-humble-you.html

176   **Even among Black Britons . . . Black, Asian and minority
       ethnic Local Political Representation Audit 2019)**: see
       Diversity UK, 'Diversity in the UK'. https://diversityuk.org/
       diversity-in-the-uk/. Also see Race Disparity Unit, 'Ethnicity facts
       and figures', HM Government. https://www.ethnicity-facts-
       figures.service.gov.uk/

179   **In 1970, for instance . . . Metropolitan Police Force**: see
       Anushka Asthana, Lanre Asthana, Lanre Bakare, Jeb Johnson and
       Franck Scully, 'The story of the Mangrove Nine', *Guardian*, 14
       October 2020. https://www.theguardian.com/news/audio/2020/
       oct/15/the-story-of-the-mangrove-nine. Also see Catherine Baksi,
       'Landmarks in law: When the Mangrove Nine beat the British
       state', *Guardian*, 10 November 2020. https://www.theguardian.
       com/law/2020/nov/10/landmarks-in-law-when-the-mangrove-
       nine-beat-the-british-state; Ursula Kenny, 'Daughters of the
       Mangrove Nine: "That passion in our parents was instilled in us"',
       Guardian, 28 November 2021. https://www.theguardian.com/
       world/2021/nov/28/daughters-of-the-mangrove-nine-protest-
       trial-steve-mcqueen

180   **A January 2021 feature in the *Guardian* . . . 'the plight of
       Black Britons'**: see Kehinde Andrews, 'Forty years on from the
       New Cross fire, what has changed for black Britons?', *Guardian*,
       17 January 2021. https://www.theguardian.com/world/2021/
       jan/17/forty-years-on-from-the-new-cross-fire-what-has-changed-
       for-black-britons

180   **Two years later, on 12 January 1983 . . . 'We were really on our
       own'**: see Emma Bartholomew, 'Benjamin Zephaniah on how
       Colin Roach's death inside Stoke Newington Police Station

sparked a movement 35 years ago', *Hackney Gazette*, 23 January 2018. https://www.hackneygazette.co.uk/news/benjamin-zephaniah-on-how-colin-roach-s-death-inside-stoke-3585066

182   **It was left to the Lawrence family . . . the conviction for murder of Gary Dobson and David Norris**: see 'What happened on Stephen Lawrence's last night alive?', BBC News, 13 March 1998. http://news.bbc.co.uk/2/hi/special_report/1998/03/98/lawrence/65060.stm. Also see Alexis Akwagyiram, 'Stephen Lawrence's killers Gary Dobson and David Norris', BBC News, 3 January 2012. https://www.bbc.com/news/uk-16097242

183   **Imran Khan, the Lawrence family lawyer . . . 'allows you to do something about it'**: see Hugh Muir, 'The Stephen Lawrence case: How it changed Britain', *Guardian*, 3 January 2012. https://www.theguardian.com/uk/2012/jan/03/how-stephen-lawrence-changed-britain

8 Black Women Are an Excellent Investment

195   **This was a point raised on the business . . . Increase the number of female VCs of colour**: see Sian Morson, 'Meet 10 kickass Black female venture capitalists you should know', UrbanGeekz, 12 December 2019. https://urbangeekz.com/2019/12/meet-10-kickass-black-female-venture-capitalists-you-should-know/

196   **The ongoing McKinsey studies . . . were up at 36 per cent in 2019**: see Vivian Hunt, Dennis Layton and Sara Prince, 'Why diversity matters', McKinsey & Company, 1 January 2015. https://www.mckinsey.com/business-functions/people-and-organizational-performance/our-insights/why-diversity-matters. Also see Vivian Hunt, Lareina Yee, Sara Prince and Sundiatu Dixon-Fyle, 'Delivering through diversity', McKinsey & Company, 18 January 2018. https://www.mckinsey.com/business-functions/people-and-organizational-performance/our-insights/delivering-through-diversity; Kevin Dolan, Vivian Hunt, Sara

Prince and Sandra Sancier-Sultan, 'Diversity still matters', McKinsey & Company, 19 May 2020. https://www.mckinsey.com/featured-insights/diversity-and-inclusion/diversity-still-matters; Sundiatu Dixon-Fyle, Kevin Dolan, Vivian Hunt and Sara Prince, 'Diversity wins: How inclusion matters', McKinsey & Company, 19 May 2020. https://www.mckinsey.com/featured-insights/diversity-and-inclusion/diversity-wins-how-inclusion-matters

197   **A 2018 paper from the International Monetary Fund . . . whole economies grow**: see Christine Lagarde and Jonathan D. Ostry, 'Economic gains from gender inclusion: Even greater than you thought', 28 November 2018. https://blogs.imf.org/2018/11/28/economic-gains-from-gender-inclusion-even-greater-than-you-thought/

198   **One statistic from a 2020 Extend Ventures . . . 0.02 per cent went to Black female founders**: see Erika Brodnock, 'Diversity beyond gender: The state of the nation for diverse entrepreneurs', Extend Ventures, November 2020. https://www.extend.vc/reports

200   **In the UK, according to the 2020 Extend Ventures . . . £1million from institutional investors**: ibid.

200   **Only one woman raised significantly more . . . also get to see a boom in their businesses**: see Steve O'Hear, 'Beautystack raises £4m seed to help beauty professionals become financially independent', TechCrunch, 23 May 2019. https://techcrunch.com/2019/05/23/beautystack/

202   **In October 2019, a study published by Bloomberg . . . strategies to attract more diverse teams**: see Collin West and Gopinath Sundaramurthy, 'Data shows that gender-inclusive founding teams have greater success in fundraising and innovation', *Kauffman Fellows Journal*, 3 October 2019. https://www.kauffmanfellows.org/journal_posts/data-show-that-gender-inclusive-founding-teams-have-greater-success-in-fundraising-and-innovation

203   **The title of the second report . . . biases are wired deep in our DNA:** see Collin West and Gopinath Sundaramurthy, 'Startups with at least 1 female founder hire 2.5x more women', *Kauffman Fellows Journal*, 17 October 2019. https://www. kauffmanfellows.org/journal_posts/female_founders_hire_ more_women

203   **In another study on ethnic diversity . . . companies with white founding teams:** see Collin West, Gopinath Sundaramurthy and Marlon Nichols, 'Deconstructing the pipeline myth and the case for more diverse fund managers', *Kauffman Fellows Journal*, 4 February 2020. https://www.kauffmanfellows. org/journal_posts/the-pipeline-myth-ethnicity-fund-managers

204   **The data that points us in a new direction . . . foster a sense of community and belonging:** see Sundiatu Dixon-Fyle, Kevin Dolan, Vivian Hunt and Sara Prince, 'Diversity wins: How inclusion matters', McKinsey & Company, 19 May 2020. https:// www.mckinsey.com/featured-insights/diversity-and-inclusion/ diversity-wins-how-inclusion-matters

205   **Although Britain ranked at number five . . . chauvinism and outright misogyny were things of the past:** see Rupert Neate, 'UK falls six places in gender equality rankings', *Guardian*, 16 December 2019. https://www.theguardian.com/world/2019/ dec/16/uk-falls-six-places-in-gender-equality-rankings. Also see Nesrine Malik, 'Britain thinks it has won the gender equality war. That's a bad sign', *Guardian*, 28 March 2021. https://www. theguardian.com/commentisfree/2021/mar/28/britain-gender- equality-war-complacency-women-pandemic

208   **Paula had distinguished herself . . . 'entrepreneurs who create jobs and build wealth':** see Charlotte Tucker, ' "It is important for those who seek social change to turn an eye toward funding entrepreneurship": Interview with Impact X's co-founder Paula Groves', EU-Startups, 8 July 2020. https://www.eu-startups. com/2020/07/it-is-important-for-those-who-seek-social-change- to-turn-an-eye-toward-funding-entrepreneurship-interview-with- impact-xs-co-founder-paula-groves/

209 **Yvonne Bajela . . . is a deal-sourcing machine**: see David
Dawkins, 'Forbes under 30 Europe: Meet the European finance
leaders of tomorrow', *Forbes*, 17 March 2020. https://www.
forbes.com/sites/daviddawkins/2020/03/17/forbes-under-30-
europe-meet-the-european-finance-leaders-of-tomorrow/?sh=
30effa9d2604

213 **Indra Nooyi, a woman of colour . . . 'improves by 144 per
cent!'**: see 'Cover story: Indra Nooyi turned around Pepsico with
strategic redirection', *Femina*, 2 August 2021. https://www.femina.
in/trending/achievers/indra-nooyi-turned-around-pepsico-with-
strategic-redirection-200175.html

9 Underdogs Become Unicorns

218 **The term was first coined in 2013 . . . how rare such
successful ventures really are**: see Aileen Lee, 'Welcome to the
Unicorn Club: Learning from billion-dollar startups', TechCrunch,
2 November 2013. https://techcrunch.com/2013/11/02/
welcome-to-the-unicorn-club/

218 **However, since that time . . . unicorn status was up at 602**: see
'What is a unicorn?', PitchBook, 19 April 2021. https://pitchbook.
com/blog/what-is-a-unicorn

218 **The path to unicorn status . . . just 0.065 per cent make it**: see
Aileen Lee, 'Welcome to the Unicorn Club: Learning from billion-
dollar startups', TechCrunch, 2 November 2013. https://
techcrunch.com/2013/11/02/welcome-to-the-unicorn-club/

219 **In my home office, between Zoom meetings . . . 'support
going hand-in-hand with health restrictions'**: see Danica
Kirka, 'UK economy suffers biggest drop since 1709', US News &
World Report, 12 February 2021. https://www.usnews.com/
news/business/articles/2021-02-12/uk-economy-suffers-biggest-
drop-since-1709

220 **In June 2020, Reuters research . . . 81.1 per cent to 79.4 per
cent**: see 'Black, minority Britons hit hardest by COVID job

losses, researchers say', Reuters, 8 June 2020. https://www.reuters.com/article/uk-health-coronavirus-britain-minorities-idUKKBN23F1X5

221 **An article about the impact . . . casualties of police brutality in the UK**: see Aamna Mohdin and Lucy Campbell, ' "So many people care!" The young Britons whose lives were changed by Black Lives Matter', *Guardian*, 13 November 2020. https://www.theguardian.com/world/2020/nov/13/how-black-lives-matter-has-inspired-a-generation-of-new-uk-activists

221 **In June 2020, the *Guardian* . . . 8 per cent of deaths in police custody**: see Nazir Afzal, 'Black people dying in police custody should surprise no one', *Guardian*, 11 June 2020. https://www.theguardian.com/uk-news/2020/jun/11/black-deaths-in-police-custody-the-tip-of-an-iceberg-of-racist-treatment

221 **Impassioned protestors carried signs . . . fifty-four per 1,000 Blacks**: see Race Disparity Unit, 'Stop and search data and the effect of geographical differences', HM Government, 31 March 2021. https://www.gov.uk/government/publications/stop-and-search-data-and-the-effect-of-geographical-differences/stop-and-search-interpreting-and-describing-statistics

221 **According to data . . . 30 per cent of Black families are home owners**: see Olivia Konotey-Ahulu, 'How London's property boom left Black Britons with nothing', Bloomberg, 18 May 2021. https://www.bloomberg.com/news/features/2021-05-18/uk-property-wealth-data-2021-show-big-gap-between-black-and-white-homeowners

222 **At the end of 2020, the *Financial Times* . . . many workers who had been furloughed were starting businesses**: see Valentina Romel, 'Pandemic triggers surge in business start-ups across major economies', *Financial Times*, 30 December 2020. https://www.ft.com/content/3cbb0bcd-d7dc-47bb-97d8-e31fe80398fb

230 **Here are some Tech Nation stats . . . received £4.2 billion by mid-2021**: see 'The future UK tech built: Tech Nation Report

2021', Tech Nation. https://technation.io/report2021/#key-statistics. Also see '2021 mid-year update of UK tech', Tech Nation, September 2021. https://technation.io/report2021/#key-statistics; Simon Neville, 'UK tech sector raised record-breaking £13.5bn in first half of 2021', *Independent*, 20 September 2021. https://www.independent.co.uk/business/uk-tech-sector-raised-recordbreaking-ps13-5bn-in-first-half-of-2021-b1923077.html

231   **Don't tell me as you look . . . the next major unicorn is a crap shoot**: see Erika Brodnock, 'Diversity beyond gender: The state of the nation for diverse entrepreneurs', Extend Ventures, November 2020. https://www.extend.vc/diversity-beyond-gender

10 Impact NOW!

233   **Shortly before I arrived at law school . . . all who seek it are involved in the daily toil for it**: see Derrick Bell, *And We Are Not Saved: The Elusive Quest for Racial Justice* (Basic Books, 1989).

234   **Other questions to ask were posed . . . *with other experts in the fields of research and advocacy?***: see Barbara Smith, 'The problem is white supremacy', *Boston Globe*, 30 June 2020. https://www.bostonglobe.com/2020/06/29/opinion/problem-is-white-supremacy/

234   **Barbara Smith followed up those 'What ifs?' . . . investing in communities of colour**: see Barbara Smith, 'How to dismantle white supremacy', *The Nation*, 21 August 2020. https://www.thenation.com/article/politics/how-to-dismantle-white-supremacy/

236   **If you have your first kid . . . currently sixteen years shy of UK retirement age**: see Office of National Statistics, 'Births by parents' characteristics', UK Parliament, 16 November 2020. https://www.ons.gov.uk/peoplepopulationandcommunity/birthsdeathsandmarriages/livebirths/datasets/birthsbyparentscharacteristics

237   **The fact that people of colour . . . should be intolerable:** see Heather Long and Andrew Van Dam, 'The black–white economic divide is as wide as it was in 1968', *Washington Post*, 4 June 2020. https://www.washingtonpost.com/business/2020/06/04/ economic-divide-black-households/. Also see Emily Moss, Kriston McIntosh, Wendy Edelberg and Kristen Broady, 'The Black–white wealth gap left Black households more vulnerable', Brookings, 8 December 2020. https://www.brookings.edu/blog/ up-front/2020/12/08/the-black-white-wealth-gap-left-black-households-more-vulnerable/

237   **Assets, according to www.Investopedia.com . . . can be converted to cash:** see Jean Folger, 'What is an asset?', Investopedia, 7 September 2021. https://www.investopedia.com/ ask/answers/12/what-is-an-asset.asp

238   **White supremacy may never be . . . 'refused to acknowledge the institution':** see Barbara Smith, 'The problem is white supremacy', *Boston Globe*, 30 June 2020. https://www. bostonglobe.com/2020/06/29/opinion/problem-is-white-supremacy/

239   **In 2020, a McKinsey study . . . shift national economies:** see Shelley Stewart III, Michael Chui, James Manyika, J. P. Julien, Vivian Hunt, Bob Sternfels, Jonathan Woetzel and Haiyang Zhang, 'The economic state of Black America: What is and what could be', McKinsey & Company, 17 June 2021. https://www.mckinsey. com/featured-insights/diversity-and-inclusion/the-economic-state-of-black-america-what-is-and-what-could-be

239   **There were a recorded 4,000 murders . . . bustling cities of the South:** see 'Lynching in America: Confronting the legacy of racial terror', Equal Justice Initiative, 2017. https://eji.org/ reports/lynching-in-america/

240   **In 2021, many in the UK . . . almost all the Black businesses were destroyed:** see Bayeté Ross Smith and Jimmie Briggs, 'Tulsa race massacre at 100: An act of terrorism America tried to forget', *Guardian*, 31 May 2021. https://www.theguardian.com/us-news/2021/may/31/tulsa-race-massacre-at-100-act-of-terrorism.

Also see Lakshmi Gandhi, 'Tulsa Race Massacre: Fact checking myths and misconceptions', NBC News, 30 May 2021. https://www.nbcnews.com/select/news/tulsa-race-massacre-fact-check-ncna1269045

240 **As described in May 2021 . . . gone by the end of the massacre**: see Yuliya Parshina-Kottas, Anjali Singhvi, Audra D. S. Burch, Troy Griggs, Mika Gröndahl, Lingdong Huang, Tim Wallace, Jeremy White and Josh Williams, 'What the Tulsa Race Massacre destroyed', *New York Times*, 24 May 2021. https://www.nytimes.com/interactive/2021/05/24/us/tulsa-race-massacre.html

240 **During this same period . . . businesses they had established**: see Virgillo Hunter, 'Britain's 1919 race riots', BlackPast, 28 November 2018. https://www.blackpast.org/global-african-history/events-global-african-history/britain-s-1919-race-riots/

240 **As recounted in the national archive . . . incredibly difficult for people of colour**: see Iqbal Singh and Kathryn Collins, 'From Cardiff to the Caribbean: The 1919 race riots', The National Archives, 24 July 2019. https://blog.nationalarchives.gov.uk/from-cardiff-to-the-caribbean-the-1919-race-riots/

242 **At a time when London . . . a marker of improved living standards**: see Anna Krausova and Dr Carlos Vargas-Silva, 'London: Census profile', The Migration Observatory at the University of Oxford, 20 May 2013. https://migrationobservatory.ox.ac.uk/resources/briefings/london-census-profile/. Also see Carly Dodd, 'The world's most multicultural cities', World Atlas, 22 September 2021. https://www.worldatlas.com/cities/the-world-s-most-multicultural-cities.html

242 **Studies reported in Bloomberg . . . proverbial gateways to opportunity**: see Richard Florida, 'How diversity leads to economic growth', Bloomberg, 12 December 2011. https://www.bloomberg.com/news/articles/2011-12-12/how-diversity-leads-to-economic-growth

242 **In the UK, many are familiar . . . easily recycled during the debate over Brexit**: see Samuel Earle, '"Rivers of Blood:" The legacy of a speech that divided Britain', *The Atlantic*, 20 April 2018. https://www.theatlantic.com/international/archive/2018/04/enoch-powell-rivers-of-blood/558344/

243 **The good news is . . . head one of the colleges at Oxford**: see 'Baroness Valerie Amos appointed as Master of University College', University of Oxford, 2 August 2019. https://www.ox.ac.uk/news/2019-08-02-baroness-valerie-amos-appointed-master-university-college

244 **In March 2021, news broke that Atmen . . . first British-led Black banking startup in the UK**: see Ruby Hinchliffe, 'UK Black-owned challenger Atmen to launch in March', FinTech Futures, 22 February 2021. https://www.fintechfutures.com/2021/02/uk-black-owned-challenger-atmen-to-launch-in-march/

248 **In September 2021 the news broke . . . tells an important story**: Sse Kai Nicol-Schwarz, 'Insurtech Marshmallow becomes just the second Black-founded unicorn in the UK', *Sifted*, 8 September 2021. https://sifted.eu/articles/marshmallow-raise/

248 **As if to remind us . . . New Cross fire, as of yet 'unsolved'**: see Kehinde Andrews, 'Forty years on from the New Cross fire, what has changed for black Britons?', *Guardian*, 17 January 2021. https://www.theguardian.com/world/2021/jan/17/forty-years-on-from-the-new-cross-fire-what-has-changed-for-black-britons

ACKNOWLEDGEMENTS

While writing this book I have been mindful of and humbled by the generations of under-represented entrepreneurs and business owners who didn't ask for permission. They leveraged their businesses to change a world that doesn't work for all.

Many people invested in this book.

The talented Transworld team, particularly co-editor Stephanie Duncan, Danai Denga, Patsy Irwin, Louis Patel, Linden Lawson and Beci Kelly.

My colleagues who daily strive to make the world a better, more equitable and just place, especially my Impact X Capital Partners colleagues: Paula Groves, Yvonne Bajela, Ezechi Britton and Erica Motley. Chief among these is Ric Lewis, the consummate ally.

Former colleagues, now friends, who invested in me: Irma Tyler-Woods, Grande Lum, Jeff Wing, Teresa Bright, Brian Woods, Arlene Brock and Rena Clark. Rich Harless, another American in Europe, is my constant confidant.

The first team I ever joined, and still my unconditional supporters, are my siblings Bradley Collins and Verna Collins Odoom. Thank you to family members past and present, with the hope that future generations will play their part in creating the world they want.

My co-investors/consistent collaborators who helped me develop the lessons of this book since childhood and throughout my formative years: Ursula Dudley-Oglesby, Andy Smith, April Young, John Horner, Scott Kim, Maurice Scott, Edward Felsenthal and Robert Buckingham.

My special thanks to my partner in toil Joe Voyticky. I have never had a friend like you. Few people have invested more in another person.

My UK family: Harry Briggs, Aarti Samani, Walter White, Amanda Foncett, Kate Grieve, Lauren Temple, Sassine Makhoul, Annette Anthony, the family of Southwark Cathedral and the Founding Members of Impact X. Special acknowledgement is needed for two of the dearest assets I have, both of whom befriended me in London and have been crucial to this book: Karen Alexander and Ursula Burns.

My best investment is my partnership with Michael. With Michael all things are possible and I never need permission.

Special thanks to Mim Eichler-Rivas, whose investment in shaping and bringing my ideas to life is all Alpha.

Black women have been the designers, engineers, architects and builders of the most impactful projects I have had the privilege to participate in. Special thanks to the three Black British women who stewarded this book from concept to completion. Andrea Henry, my publisher and editor, whose intelligence, clear-eyed guidance and care made this writing endeavour such a good investment. Natalie Jerome is the book agent who took me on and found this book the right home. Without her business savvy and love for what she does this process would not have yielded returns. Eva Simpson, my chief strategist and a great tactician, who makes anything happen.

Finally, thank you the reader for applying what you will derive from this book. I am excited to see the disruptive changes you cause in the world, for good.

INDEX

non-disruptive 38
wealth inequality 42–3
support and investment for 4
turnaround 145
in the UK 40–41
Black consumers 162
Black deaths
from Covid-19 2, 3, 220
in police custody 221
Black empowerment
corporate pledges and 125–6
economic 11, 20, 49
education 73–4
financial commitment 127
financial literacy 34
impacting change 62
money and 42, 43
resources and user-friendly
strategies 74–5
self-determination 36
steps for 6, 10, 253–6
venture capital 7, 24
Black Enterprise 25, 26, 27, 32
Black entrepreneurs
barriers to entry 68
beating the odds 71
Covid-19 pandemic 123
graduate-level degrees 73
lowered expectations, rising
above 74–5
origin stories 72
personality traits 75–6
security 75
seeking investment
building working relationships
223
preparation for 222–3
recruiting allies 223–30, 244–5
two-pronged strategy, failure
of 27

visionaries 49–52, 52–3, 54–8,
60, 68–9
waiting for permission 27
Black entrepreneurship 7, 8
achieving equality 46
education and experience 36
ideologies 75–6
social mobility 75
Black fashion 51
Black founders
careful selection of funders 245
considerations for investment
147–8
education 73
exit strategies 154–6
incremental approach 63
outperforming non-diverse
peers 96–7
personality traits 76
pragmatism 62
staying lean 198–9
tenacity 198
thinking bigger 67
transitioning between parent
companies 155, 156
under-representation 66, 67, 91,
96–100, 195–6
venture capital 5
vision 62, 66
Black Hand Gang 18, 206
Black Heart Foundation 36
Black innovation 80
Black Lives Matter 4, 5, 32, 125,
164, 182, 220, 237
Black models 51
Black music 30
Black Panther 113
Black people
denial of opportunities 16
education 34

Health & Her 213, 247
Heath, Nick 66
Hendrix, Jimi 179
Henry, Sir Lenny 18, 92, 206–7, 210
Hill, Dr Amber Michelle 212
hiring 202, 203–4
history
    Black *see* Black business:
        history
    importance of 129–32
    learning from 129, 131
Hollis, Michael R. 49, 52–3, 54
home ownership 19, 221–2
hope 21
Hope Not Hate 4
Hopper, Andy 66
*How the Internet Happened: From
    Netscape to the iPhone*
    (McCullough) 130–31
Howard University 60, 105
Howe, Darcus 179
Hudson, Jennifer 98, 99
Hughes, Cathy 105–6, 197
Hunt, Vivian 145
hustle and action 44, 80–87, 97

Ilube, Tom OBE 191, 207
    achievements 17–18
    meeting of influential Black
        people 18–19, 20–21, 22
imagination 71–2, 76
Immigration Advice Service report
    (2015) 161
impact 62, 233–50
Impact X Capital Partners LLP
    22–3, 50
    allies 246
    board 208–11
    capital 251
    Covid-resistant projects 247

diversity and under-
    representation 207
infrastructure of 249
investment
    characteristics for 209
    guidelines for 209, 217,
        247–8
    in under-represented
        entrepreneurs 195–6, 197
    mission 23
    planning phase 212
    thesis 207–8
    validation 251
Impact X Studios 213
indenturing 37–8, 38–9
Independent 4, 19
indie films 101, 113
inherited wealth 42–3
institutionalized racism 183
insurance policies 50
insurance sector 247–8
International Monetary Fund
    (IMF) paper (2018) 197
internet 64
    users 131
    websites 131
intrapreneurs 216–17
investment
    Alpha 194–5
    in Black entrepreneurs 222–30,
        244–5
        women 195, 197–8, 199–200,
            212–13
    considerations for 147–8
    diversity and 205
    from others 194
    selection bias problem 203–4
    social-impact 208
    in yourself 194
    see also venture capitalism (VC)

investment 195–6
women 138, 140
unicorns 218
definition 215
marketing for 225–31
in the UK 230–31
Unilever 174
'Unite the Right' rally (2017) 14
United States of America (USA)
Constitution 39
far right organizations 14
Great Migration 241–2
Jim Crow laws 239, 242
Tulsa massacre 240
university education 34, 35, 36
University of Warwick 160
Urban One 26
UrbanGeekz 80
USP (unique selling proposition)
137, 143

Vaz, Keith 164
Venice Film Festival 114
venture capitalism (VC) 4–5
Black empowerment 24
for Black entrepreneurs 5, 198
Black-founded businesses 5, 25
investment
in all-female founders 203–4
in all-male founders 203–4
belonging through diversity
205
in Black-owned businesses
5, 198
in Black women 197–8,
199–200
equality of opportunity 204
openness 204
tackling microaggressions
204–5

in the UK 230
virtuous circle 200–202
success of 25
in the US 5
value of 24–5
venture capitalists (VCs)
Black
female 195
lack of 5, 25–6
degrees of separation 244–5
disruption 26
interests and objectives 119
investment in startups 5, 124–5
predators 24
risk takers 24–5
supporting Black businesses 127
win-win scenarios 82
women 202–6
Verd, Nicky 29
Verizon 174
Viacom 105
video rental 114
Vikings 40
Virgin Airlines 153
Virgin Atlantic 153
Virgin Records 153
virtual meetings 246
virtuous circle 200–202, 208
visionaries 49–52, 52–3, 54–8, 60,
68, 68–9
visions 83–4, 223
Vox 70
Voyticky, Joe 112

Wallace, Governor George 44
walled gardens 171
Walmart 151, 174
Warner Music 134
Washington, Booker T. 46
Washington, Denzel 98, 101

Eric Collins is a technology executive and serial entrepreneur. In 2011, President Obama appointed him to the Small Business Administration's Council on Underserved Communities. In 2018, Eric became part of a prominent group of Black European and US founders of Impact X Capital Partners. The *Financial Times* named him among the UK's top 100 BAME leaders in technology. Since 2019 he has been voted one of the most influential Black people in Britain on *The Power List*. Eric has appeared on Radio 4 and Sky News, and has been featured in the *Financial Times, Guardian, Times* and *Sunday Times*. Eric hosts Channel 4's award-winning business reality series *The Money Maker*.